OWL

D1486354

0

- 2

2002

03

NOV 1991

Strategic Corporate Facilities Management

Other McGraw-Hill Books of Interest

Strategic Corporate Facilities Management

Stephen Binder

McGraw-Hill, Inc.

New York   St. Louis   San Francisco   Auckland   Bogotá
Caracas   Lisbon   London   Madrid   Mexico   Milan
Montreal   New Delhi   Paris   San Juan   São Paulo
Singapore   Sydney   Tokyo   Toronto

Library of Congress Cataloging-in-Publication Data

Binder, Stephen.
    Strategic corporate facilities management / Stephen Binder
        p. cm
    Includes index.
    ISBN 0-07-005306-5
    1. Facility management. 2. Plant engineering. 3. Business
relocation—Management. I. Title.
TS177.B563   1992
658.2—dc20   92-6403
                                                             CIP

1 2 3 4 5 6 7 8 9 0   DOC/DOC   9 8 7 6 5 4 3 2

ISBN   0-07-005306-5

*The sponsoring editor for this book was Joel Stein, the editing
supervisor was Paul R. Sobel, and the production supervisor was
Pamela A. Pelton. It was set in Century Schoolbook by McGraw-Hill's
Professional Book Group composition unit.*

Printed and bound by R. R. Donnelley & Sons Company.

Contents

Preface

We spend most of our management time asking questions and listening to answers; or, being asked questions and answering them. Here are some questions and answers:

Which book do I read first? *Corporate Facility Planning* or *Strategic Corporate Facilities Management*? That is like asking the question: What came first, the chicken or the egg? *Corporate Facility Planning* deals with establishing yourself as a facility manager. This book covers your role as a facility manager through the normal phases of an interior design project: space planning; setting and selling standards; project management; design management; furniture management; and construction management.

How did you get to do the interior planning unless you physically moved from another location; or, managed a new building which needed to have the space within it planned and designed? So read the second book first. *Strategic Corporate Facilities Management* follows your growth as a facility or project manager into an asset manager. This book covers your role managing the relocation of your corporate office through these phases: strategic and tactical planning; site and building selection; lease negotiations; managing implementation; and managing beyond occupancy through preventive maintenance. Your next steps in your facility management career depend upon your success in handling the major new site project for your company. It's absolutely essential for you to understand the criteria of strategic planning so that you can develop the tactical plan to provide the best facility for your corporate businesses. However, you do not "graduate" to this level of project complexity and corporate responsibility without having first successfully managed interior design renovation projects. So read the first book first.

Why only four chapters? Because I couldn't fit the contents into three chapters.

Where does the humor come from? Now that I clarified the chicken and egg question, let me outline some points to look for in this book. (You might as well read this book now since you've just purchased it.) As my students, colleagues, staff, and friends know, I maintain a wry sense of humor. I never have to make a joke about our careers because there is so much humor just working in the profession. I mentioned in my first book that if you do not keep a sense of humor about yourself, you will end up managing from that field office in the sky.

Who succeeds first? I have planned, designed, built, and furnished millions of square feet. I have moved tens of thousands of staff; and, saved my corporation millions of dollars through good management practices. Let's revisit the chicken and egg question.

Who is successful first: the manager or the staff member? As usual, it is my staff that makes me a success. Perhaps, I add rational thinking, logic, and a spark to their desire to attain new heights. In any event, it is Yourco that succeeds first. That is what it is all about.

What preparation do I need? You probably should have five to ten years of experience in facility management experience. At this point in your career, you should be responsible for your corporation's assets. When you reach this level of management, you especially need to be comfortable with finance and contract administration. You'll note I didn't mention architecture or engineering. I think I spend more time in evaluating financial impacts, net present values, payback analyses, contract clauses, and negotiating agreements; then in developing strategic and tactical plans. I pay tribute to all my colleagues who are contract employees; and those of us who negotiate contracts.

What do the symbols mean? Look for the symbols '■' and '✔' throughout the text. '■' reflects the normal facility and asset solution. In terms of the sample contracts throughout the book, the symbol represents the normal terms requested by "the other side." While these terms are probably acceptable, you can usually do better. '✔' reflects further hints, pointers, or terms that asset, realty, and facility managers may achieve in negotiating on behalf of Yourco.

How did you get "column H"? There are numerous tables throughout the book which provide sample analyses. Where appropriate, the columns are labeled with letters to help you decipher the mathematical relationship of the columns. My daughter, Kasi Nicole Binder, is now in college with a scholarship in mathematics. I will leave it to her to figure out if the formulas and assumptions are correct.

Why case work studies? Social work is where a worker investigates a case of personal or family maladjustment, and gives advice and guidance. Welcome to the realty and facility family.

You will easily identify with the real-life situations outlined in the case work studies scattered throughout the book. Each case work study is real, and is based on actual problems encountered by *you* working at Yourco. Case work studies are organized as follows: Pertain to the section immediately preceding them; offer pertinent Yourco information and disinformation (factual but not necessarily relating to the case study); there is no misinformation; suggestions to be considered (three or four suggested answers); discussion points for each suggested answer; analysis points for each suggested answer; and answers for those who refused any of the above.

What is the answer? If I only knew the answer first, it would make the question so much easier. Fans of *Jeopardy* would probably disagree. Unfortunately in our business, there is usually more than one answer or direction. Answers depend upon your own comfort level, expertise, corporate policies, and personal attitudes as well as those of your supervisor. I don't necessarily suggest that any answer given in these case work studies is the "right" one. Wherever possible, I point out why the particular answer shown is correct for the circumstances involved. Since this is an instructional text, your professor and your professional associates in class will discuss the reasoning behind their personal response. I have taught three different courses at Pratt Institute's graduate degree program in Facility Management: *Integrative Seminar* (a class on how to benchmark facility attributes during on-site visits to corporations), *Principles of Facilities Management*, and *Strategic Planning and Management*. As they earn their Masters of Science in Facility Management, the professionals who have attended my courses all know the "right" answer in advance: It Depends.

What about time? First old saying: "There is never enough time to do something right, but there is always enough time to do it over." My colleagues at Meadows Office Furniture received a Yourco purchase order with the following note: "This is the revised revision of the amended original." Don't miss deadlines; on the other hand, why foulup? What are the chances that the right furniture items get purchased and installed? Second old saying: "It is easier to apologize than to seek permission." In August 1991, a design firm sent me a letter that began: "Yes, yes, I know, I know. It has taken me a long time to get this in the mail. But at least I've caught up to my requests of November 1990. I'm sure you've had other things to do while waiting for this set of drawings you asked for, so my conscience isn't bothering me too badly." This is stretching the point a bit. Keep these in mind during your career development. Incidentally, I did have other things to do— namely, hire another design firm.

What is Yourco? This hypothetical company is derived from YOUR COrporation. Yourco is a hybrid of corporations, financial institutions, nonprofit institutions, educational bodies, governmental agencies, health care facilities, and small businesses. No resemblance to any one company is implied. Yourco is based on my listening to the thousands of professionals I have taught and with whom I have spoken. The problems, frustrations, policies, and attitudes expressed in this instructional text are a composite of us all.

What computer programs did I use? All the text was typed using WordPerfect. All the tables were done with Wingz. The flow charts were done with MacProject II. Sample letters were composed utilizing QuarkXPress.

What's my line? In the 1960s we used to be known as office managers. In the 1970s we used to be known as operation officers. In the 1980s we used to be known as facility or project managers. In the 1990s we are known by our specialty: realty manager, space planner, building manager, facilities specialist, CAD operator and construction manager. We are nearing 2000. Let's not wait for the new century. We are asset managers.

Acknowledgments

Thanks are due to the following:

Valerie Hail, my researcher, who was a tremendous help in the preparation of this book

Harriet Binder, my mother, for finally realizing that working for a bank doesn't mean one sits behind a teller's cage

Joel Stern, my lawyer, for attending to my personal matters which allowed me to concentrate on this book

Thunder and Tubes, siamese cats, who supplied endless typographical errors by padding across the keyboard and nuzzling the mouse

Finally, my staff, for learning these principles and effectively converting them into practice

Stephen Binder

Strategic Corporate
Facilities Management

1

Strategic and Tactical Planning

Introduction

In *Corporate Facility Planning,* I wrote that space was the first frontier (unlike a popular science fiction series in which it is deemed the
final frontier). Since the book's publication, space has received a lot of
attention. The lead editorial on *The New York Times* op-ed page of
July 21, 1990, read:

Rethink Space

The editorial stated that a sensible plan had been presented to the
White House to rescue the space program from decay. Some five
months later, on December 12, another *Times* op-ed headline declared:

How to Put Space in Its Place

Whereas these headlines refer to outer space, our concern is with in-
ner space. In our progression up the corporate ladder, we move beyond
our concerns for space and interior design processes.

The master space plan is only the implementation of a greater
scheme—the strategic and tactical plan. To start, we need to define
some terms.

Definitions

Strategic (adjective)	critical, crucial, essential, important, vital; characterized by sound strategy
Tactic (noun)	approach, maneuver, method, procedure, plan, system, stratagem
Tactical (adjective)	characterized by or showing cleverness and skill in tactics

Plan (noun)	conception, design, strategy, method, pattern, system, blueprint, diagram, sketch, ambition, intention, purpose; a scheme for making, doing, or arranging something: a project, program, or schedule

The theme of my speeches, books, articles, and management style is the use of a common language. No, it is not English, French, or Spanish. It is the local currency—in my case, dollars and cents. All too often, we talk to one another and to senior management using transactional language. Senior managers think in terms of the corporate bottom line: profit and loss, earnings per share, return on assets, and return on investment.

We call ourselves facility managers, project managers, real estate managers, project directors, et cetera. Our titles are of minor consequence compared with our common goals as managers of corporate assets. Those of you who perform this same service as consultants to Yourco are also asset managers. Those of you who provide a product to Yourco are asset managers as well.

The terms *facility, project,* and *asset* may be used interchangeably throughout the book or from corporation to corporation. Start thinking of yourselves as Yourco's asset manager.

Definition

Assets (noun)	all the entries on a balance sheet showing the entire property of a business as cash, inventory, equipment, and real estate

Let's view our own personal strategic plans. At the end of the book, we will review those plans.

Where we are

We talk to senior management in terms of our transactions.

Examples

- Hired the consultant for $3.00 per usable square foot.
- Bought 500 desks.
- Installed 100,000 square yards of carpeting.
- Moved 5000 boxes.
- Managed 1 million rentable square feet of space.

- Managed four buildings, each with 250,000 square feet and "co-gen" (your own co-generation electrical plant).

Where we want to be

We want to use asset management as our common language.

Examples

- Managed a consultant with a $150,000 contract.
- Responsible for purchasing $1.25 million worth of furniture.
- Responsible for $300,000 carpeting installation.
- Managed the timely relocation of 1000 employees to minimize lost efficiency of the $50 million corporate payroll.
- Managed corporate space with an annual expense of $30 million.
- Managed corporate real estate assets with a book value of $750 million and a market value in excess of $1 billion.

How we get there

To get there, we need to start converting transactions into dollars and cents (or local currency). Initially, we will use both transactions and corresponding asset values; then, we will use asset values and corresponding transactions. Eventually, we will use only asset values. Finally, we must communicate the value of our business to senior management.

Examples

- Wait, I'm getting ahead of myself.
- Follow the approach in the rest of the book.
- Learn how to manage building your own strategic plan as you develop Yourco's.
- Make sure that everything you do is derived from a strategic and tactical plan.

Fairy tales revisited

Examples of strategic and tactical plans in action appear where you least expect them. At a recent speech, I asked the audience of professional facility managers, architects, engineers, and designers the following:

- How many of you have children?
- How many of you have neighbors who have children?
- How many of you have been a child?

Surprisingly, not everyone raised a hand on that last question. So I requested that people go back and check their past.

As a child, you probably listened to and, eventually, read for yourself famous fairy tales like *Little Red Riding Hood* and *Snow White*. Did you realize these tales were not about good versus evil? In fact, almost all are strategic corporate facilities management stories. Each story relates the strategic plan of one of the characters and how it was carried out (tactical plan).

Sometimes the plan is successful. Sometimes the character doesn't survive the tale. Here are just a few examples of how a strategic and tactical plan, successfully executed, can be crucial.

Little Red Riding Hood

Story

- Wolf developed strategic and tactical plan to consume the Hood clan.
- Wolf cleverly outlined an action plan.
- Plan included interviewing Miss Hood for her business plan.
- Wolf took short cuts to get to Miss Hood's relocation site (grandma's house).
- Plan was unsuccessful due to big eyes, big mouth, and overanxiety to succeed.
- Wolf tried to implement the plan all alone.
- Chief executive officer, disguised as a woodcutter, ruined the plan by cutting Wolf's employment (and life).

Moral

- ✔ Next time, let Wolf alert the CEO to the plan.
- ✔ Let Wolf improve on the schedule.
- ✔ Wolf had no standby plans.
- ✔ Wolf never "got with the program!"

Snow White and the Seven Dwarfs

Story

- Dwarfs' strategic implementation plan was based on past occupancy.
- Their home had enough space to house existing staff of seven.
- Dwarfs did not foresee their own growth properly.
- Their tactical facility plan failed.
- They added one person to the cottage, Snow White, and had a space problem.
- Subplot: Snow White did not secure three bids for that apple, as required by the king's audit division.
- Snow White nearly "paid the price" for not analyzing the quality of her selection.
- Name the seven dwarfs. (See end of section for answers.)

Moral

- Relocation to a larger facility might have been appropriate.
- Relocation to a cottage closer to the mine would have reduced commutation time.
- Snow White should have taken three bids on the apple.
- Nothing that happened to the dwarfs had ever happened before.
- As a result of rightsizing (or "dumb luck"), the dwarfs ended up with exactly the right space after all.

Goldilocks and the Three Bears

Story. Bears lacked foresight in assuming that their equipment needs would not change. When an unfriendly merger occurred with another party (Goldilocks):

- dining facilities were insufficient.
- furniture was of an inferior quality.
- housing accommodations were inadequate.
- security system was nonexistent.

Bears showed no evidence of strategic planning.

Moral

✔ Simplest solution: Invest in a good security system.

✔ Suggest a coded-entry device or "smart" card system.

✔ No suppositions were made by the bears.

✔ Bears never had these problems before.

The Three Little Pigs

Story

▪ Three equally ranked pigs could not agree on a new building site.

▪ All three were aware of fierce competition from the Big Bad Wolf.

▪ First pig sought a quick-fix solution by erecting a straw house.

▪ First pig did not bother with an environmental impact study.

▪ Second pig realized a tactical plan was required.

▪ Second pig took a brief period of time to build a house of wood.

▪ Third pig took the longest time but read this book and wrote a strategic and tactical plan.

▪ Third pig built a brick house according to local building codes.

▪ First two pigs laughed at the length of time the third pig was working.

▪ Wolf quickly overcame the first two pigs with some huffing and puffing.

▪ Wolf could not blow down the third pig's brick house.

▪ Wolf tried something new—a shortcut down the chimney.

▪ Wolf burned up in the chimney.

Moral. Good planning, carefully executed, is often mistaken by others as dumb luck.

Fairy tales can come true

As you read through the rest of this book, you'll identify other fairy tales that relate to the asset or facility management topic being covered. For example:

Chapter 2

Site Environmental Concerns   *Jack and the Beanstalk*
Lease Negotiations   *The Old Lady Who Lived in the Shoe*

Chapter 3

Hiring the Professional Team   *The Pied Piper*
The Moving Experience   *The Wizard of Oz*

Chapter 4

Maintenance and Operations   *Old Mother Hubbard*
Headhunters, Résumés, Career Paths   *Hansel and Gretel*

These tales are not expressly related in this book, as either references or case studies. However, the next time *you* are a child, or are reading a fairy tale to a child, you will be able to deduce the strategic and tactical plan that the characters were attempting to implement. More important, you will be able to figure out the proper action plan and carry that information back to Yourco for implementation.

Strategic Business Planning

S · S · S · S · S · S · Strategic plan

Statement Strategies Suppositions Specifics Strengths Standbys Stengel

It's so simple when creating a strategic plan. It's all in the letter S. If you can remember the seven S's of strategic planning you should be able to succeed every time.

A good investigative reporter will ask the right types of questions. Name the seven basic "W and H" questions. (See end of section for answers.) The strategic plan answers these questions. Here are what the S words mean. A facility-related example is included for each.

Statement.   Begin by stating the mission of the business and its long-range goal. Write short, succinct, comprehensive sentences. Remember that *your* business mission is related to facility management. Your client's mission is *not* facility-related; it is whatever business the client is performing.

Do not relate the statement to timeliness, individuals, or locations. Be generic in scope but all-encompassing in breadth and depth.

Examples

- To provide facility and asset management for Yourco-occupied properties.
- To ensure the highest and best usage of space in Yourco facilities.

- To provide management of the professional disciplines required to plan, design, construct, and furnish Yourco facilities.

Strategies. Outline where the business should be and state the basic objectives you wish to follow. One Sunday comics' character stated a short-term goal of getting through the workday from 9:00 A.M. to 5:00 P.M. The character's long-term strategy was to string together a series of short-term goals! Point: Do not write a series of short-term goals and call it a strategy.

Examples

- To handle all facilities requests regardless of staffing levels.
- Overcome lack of communication to clients (users).
- To leverage external consultants for maximum savings to Yourco.
- To enter all floor plans onto computer-assisted design equipment.

Suppositions. List which tasks must be accomplished to achieve your strategies. Include assumptions for risks and opportunities to achieve the strategies. List impediments along the way. Finally, quantify risks and opportunities. Include such variables as market conditions, legal and regulatory constraints, and trade barriers.

Examples

- Forecast new staff count and salary expenses for next year's budget.
- New staff will require an "in-house proficiency plan" (discussed later in this chapter).
- If new staffing is unrealistic, communicate the cost of projects, including external consultant expense, to clients (users).
- Clients have no accurate forecasts of next year's facility projects.

Specifics. Devise a specific action plan to achieve the strategies. Include when tasks will be achieved and who is responsible for them.

Do tasks include personnel or production activities beyond your management sphere? How will you manage the performance of others required to achieve your plan? Determine the costs of the plan and schedule review dates for tracking completion.

Examples

- Assign Yourco administrator to develop in-house proficiency plan.

- Assign senior project manager to investigate computer-assisted design equipment.
- Develop new communications plan.
- Develop new project-tracking system.

Strengths.   Define the areas of effectiveness and vulnerability in your plan. Include courses of action to fortify the weak areas and capitalize on the strong areas. What are the critical performance strengths of the assigned staff?

Examples

- Clients have previously criticized staff for lack of communication.
- Corporate expansion program throughout North America requires our division to communicate its skills.
- Current staff is not familiar with code issues in other states and in Canada.

Standbys.   List alternative actions in the event of not achieving specific tasks. These actions should depend on suppositions. A detailed backup program is critical.

Examples

- If new in-house staffing is not approved, expand leveraged external consultant program.
- Contact various professional associations and facility colleagues for recommendations of external consultants.
- Plan a proactive campaign to solicit information for divisional business plans for the next 12 to 24 months.
- Have staff members arrange meetings with their respective contacts.

Stengel.   Four points of view to keep in mind while developing a strategic plan:

Casey Stengel, baseball player, manager, and philosopher

Yogi Berra, baseball player, manager, and philosopher

George Carlin, comedian

Miss Humphreys, eighth-grade English teacher

Stengel's definition of strategic planning. "If you don't know where you're going, you'll wind up somewhere else!"

Stengel makes an important point. You cannot write and implement a successful plan unless you have worked out where you are, where you want to be, and how you are going to get there. Figure it out at the outset—or end up *working* somewhere else.

Berra's definition of strategic planning. "It's déjà vu, all over again."* Yes, Yogi, history does repeat itself, and it's essential to learn from the past. How will you apply those history lessons to your strategic plan?

Carlin's definition of strategic planning. "It's dévu ja. Everything that is happening now never happened before!" Or did it? All new business ventures rely on past methodologies and planning techniques to achieve success. It is highly unlikely that your strategic plan is so new that none of the S's previously occurred. Check.

Miss Humphreys' definition of strategic planning. "First, you tell them what you're going to tell them. Second, you tell them what you're telling them. Third, you tell them what you told them."

Repetition of salient points is important, so be redundant, but don't be obvious about repeating yourself. Get it? Senior managers get there by being somewhat astute.

Examples. If your strategic plan is not accepted by senior management, you probably didn't follow one of the four principles:

- Stengel: Didn't develop a true mission statement and strategy.
- Berra: Didn't learn from past mistakes for future use.
- Carlin: Didn't think anything next year would relate to the past.
- Humphreys: Didn't tell them, again.

If you feel the S · S · S · S · S · S · Strategic Plan is difficult to remember, then try another mnemonic. Kreon Cyros, director of facilities at the Massachusetts Institute of Technology, speaks of the six P's of strategic planning:

Prior Planning Prevents Pretty Poor Projects

It's your choice of how to remember the criteria for writing a successful plan:

*According to William Safire, *New York Times* columnist, this is only attributed to, not stated by, Yogi Berra. In other words, it's a Yogi-ism.

S · S · S · S · S · S · Strategic Plan or Strategic P · P · P · P · P · Plan

Strategic Reasons for Corporate Moves

Surveys of over 100 corporate moves during the late 1980s reflect some interesting statistics.

- Over 75 percent of the relocations included fewer than 600 employees.
- Over 75 percent of the firms making relocations had gross revenues in excess of $1 billion.
- Some 40 percent of all moves were due to corporate restructuring.
- Improved operational efficiencies was the number-one reason for relocation among 86 percent of the companies surveyed.
- Expanding or penetrating new markets was the prime reason for relocation among 90 percent of the companies surveyed.

Every strategic plan should heed the rationale for corporate relocation. Through decision seeking, we can delve further into the strategy utilized by facility and asset managers. Acquisitions and divestitures, downsizing, expansion, mergers, reorganization, restructuring, and rightsizing can lead to one or more of the following:

- Leasing or deleasing of facilities
- Relocation of all facilities
- Relocation of selected facilities
- Restacking of existing facilities
- Start-up of new operational facility

Strategic reasons for these changes include:

- Centralization or decentralization
- Cost containment
- New or expanded market potential
- Operational efficiencies
- Rightsizing or downsizing initiatives
- Work force opportunities

Saving a strategic plan

Here is a classic case of a strategic plan "saved" by asset management.

The strategic plan was to house the ever-growing number of prisoners in New York State's medium-security sites. The tactical plan reflected a serious lack of room in state prisons for inmates awaiting transfer from local jails. In 1990 there were over 52,000 such inmates, almost double the number from 1983. In all cases, new beds would be required for the prisoners, and timing was critical.

Standby 1: Build a new prison facility. Financial difficulties in New York State severely limited this option. The timing required to find a site and erect a new facility would be too long, and the additional cost of personnel in a new prison would be prohibitive.

Standby 2: Relocate medium-security prisoners to an existing facility. Using an existing empty state-owned facility (such as a gymnasium from a closed school) and converting it to a barracks-type jail requires capital investment in a new infrastructure as well as hiring additional security and administrative personnel.

Standby 3: Change the space standards per prisoner. The average cell is 10 feet deep and 12 feet wide (120 net usable square feet per prisoner). This solution calls for taking the space occupied by two consecutive cells (10 feet deep and 24 feet wide) and moving the center wall 4 feet in one direction. Then add another wall to divide the space into three cells, each 10 feet deep and 8 feet wide (80 net usable square feet per prisoner).

This approach requires no major increase in security personnel. However, substantial capital investment is needed and implementation costs are high: plenty of construction, plus the purchase of one new cell door for each existing two cell doors.

Standby 4: Double-deck existing prison cells. As announced in the newspapers on March 1, 1990, New York State finally figured out a way to double the capacity of its medium-security prisons with minimal capital investment: bunk beds! What a creative solution. The average cell space of 120 net usable square feet would now be occupied by two prisoners, creating a new space standard of 60 net usable square feet per prisoner. This solution requires no new doors, walls, or other structures and no major increase in security personnel. Presumably the single beds would be "recycled" to high-security prisons.

Lesson learned

This case doesn't necessarily translate to double-decking office desks. However, sometimes you must step back from the immediate problem and try to see the larger issues. The not-so-obvious solution may be the simplest one. Don't be so anxious to go with the standby throw-dollars-at-it alternative.

Seeking Management Approval

The strategic plan always requires senior management approval. (Chapter 2 discusses techniques in selling management.) It is important to be aware of reasons that the strategic plan may not be well received. If a plan is not supported, it is usually due to *your* failure to overcome management's attitude. Objections typically fall into two categories: the "nevers" and the "always." Here are a few examples.

The nevers

- Never had a correct plan before
- Never have time to implement
- Never required for a steady-state company like ours
- Never any different than your master space plan
- Never asked if we wanted one
- Never asked what our business plans are
- Never got each of us to agree to it
- Never got any of us committed

The always

- Always great style but no significance
- Always great financial information but no flash
- Always optimistic
- Always great detail for immediate future
- Always loses focus on longer-range strategies
- Always excludes senior management from the process

ANSWERS:

The names of the seven dwarfs are:

Bashful Doc Dopey Grumpy Happy Sleepy Sneezy

The seven basic investigative reporter "W and H" questions are:

What When Where Which Who Why How

If you can remember those names and questions, remember the seven S's:

Statement Strategies Suppositions Specifics Strengths Standbys Stengel

First strategic test. If you feel that you are now a strategic thinker, try the test in Figure 1.1. Simply connect the nine dots using four straight lines without lifting your pencil. Caveat: If you draw in the book, it will be hard to resell! The solution is given in Chapter 4.

Tactical Facility Planning

W^2A—where we are

Your initial goal in strategic planning is to figure out where you are starting. You can consolidate your points into three categories: management, finance, and technology. Surveys of asset managers reveal the following W^2A concerns:

Management

- Inability to control government regulations
- Inability to maintain current services with rising costs and declining resources

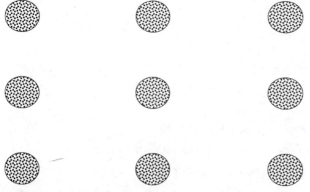

Figure 1.1 Strategic thinking test. Connect the dots using four straight lines without lifting your pencil.

- Crisis management mode of operation
- Hazardous wastes costs: "make them disappear"
- Insufficient planning time
- No management enforcement of standards
- Organizational changes too frequent
- Unpredictable growth
- "User" changes mind

Finance

- Accurate cost accounting not available
- Antiquated budgeting process
- Benefits analysis of facility decisions inconclusive and inconsistent
- Lease renewals market-dependent
- Space utilization and allocation policy for "charges" not strong enough

Technology

- Aging facility not in tune with new technology
- Business managers unfamiliar with energy requirements
- Facility automation almost nonexistent
- Insufficient funds to understand existing conditions
- No funds for necessary wire management

W^3TB—where we want to be

Next, you figure out what your final goal is—where you want to be. Surveys of facility managers showed these W^3TB concerns:

Management

- Active management role in managing government regulations
- Less management involvement
- Lack of strategic and tactical plans
- Minimal "user" changes
- Management and community support to find "right" future sites
- New work force, with new ideas and energy

Finance

- Creative solutions needed to meet rising facility and occupancy costs
- Leverage needed in contracts to minimize bidding and negotiating
- Real estate and lease management should be considered *our* business

Technology

- New facilities services required for new technologies
- Funding within each project to cover technology
- Increased staff education on new technologies

HWGT—how we get there

The key to success in real estate is location, location, location. The key to success in facilities is planning, planning, planning. Remember the six P's. A quick checklist of facility planning steps is given below and discussed in more detail throughout the book. The three basics for the asset manager are: Be a planner. Be a provider. Be proactive.

Checklist for being a planner

Review business plan for facility implications.   Review the business plan with the "local" business manager who approved it. Determine a working budget, space requirements, and needs requirements, including business change (expansion or contraction), co-location with another corporate entity, and market study of locations. Then prepare a preoccupancy evaluation.

Appoint an in-house project team.   The project team should include:

- Project manager
- Client coordinator
- Realty manager
- Space planner
- Architect/design manager
- Engineering manager
- Purchasing agent
- Financial analyst
- Security manager

Translate the business plan into space and location plan. Undertake a series of demographic studies, including an assessment of urban versus suburban locations and the availability of transportation, utilities, and services (e.g., postal, food).

Determine requirements not covered by existing facility. Develop a program of current plus future needs and analyze special requirements that are not available. For example:

- Raised flooring
- Data center
- Telecommunications
- Uninterrupted power supply (UPS)
- Sufficient utilities (electric, gas, water)
- Security

Identify alternatives for consideration. The six most common options are:

- Continue with business-as-usual (no change).
- Renovate existing facilities.
- Expand existing facilities.
- Relocate (fully or partially) to an existing building or a new building.
- Buy, build, or lease space to accommodate the business plan.
- Set up joint or solo venture for new building.

Make a cost analysis. Determine business-as-usual costs as benchmark for cost comparisons. Then determine costs for each viable alternative and associated incremental expenses for each. Next, consider variable costs for each alternative, including:

- Initial start-up and ongoing expenses
- Cost impact of time (cost of money, ongoing lease expenses)
- Complexity and logistical impact
- Market risks
- Disruption costs
- Write-offs of undepreciated assets and leasehold improvements
- Impact of zoning restrictions on schedule and budget

- Taxes (occupancy taxes; land taxes; federal, state, city taxes)
- Environmental studies and remedies

Calculate impact from a business not a facility perspective, including:

- Per capita earnings
- Return on assets
- Return on investment
- Payback period
- Earnings per share
- Profit and loss
- Hurdle rate
- Basis points

Issue your recommendation. Determine which alternative is the best solution by listing the advantages and disadvantages of each. Utilize objective information determined from the steps listed above as well as subjective information determined above your shoulders. Score each alternative in a weighted analysis. Then write a one-page outline of the problem, your recommendation, and how you arrived at the recommendation.

Checklist for being a provider

Secure approval. Prepare a request for capital appropriation with all expected costs and assumptions. Do not exceed any interim funding allocation that helped "seed" the project. Sign the document and manage its passage through all required levels of management.

Finalize the project team, including the external consultants required to complete the project. Make sure that the financial control system is ready to monitor project expenses as they are received. When you receive the approved capital appropriations form, distribute copies to all pertinent units. Check with the auditing department to determine who retains the original signed copy.

Manage design. At the project start-up meeting, establish preliminary budgets for each discipline, interview key staff, and develop a project program. Develop a site plan; architectural, design, and engineering plans; interior design plans, including furniture; and a security plan. Obtain initial cost estimates and review them.

Obtain all approvals on plans as you go along. Make changes in plans and seek a "freeze" date on further alterations. (Freezing changes is easier said than done.) Develop working or contract drawings and specifications (contract documents). Remember that the client is part of the project team.

Award contracts.   Develop a request for proposal (RFP) for bid items in construction, furniture, telecommunications, and so on. Evaluate, negotiate, and award contracts. Be sure to call the unsuccessful firms and tell them why they did not get the award. (An informed bid loser will either improve or not bother taking up your time in the future.)

Finalize the project budget on the basis of actual prices received. Obtain extra funding or project reduction in scope or quality, as required. Reaffirm the project schedule.

Implement the project.   Issue purchase orders to all successful bidders and start the construction process. Review requisitions for payments and process them, less retainer. Monitor and supervise all construction in progress. Coordinate telecommunications equipment, wiring installations, and security implementation. Review furniture, furnishings, and equipment vendor acknowledgments for accuracy versus purchase order and contract documents.

Complete construction, security installation, telecommunications installation, and carpet installation. Install all furniture and furnishings as well as all signage. Manage a punchlist of the facility.

Make sure all desk and office accessories that easily "walk" are in a secure room until the day before occupancy. Make sure the mover is on schedule and ensure proper operation of all subsystems. Conduct tours for affected personnel in the new facility. Move contents from the old facility to the new facility. Lay out desk and office accessories and make sure that a pamphlet outlining how furniture and equipment work is accessible to all. Arrange for cleaning the night before occupancy.

On occupancy day (Monday, usually), be on hand for staff questions. Have the mover or extra porters on hand to remove packing boxes promptly. Walk through the facility with the mover to agree on a "clean" move or to assess damages.

Okay, take Wednesday off.

Make final payments and get a sign-off from each discipline that all items are received and paid. Close the project. Do not keep it open just because you are under budget. Do not allow the client to have an open-ended project.

Checklist for being proactive

Facility management. Start routine facility churn work and perform preventive maintenance work. Prepare your post occupancy evaluation (POE). (Wait at least three months after the move-in before conducting your POE.)

Education. Maintain an active participation with the business manager during ensuing business planning cycles. Do not be reactive and wait for business to call with a project. Keep updated on new ways and methods to solve old and new problems. Continue educating yourself through:

- Seminars and expositions
- New vendor products
- Continuing education courses
- Degree-related graduate programs
- Trade magazines
- Professional associations
- Your colleagues at other corporations
- Rereading this book

Always pass on salient ideas to your client, the business manager. Start all over again with the next major business change. Figure 1.2 illustrates a typical Yourco tactical plan.

Case work study: Business to tactical plan

Yourco information. The director of Yourco's credit division has sent you an advance copy of the unit's business plan. The plan is to be presented to senior management at the annual review, which is four months away. You need this department's staff forecast now to complete the tactical plans for Yourco's relocation and to decide on whether to commit to the new lease.

Credit is the largest division. The number of staff is completely inconsistent with that of the other divisions. The credit director's plans appear to be suspiciously high in number of staff. The director is on the same level as your BIG boss (two levels above you).

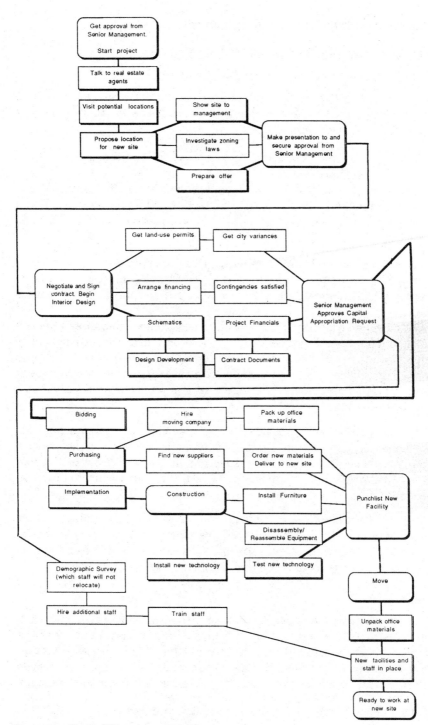

Figure 1.2 Typical Yourco tactical plan.

Among the alternatives to be considered are:

- Go to the director and review the staffing forecast.
- Go to your supervisor and review the forecast.
- Proceed with the tactical plans on the basis of what you received, including signing the new lease. After all, the business plan was signed by a director.

What is your recommendation? (Analysis of the choices is given at the end of this section.)

As usual, you as facility manager are caught in the middle. If you raise doubts about the plan, you may be deemed a police officer. If you do not raise a concern—and the plan is wrong—you have failed to do your job.

Go to the director.   If your responsibilities include signing the lease, you should be certain of your facts. This is not a matter of a lower-level staff member dealing with a senior staff member. It is a business discussion.

Know your own company protocol. In most open companies, this is a quick telephone call conversation. The credit director will normally appreciate the fact that you have reviewed the plan and are calling to verify the information. The director can reassure senior management that facility management has taken into account the credit division's new business plans.

Go to your supervisor.   There is no way that you can go to the big boss two levels up. It's just not "right." That's why you have a supervisor. Your supervisor may have a perspective on unusual growth that you do not know. Also, your supervisor is paid the "big bucks" to question a director.

Proceed with tactical plans.   You didn't question other business plans that showed downsizing, so why are you questioning substantial growth? The credit director is considered a senior manager and you do not have the time to wait for the senior management review.

Analysis

Those who selected going to the director.   If Yourco is an entrepreneurial company, you should consider your position as equal to that of the director for purposes of information gathering. You have every prerogative to call or meet to verify data, not to question. Companies that do not encourage information seeking should learn the current trends.

✔ This is correct for the proactive facility manager.

Those who selected going to your supervisor. You may be less experienced or more timid than your colleagues. Also, Yourco may not permit such level-differential discussions, or may permit them only after consulting with your supervisor.

✔ This is correct for the reactive facility manager.

✔ This is correct for the proactive facility manager with a reactive supervisor.

Those who selected proceeding with tactical plans. If you legitimately are concerned with information you received, why proceed? On the other hand, you are accountable for signing a lease for space on the basis of all the business plans you received. You can tell your supervisor and senior management that your calculations were based on plans received from the director level.

✔ Storks stick their head in the sand, too.

✔ This is correct for all inactive facility managers. They are neither reactive nor proactive.

Organizational Approaches

Team approach

Yourco always is the team leader. In other words, as the owner's representative you are the final point of approval for all external consultants. The manner in which you set up the team relationship below you will vary from project to project and company to company.

Team members

The team consists of Yourco employees and members of external firms.

Yourco employees

- Senior manager
- Client contact
- Project manager
- Real estate manager
- Strategic planner
- Human resources manager

- Architect
- Interior designer
- Construction manager
- Financial accountant
- Purchasing agent
- Telecommunications manager
- Building manager (not shown on the organizational charts)

External firms

- Realty
- Relocation
- Architect
- Interior design
- Electrical engineer
- Mechanical engineer
- Structural engineer
- Construction
- Telecommunications
- Subcontractors

Organizational structural

All combinations of organizational structure are possible. You may find that one structure works well on smaller projects while another approach works well on larger projects. If you are not sure, try one of the approaches and see how it works out for you. Below are four major approaches. In reality, there are over a dozen equally valid organizational structures.

Management by in-house staff. Under this approach, each in-house discipline is responsible for managing any and all external consultants under its expertise. In all cases the in-house staff reports to the team leader, the project manager. All the in-house staff shown on the same line as the project manager may be "equal" or they may report to the project manager. Figure 1.3 is one example of an in-house organizational chart.

Management by lead professional firm. Each professional firm is hired by or reports through a designated lead professional firm. This ap-

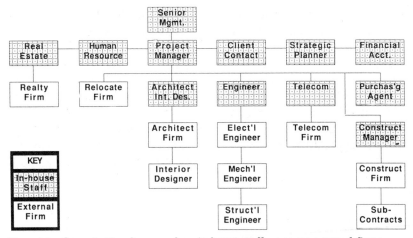

Figure 1.3 Organizational approaches: in-house staff manages external firms.

proach leads to as many variations as there are firms. If the external architect is the lead firm, engineers and contractors all report through the architect. If the electrical engineer is the lead firm, other firms report through the engineer. Figure 1.4 is an example of when construction is the lead firm.

The design-build organization. Under the design-build approach, a professional firm combines all or many of the disciplines within one company. The firm usually offers architecture, engineering, telecommunications, and construction and also hires the subcontractors. At the

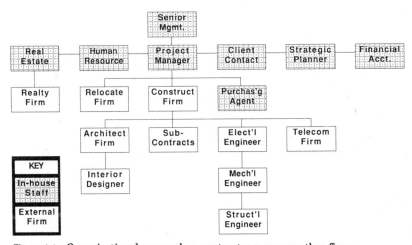

Figure 1.4 Organizational approaches: contractor manages other firms.

client's discretion, the firm may do all the purchasing for the project. Figure 1.5 is an example of a design-build organization.

The joint venture. In a joint venture, the client retains two large firms to split responsibilities. The two firms manage all disciplines within the project and serve as a check and balance on each other. Half of the venture usually includes architectural and engineering disciplines. The other half usually includes construction, purchasing, and communications. Figure 1.6 is an example of a joint venture organization between construction and architectural-engineering (A/E).

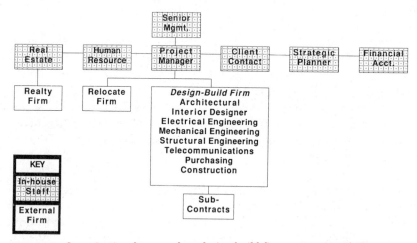

Figure 1.5 Organizational approaches: design-build firm manages project.

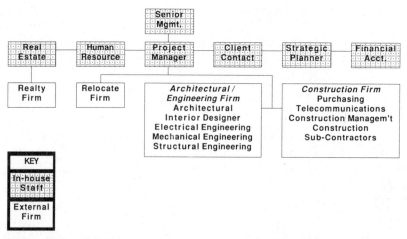

Figure 1.6 Organizational approaches: joint-venture partnership manages project.

Understanding the Need for a Facility Organization

In-house staff versus external consultants

All facility professionals face the dilemma of staffing internally for the peaks, valleys, or in-betweens of corporate facility work. There is no question that an in-house facility professional reading this book will see the merits of the facility management disciplines being performed by in-house staff. Similarly, a consultant reading this book will see the merits of keeping the in-house staff small and maximizing the use of external staff.

No sense seeking to solve this "chicken and egg" type of problem. Instead, a clear statement of the advantages and disadvantages of each approach is called for. The best method to analyze the cost effectiveness of in-house staff versus external consultants is a *proficiency plan,* which couples productivity and costs with revisions and anticipated workload.

A proficiency plan for the architectural and interior design disciplines is presented below. My earlier book, *Corporate Facility Planning,* outlines the steps to follow for determining whether to utilize computer-assisted drafting (CAD) if you maintain in-house staff. Note that the analysis involves two sets of factors: financial and qualitative.

The same analysis may be utilized for any other service, including real estate, space planning, project management, engineering, purchasing, construction management, and building management. In these cases, additional questions as to corporate financial integrity are appropriate.

In-house architectural design staff

Financial considerations

- Assuming the salary rates are the same for both external and in-house employees, in-house staff salary may be multiplied by fixed overhead (about 20 percent) and Yourco benefits (in this sample at 30 percent). These are additive, totaling a salary factor of 1.5.
- Salary paid is an annual expense for Yourco.
- Salary invariably increases through normal raises.
- Salary is paid whether the corporate workload is high or low.
- Generally the total employee expense base may be subtracted from gross revenues for tax purposes.

- The higher the payroll, the lower the bottom line.
- Overall cash outlay is lower.

Qualitative considerations

- Quicker turnaround to start a project
- Project start-up not subject to consultant's workload
- Quality control improved with direct supervision
- Workload balancing faster
- Quicker response to emergency or special projects
- No contracts, invoicing, or vouchers required
- Not reliant on external market conditions

External architectural design consultants

Financial considerations

- External staff's base salary is multiplied by a factor of about 3.25. (See Chapter 3 for a fuller explanation.)
- Factor includes consultants' actual salary costs, fixed overhead, benefits, and profit.
- Yourco incurs expenses only when work is to be performed.
- Peaks and valleys in workload are nullified.
- Yourco may capitalize (depreciate) consultant expenses over the project's life.
- Corporate building, depreciable life is up to 50 years (one-fiftieth of the expense to be deducted from gross revenues).
- Interior renovation, depreciable life is generally 10 years (one-tenth of the expense to be deducted from gross revenues).
- The lower the expenses, the higher the bottom line.

Qualitative considerations

- Scheduling is not a problem when more than one firm is used.
- Consultants are called in only when needed.
- Need for in-house quarterly staff reviews is eliminated.
- Sick leave and vacation downtime for in-house staff are avoided.
- Minimum number of in-house staff is required regardless of workload.

- Professional staff is managed by full-time professionals.

- Engineering may require minimum staffing for specialty work (mechanical, electrical, plumbing, structural).

In-house proficiency plan

How many in-house staffers do you need to accomplish the work?

How much work do you have?

How do you equate varying projects—by dollar volume, complexity, size?

How do you factor in revisions?

The proficiency plan is an analytical method of determining the average number of staff workdays required over a fixed period of time for the anticipated project. This plan will reflect how many staff members will be required and the cost to Yourco. The workload projection may be used to calculate the same cost if external consultants were utilized.

Assumptions

Definitions of work

- All calculations will be based on design work and in usable square feet.

- Feasibility: planning studies, block allocations, and preliminary layout and design.

- Schematic design: furniture, equipment and partition plans.

- Design development: color schemes, furniture selection, fabrics and finishes.

- Contract documents: detailed specifications including demolition and construction plans, telephone and electric plans, reflected ceiling plans, finish plans, elevations and detailing plans, furniture placement and move plans.

- Other project work, including supervision to be performed by facility, project, and/or construction managers.

- A workday is one individual working 7.5 hours a day and excludes lunch.

Required analyses

- Revision rate and drafting speed

- Workload forecast
- Workday analysis and consultant costs
- New hires analysis
- In-house versus external consultants

Revision rate and drafting speed (Table 1.1)

Revision rate. The revision rate is the percentage of change experienced during each phase of a project. To arrive at an average rate, Yourco experience and those of three external consultants were solicited.

Drafting speed. The drafting speed is the rate at which a draftsperson can draw during each phase of work. Productivity is measured in usable square feet of drawing produced. To arrive at an average speed, Yourco experience plus those of three external consultants were solicited.

Workload forecast (Table 1.2)

Square-foot projects. Projects are listed by location and usable square feet. They include all projects planned and/or estimated during the next time period (two years in this sample).

Workday projects. Projects not measurable in usable square feet are listed separately. These projects require your best estimate for workdays to accomplish.

Workday analysis and consultant costs (Table 1.3)

Table 1.3 combines number of usable square feet forecasted (Table 1.2) times revision rate (Table 1.1) divided by drafting speed (Table 1.1). The number of workdays required for the square-foot projects are totaled. Usable square feet are multiplied by the applicable consultant costs to determine external costs for square-foot projects. Workdays are then added to the workday projects (Table 1.2) to arrive at total workdays required. Consultant costs are divided by workdays to arrive at per diem cost, which is applied to workday projects. The average number of workdays per month is also generated from this table.

New hires analysis (Table 1.4)

A detailed analysis is made of all available workdays less non-workdays for existing staff. Productivity rate of performed work is

TABLE 1.1 Proficiency Plan Revision Rate and Drafting Speed

Revision rate	Yourco	Cons. A	Cons. B	Cons. C	Mean rate	Average rate
Feasibility	75%	85%	100%	95%	88.8%	90%
Schematic	35%	40%	30%	25%	33%	33%
Design development	25%	30%	30%	35%	30%	30%
Contract documents	20%	15%	25%	20%	20%	20%
			Drafting Speed			
Feasibility	5000	5000	6000	6000	5500	5500
Schematic	4000	4500	5000	5000	4625	4600
Design development	3000	3000	1800	2000	2450	2500
Contract documents	1500	1000	750	1250	1125	1100
Cost of service	TBD	$3.00	$4.00	$3.50	$3.50	$3.50
			Definitions			

Revision rate   Percentage of change experienced during a particular phase
Drafting speed   Measured in usable square feet produced per workday

TABLE 1.2 Proficiency Plan Workload Forecast

Square-Foot Projects

Next 2 years	Projects	Design usable square footage projections			
		Feasibility	Schematic	Design dev.	Contract
Building 1	55	600,000	500,000	450,000	450,000
Building 2	31	300,000	250,000	225,000	225,000
Building 3	3	50,000	50,000	50,000	50,000
Building 4	10	45,000	45,000	45,000	45,000
Building 5 (new)	1	450,000	450,000	450,000	450,000
Total	100	1,445,000	1,295,000	1,220,000	1,220,000

Work Day Projects

	Work days
Asbestos abatement	325
Sprinkler project	275
Master space plan	225
Telephone system	175
Landscaping upgrade	125
New space standards	75
Total	1,200

Definitions

No. of projects	Compile list of all known capital and expense projects
Phases	Not all projects require work in each phase

TABLE 1.3 Proficiency Plan Workday Analysis and Consultant Costs

			Work days and consultant cost analysis			
	Usable square feet (Column A)	Revision rate (Column B)	Total usable square feet (Col. A × B = C)	Design speed per work day (Column D)	Work days required (Col. C ÷ D = E)	Actual rate (Column F)	Consultant cost (Col. A × F = G)
Feasibility	1,445,000	1.9	2,745,500	5500	499	$0.35	$ 505,750
Schematic	1,295,000	1.33	1,722,350	4600	374	$0.88	$1,133,125
Design devel.	1,220,000	1.3	1,586,000	2500	634	$0.53	$ 640,500
Contract doc.	1,220,000	1.2	1,464,000	1100	1331	$1.75	$2,135,000
Total					2838	$3.50	$4,414,375
Consultant per diem					4,414,375 ÷ 2,838 =		$1,555

		Workdays required			
	Work days	Per diem	Months	Average monthly demand	Consultant expense
Square-foot projects*	2838	N/A			$4,414,375
Workday projects†	1200	$1555.45			$1,866,543
Total	4038		24	168 Work Days	$6,280,918

*Square-foot projects: From analysis above.
†Workday projects: From workload forecast.

TABLE 1.4 Proficiency Plan New Hires Analysis

	Workdays (Column A)	Existing staff (Column B)	Available workdays (Cols. A × B = C)	Nonproductive days — Vacation (Column D)	Sick (Column E)	Other (Column F)	Net available workdays (Cols. C − D − E − F = G)	Productivity @95% (Col. G × 0.95 = H)	Performance criteria (Cols. H + B = I)	Avg. monthly demand (Column J)	Demand (O)/U productivity (Cols. J − H = K)	New hires required (Cols. K + I = L)
Year 1												
January	21	3	63	0	2	0	61	58	19	168	110	5.70
February	18	3	54	10	1	1	42	40	13	168	128	9.63
March	23	3	69	5	2	0	62	59	20	168	109	5.56
April	20	3	60	0	1	1	58	55	18	168	113	6.15
May	22	3	66	0	2	0	64	61	20	168	107	5.29
June	22	3	66	5	1	1	59	56	19	168	112	5.99
July	20	3	60	0	1	1	58	55	18	168	113	6.15
August	23	3	69	10	2	0	57	54	18	168	114	6.31
September	20	3	60	5	1	1	53	50	17	168	118	7.01
October	21	3	63	0	2	0	61	58	19	168	110	5.70
November	20	3	60	0	1	1	58	55	18	168	113	6.15
December	20	3	60	10	2	0	48	46	15	168	122	8.05
Total	250	36	750	45	18	6	681	647	214	2016	1369	6.40
Year 2												
January	22	3	66	5	1	1	59	56	19	168	112	5.99
February	18	3	54	10	2	0	42	40	13	168	128	9.63
March	22	3	66	0	1	0	65	62	21	168	106	5.16
April	21	3	63	0	2	1	60	57	19	168	111	5.84
May	22	3	66	0	1	0	65	62	21	168	106	5.16
June	21	3	63	10	2	0	51	48	16	168	120	7.40
July	21	3	63	10	1	1	51	48	16	168	120	7.40
August	23	3	69	5	2	0	62	59	20	168	109	5.56
September	19	3	57	0	1	1	55	52	17	168	116	5.65
October	22	3	66	0	2	0	64	61	20	168	107	5.29
November	19	3	57	5	1	1	50	48	16	168	121	7.61
December	20	3	60	0	2	1	57	54	18	168	114	6.31
Total	250	36	750	45	18	6	681	647	216	2016	1369	6.34*

Definitions

Workdays: Excludes 10 legal holidays

Nonworking time: 15 days vacation, 6 sick days, 2 other non-work days per employee

*Two Year Average Need 6.37 Workers, say, 6 New Hires

TABLE 1.5 Proficiency Plan Final Cost Comparison: In-house versus External Consultants

New hires required	Quantity (Column A)	Actual salary (Column B)	Overhead @0.20 (Col. A × 0.2 = C)	Benefits @0.30 (Col. A × 0.3 = D)	Compensation package (Cols. B + C + D = E)	Total compensation (Cols. A × E = F)
			Year 1: Start January 2			
Chief architect	1	$45,000	$9,000	$13,500	$67,500	$ 67,500
Job captain	1	$40,000	$8,000	$12,000	$60,000	$ 60,000
Draftsperson	4	$30,000	$6,000	$ 9,000	$45,000	$ 180,000
Total year 1	6					$ 307,500
			Year 2: Assume 5% Increase			
Chief architect	1	$47,250	$9,450	$14,175	$70,875	$ 70,875
Job captain	1	$42,000	$8,400	$12,600	$63,000	$ 63,000
Draftsperson	4	$31,500	$6,300	$ 9,450	$47,250	$ 189,000
Total year 2	6					$ 322,875
New hires two-year cost						$ 630,375
Consultant expenses						$6,280,918
Two-year cost (10-year depreciable life)						$1,256,184

95 percent. (See productivity discussion below.) Actual work performed is deducted from average monthly demand to arrive at the shortfall of workdays to be performed. The shortfall is divided by average actual workdays to arrive at the number of new hires required per month. From this, a two-year average of new hires is determined.

Cost comparison: in-house versus external consultants (Table 1.5)

The final cost comparison requires a decision on which levels of individuals will perform the work. In this sample, a chief architect, job captain, and four draftspersons are selected, with a starting salary estimated for each one. (See Chapter 4 for sample salaries.)

The complete compensation package is determined and totaled for a two-year period. Two-year consultant costs are 20 percent of the total cash outlay and are assumed to be depreciated over ten years. In-house costs are compared with consultant costs for the same two-year period.

And the answer is...
Financial considerations

- In-house staff costs are $630,375.
- Total consultant costs are $6,280,918.
- Since consultant costs are usually written off over a ten-year period, the two-year consultant cost is $1,256,184.
- There is no question that in-house staff costs less, initially.

Qualitative considerations. *No more work?*

- In-house staff will be released (fired).
- Severance costs are not included in the analysis.

More work than anticipated?

- External consultants will still be needed.
- Clearly, in-house management carries potential risks and explanations for your inaccurate forecast of work.

Productivity. Do you feel that a 95 percent productivity rate is too high? According to a *New York Times* survey in July 1991, engineers estimated that the true engineering portion of their work accounted for under 20 percent of their time. The unproductive time covered paperwork, meetings, and other administrative duties.

If the productivity rate were lowered to only 20 percent in the new hires analysis (Table 1.4), the number of new hires would grow from 6 to 42—and Yourco costs would leap from $630,375 to $4,043,625 for the two-year period. If your productivity rate was that far off in your estimate, you are clearly not managing well.

Unsuccessful managers should read about headhunters in Chapter 4.

Case work study: organizing your workload

Yourco Information. At Yourco, directors are authorized to sign for projects up to $250,000. Projects over $750,000 require senior management concurrence.

You assign new work to your next available staff member.

- With projects under $300,000, you prefer to manage with in-house staff.
- With projects around $750,000, you prefer to manage with the architect or engineer as lead professional firm.
- With projects over $1,000,000, you prefer to manage with a design-build firm.

Credit is the most active division at Yourco. Over the last six weeks, the credit division director has sent you three project requests at exactly $250,000 each. Today, the fourth credit division project, also for $250,000, arrives on your desk. You believe these requests are really one massive project. The credit director appears to be circumventing Yourco's approval process.

Among the alternatives to be considered

- Continue working on four properly authorized projects with an in-house staff approach on all four.
- Change your organizational approach on three recent projects to effect economic savings and tie together with the fourth project.
- Refuse to proceed until the credit director gets approval from senior management for the full $1 million.

What is your recommendation?

Discussion. What annoys you the most? Is it that the credit director appears to be getting around Yourco's policy? Is it that you would have just one project manager handling a massive project instead of tying up several staff? Is it that you would have preferred managing a design-build firm in lieu of bidding out four smaller projects?

Continue working. Quick business changes, reorganizations, new client needs—all these things happen. Perhaps the credit director just didn't realize the extent of all the changes. In any case, it counts as four projects on your list of things to do. Moreover, work has been slow, and smaller projects keep several staff members busy. Finally, since the director can properly sign for up to $250,000, there is no question of violation of Yourco policies.

Change your organizational approach. You look forward to an opportunity to go with a design-build organizational approach. Stopping the bidding and going with one firm should make things easier. Of course, you'll have to find work for the extra staff not required to handle the canceled smaller projects. But Yourco should save money by leveraging its purchasing power.

Handle as one major $1 million project using the four $250,000 project authorizations, there is no need to wait for senior management approval.

Refuse to proceed. You are convinced that this is a subterfuge by the credit division director. You have a fiduciary interest to Yourco to ensure proper facility expenditures. You also feel it is not a good idea to have several different staff members working on projects in the same division. You'll reorganize assignments if and when the credit division gets senior management approval.

Analysis

Those who selected continuing working. Yourco must have a high level of unbudgeted projects. This is simply business as usual. As a manager, you are probably reactive: You handle work as it comes in and don't want to create waves. You also feel "it's not my job" to question such multiple authorizations.

✔ This is correct for organizations that are transactional in lieu of entrepreneurial.

✔ This may be correct in health care organizations and government agencies.

Those who selected changing your organizational approach. Why should the credit division upset the way you run your projects? A slight delay now in the first few projects will result in some additional cost savings overall. Some of your staff will be upset at "losing" a project, but others will be pleased with increased responsibilities.

✔ This is correct when Yourco facility management "holds" the costs for renovation in lieu of charging back costs to the credit division.

✔ This is correct when each division is entrepreneurial and does what is best for itself.

Those who selected refusing to proceed.   You have seen this a hundred times: Divide up the work to avoid the longer approval process. You feel that it is more impressive to manage a "super-project," and that a series of small projects in the same division is not a good use of staff or of Yourco funds. You will probably reorganize and continue bidding while seeking proper authorization.

✔ This is correct for cost-conscious organizations.

✔ This is correct for proactive facility managers.

Roles and Responsibilities of the Asset Manager

Each project phase requires Yourco team members to be responsible (usually one individual), to approve the transactions (usually one or two individuals), and to participate in achieving the objective of the phase (as many individuals as required).

Figure 1.7 highlights the key team members' roles and responsibilities during the life cycle of a project.

Key team members

Key team members include senior management, business management, and facility management.

Senior management

- Senior manager

Business management

- Client contact (user)
- Relocation specialist
- Human resources

Objective	Senior Manager	Client Contact	Real Estate	Strategic Planner	Project Manager	Designer Engineer	Purchasing Agent
Strategic Plan	APPROVE	PARTICIPATE	PARTICIPATE	RESPONSIBLE	PARTICIPATE		
Tactical Plan	APPROVE	APPROVE	PARTICIPATE	RESPONSIBLE	PARTICIPATE	PARTICIPATE	PARTICIPATE
Organization	APPROVE	PARTICIPATE	PARTICIPATE	PARTICIPATE	RESPONSIBLE		
Pre-Occupancy Evaluation	APPROVE	PARTICIPATE			RESPONSIBLE		
Needs Analysis		APPROVE		PARTICIPATE	RESPONSIBLE	PARTICIPATE	PARTICIPATE
Existing Facilities		APPROVE	PARTICIPATE	PARTICIPATE	RESPONSIBLE	PARTICIPATE	
New Facilities		PARTICIPATE	APPROVE	RESPONSIBLE	PARTICIPATE	PARTICIPATE	
Site Selection	APPROVE	PARTICIPATE	RESPONSIBLE	PARTICIPATE	PARTICIPATE	PARTICIPATE	
Labor Market		APPROVE			PARTICIPATE		
Programming		APPROVE			RESPONSIBLE	PARTICIPATE	PARTICIPATE
Master Space Planning	APPROVE	PARTICIPATE	PARTICIPATE	RESPONSIBLE	PARTICIPATE	PARTICIPATE	
Employee Skills Assessment		RESPONSIBLE					
Policy Development	APPROVE	PARTICIPATE	PARTICIPATE	PARTICIPATE	PARTICIPATE		PARTICIPATE
Communications	APPROVE	PARTICIPATE		PARTICIPATE	PARTICIPATE		
Financial Analyses	APPROVE	PARTICIPATE	PARTICIPATE	PARTICIPATE	PARTICIPATE	PARTICIPATE	PARTICIPATE
Counseling/Training	APPROVE	PARTICIPATE					
Selling Management/Approval	APPROVE	RESPONSIBLE	PARTICIPATE	RESPONSIBLE	RESPONSIBLE		
Planning		PARTICIPATE	PARTICIPATE	RESPONSIBLE	PARTICIPATE	PARTICIPATE	PARTICIPATE
Hiring Professional Team		PARTICIPATE	PARTICIPATE	PARTICIPATE	RESPONSIBLE	PARTICIPATE	PARTICIPATE
Design/Engineering		PARTICIPATE			APPROVE	RESPONSIBLE	PARTICIPATE
Estimating		PARTICIPATE	PARTICIPATE		APPROVE	PARTICIPATE	RESPONSIBLE
Request for Proposals			PARTICIPATE		APPROVE		RESPONSIBLE
Bidding		PARTICIPATE	PARTICIPATE		APPROVE		RESPONSIBLE
Negotiating/Awarding Contracts					APPROVE		RESPONSIBLE
Construction Process		PARTICIPATE			APPROVE	PARTICIPATE	RESPONSIBLE
Interior Furnishings		PARTICIPATE			APPROVE	PARTICIPATE	RESPONSIBLE
Punchlist		PARTICIPATE			APPROVE	PARTICIPATE	PARTICIPATE
Relocation and Occupancy		PARTICIPATE		PARTICIPATE	APPROVE	PARTICIPATE	PARTICIPATE
Project Close-Out		APPROVE			RESPONSIBLE	PARTICIPATE	PARTICIPATE
Financial Closing		PARTICIPATE			APPROVE	PARTICIPATE	PARTICIPATE
Post-Occupancy Evaluation	APPROVE	PARTICIPATE			PARTICIPATE		
Maintenance and Operations		PARTICIPATE			APPROVE		
Preventive Facility Management		PARTICIPATE			RESPONSIBLE		
Starting All Over	APPROVE	PARTICIPATE	PARTICIPATE	RESPONSIBLE	PARTICIPATE		

Figure 1.7 Roles and responsibilities of key team players.

Facility management

- Real estate
- Strategic planner
- Project/asset manager
- Designer/engineer
- Purchasing agent
- Construction manager
- Telecommunications manager
- Financial analyst
- Building manager

The project life cycle
Be a planner
- Strategic plan–business plan

Objective	Construction Manager	Telecom Manager	Financial Analyst	Relocation Specialist	Human Resources	Building Manager
Strategic Plan			PARTICIPATE		PARTICIPATE	
Tactical Plan	PARTICIPATE	PARTICIPATE	PARTICIPATE	PARTICIPATE	PARTICIPATE	PARTICIPATE
Organization					PARTICIPATE	
Pre-Occupancy Evaluation					PARTICIPATE	
Needs Analysis	PARTICIPATE	PARTICIPATE		PARTICIPATE	PARTICIPATE	PARTICIPATE
Existing Facilities			PARTICIPATE	PARTICIPATE	PARTICIPATE	PARTICIPATE
New Facilities	PARTICIPATE	PARTICIPATE	PARTICIPATE	PARTICIPATE	PARTICIPATE	PARTICIPATE
Site Selection			PARTICIPATE	PARTICIPATE	PARTICIPATE	PARTICIPATE
Labor Market			PARTICIPATE	PARTICIPATE	RESPONSIBLE	
Programming		PARTICIPATE		PARTICIPATE	PARTICIPATE	
Master Space Planning			PARTICIPATE	PARTICIPATE	PARTICIPATE	
Employee Skills Assessment					APPROVE	
Policy Development	PARTICIPATE		PARTICIPATE		RESPONSIBLE	
Communications				PARTICIPATE	RESPONSIBLE	
Financial Analyses	PARTICIPATE	PARTICIPATE	RESPONSIBLE	PARTICIPATE	PARTICIPATE	PARTICIPATE
Counseling/Training					RESPONSIBLE	
Selling Management/Approval			PARTICIPATE		PARTICIPATE	
Planning	PARTICIPATE	PARTICIPATE	PARTICIPATE	PARTICIPATE	PARTICIPATE	PARTICIPATE
Hiring Professional Team	PARTICIPATE	PARTICIPATE	PARTICIPATE	PARTICIPATE		
Design/Engineering	PARTICIPATE	PARTICIPATE	PARTICIPATE	PARTICIPATE		
Estimating	PARTICIPATE	PARTICIPATE	PARTICIPATE	PARTICIPATE		PARTICIPATE
Request for Proposals	RESPONSIBLE	RESPONSIBLE	PARTICIPATE	PARTICIPATE	PARTICIPATE	PARTICIPATE
Bidding	RESPONSIBLE	RESPONSIBLE	PARTICIPATE	PARTICIPATE		PARTICIPATE
Negotiating/Awarding Contracts	RESPONSIBLE	RESPONSIBLE	PARTICIPATE			PARTICIPATE
Construction Process	RESPONSIBLE	RESPONSIBLE	PARTICIPATE	PARTICIPATE		PARTICIPATE
Interior Furnishings			PARTICIPATE			
Punchlist	PARTICIPATE	PARTICIPATE	PARTICIPATE	PARTICIPATE	PARTICIPATE	PARTICIPATE
Relocation and Occupancy	PARTICIPATE	PARTICIPATE	PARTICIPATE	RESPONSIBLE	PARTICIPATE	PARTICIPATE
Project Close-Out	PARTICIPATE	PARTICIPATE	PARTICIPATE	PARTICIPATE	PARTICIPATE	PARTICIPATE
Financial Closing	PARTICIPATE	PARTICIPATE	RESPONSIBLE	PARTICIPATE	PARTICIPATE	PARTICIPATE
Post-Occupancy Evaluation				RESPONSIBLE		
Maintenance and Operations						RESPONSIBLE
Preventive Facility Management						PARTICIPATE
Starting All Over			PARTICIPATE		PARTICIPATE	

Figure 1.7 (*Continued*)

- Tactical plan–facility plan
- Organizational-approach to manage project
- Preoccupancy evaluation—survey of existing employee opinions
- Needs analysis—initial analysis of project scope
- Existing facilities—survey of conditions
- New facilities—survey of future buildings
- Site selection—survey of future sites
- Labor market—in new location
- Programming—staff projections
- Master space planning—space assignments, stacking
- Employee skills assessment—which staff should relocate
- Policy development—changes in hours, working policies
- Communications—inform staff of ongoing process
- Financial analyses—what is financial impact on Yourco

- Counseling/training staff for new assignments

Be a provider

- Selling management/approval—go versus no go
- Planning—start implementation process
- Hiring professional team—combination of in-house staff and external consultants
- Design/engineering—actual design
- Estimating—comparing design with original budget
- Request for proposals—outline of needs
- Bidding—securing actual prices
- Negotiating/awarding contracts—selecting best firm and price
- Construction process—build out
- Interior furnishings—installation
- Punchlist—checking for missing, damaged, or poorly installed items
- Relocation and occupancy—move-in
- Project closeout—installation and completion of outstanding items
- Financial closing—no more expenditures allowed

Be proactive

- Postoccupancy evaluation—survey staff reaction to new site
- Maintenance and operations—maintain facility in same condition as move in
- Preventive facility management—invest in small costs each year to avoid higher costs in the future
- Starting all over—expansion and contraction require relocation sooner or later

Viewpoints

Team members have occasionally expressed their viewpoints on achieving their objectives during each phase. My own observations and those of my colleagues suggest a number of oft-repeated views. The comments of senior management, business management, and facility management are captured in Figures 1.8 to 1.10.

Activity	Senior Management
Strategic Plan	Good to have
Tactical Plan	Keep it on schedule and budget
Organization	Let the business managers decide
Pre-Occupancy Evaluation	Don't upset the employees
Needs Analysis	Let the business managers decide
Existing Facilities	We have that many sites?
New Facilities	I do want to limit my travel time
Site Selection	I do want to limit my travel time
Labor Market	Human resources will handle this
Programming	What channel?
Master Space Planning	Get a top notch firm
Employee Skills Assessment	Human resources will handle this
Policy Development	Let the business managers decide
Communications	Get a top notch firm
Financial Analyses	That's why we have a CFO
Counseling/Training	Human resources will handle this
Selling Management/Approval	I am not spending too much this year
Planning	Let the business managers decide
Hiring Professional Team	Get a top notch firm
Design/Engineering	Get a top notch firm
Estimating	I am not spending too much this year
Request for Proposals	Why am I getting vendor complaints?
Bidding	Why am I getting vendor complaints?
Negotiating/Awarding Contracts	Why am I getting vendor complaints?
Construction Process	I approved that a long time ago
Interior Furnishings	Make sure I get the cherry wood
Punchlist	Punch who?
Relocation and Occupancy	Tell me when it's over
Project Close-Out	They moved already
Financial Closing	I didn't approve that much
Post-Occupancy Evaluation	They're happy, why bother?
Maintenance and Operations	Too much dust
Preventive Facility Management	Defer that expense till next year
Starting All Over	Never again

Figure 1.8 Strategic plan viewpoints senior management.

Time management

Playing telephone tag. Visitors to my office state that they are impressed with how well organized I am. Yet I feel I still have a long way to go. My files are down to four drawers from eight; and further reductions are planned.

My telephone messages are in a neat little holder. I still return every call I receive. I would rather spend a few minutes in a straightforward discussion with a vendor on my reasons for not using its services now than be swamped by endless follow-up calls. My colleagues who claim that sooner or later the vendor "gets the message" miss an im-

Activity	Business Management
Strategic Plan	I'll assign a junior officer
Tactical Plan	Not against my department
Organization	I make the most PCE, I'll head it
Pre-Occupancy Evaluation	I'll assign a junior officer
Needs Analysis	I'll decide this
Existing Facilities	I never liked my space
New Facilities	I do want to limit my travel time
Site Selection	I do want to limit my travel time
Labor Market	Human resources doesn't understand
Programming	I'll assign a junior officer
Master Space Planning	View and higher floors for us
Employee Skills Assessment	I'll decide this
Policy Development	I'll decide this
Communications	I'll assign a junior officer
Financial Analyses	The CFO rigs the numbers
Counseling/Training	I'll assign a junior officer
Selling Management/Approval	Not my job
Planning	I'll assign a junior officer
Hiring Professional Team	Get a top notch firm
Design/Engineering	Get a top notch firm
Estimating	Not against my department
Request for Proposals	Why am I getting vendor complaints?
Bidding	Why am I getting vendor complaints?
Negotiating/Awarding Contracts	Why am I getting vendor complaints?
Construction Process	They'll never make it
Interior Furnishings	Make mine like senior management's
Punchlist	Can't we move, it looks done
Relocation and Occupancy	I can't move this week
Project Close-Out	Don't have the time to go over the list
Financial Closing	Not against my department
Post-Occupancy Evaluation	I'll assign a junior officer
Maintenance and Operations	Too much dust
Preventive Facility Management	Not against my department
Starting All Over	Never again

Figure 1.9 Strategic plan viewpoints business management.

portant one themselves. All those follow-up calls tie up a key member of your team—your secretary.

A well-educated secretary can not only screen your calls but give a polite reply when the vendor does follow up. In addition, your secretary can redirect calls that belong elsewhere among your staff. By returning my own calls, I free up my secretary for other duties.

The best time-saving device for returning calls is to bunch together nonemergency calls for a free period and return all the calls at once—for example, during the hour before or after lunch. I always try to leave a message why I am calling when I call, and ask that you spread this advice. Too many callers refuse to heed a secretary's advice to leave a message. Doing so is a real time saver.

Activity	Facility Management
Strategic Plan	Essential to have
Tactical Plan	Not enough money
Organization	I am the team leader
Pre-Occupancy Evaluation	I can do this myself
Needs Analysis	I can't believe the business manager
Existing Facilities	Piece of cake-it's in the PC
New Facilities	Time for a demographic study
Site Selection	Need an environmental impact study
Labor Market	Call the chamber of commerce
Programming	I can do this myself
Master Space Planning	I can do this myself
Employee Skills Assessment	This is not mine
Policy Development	I can do this myself
Communications	I can do this myself
Financial Analyses	Let's do NPV
Counseling/Training	Get a top notch firm
Selling Management/Approval	I read Binder's book
Planning	I can do this myself
Hiring Professional Team	Get a top notch firm at low price
Design/Engineering	Get a top notch firm at low price
Estimating	I can do this myself
Request for Proposals	I need to limit the RFP list
Bidding	I need to limit the bid list
Negotiating/Awarding Contracts	But it's a quality firm and low bid
Construction Process	Who selected this firm?
Interior Furnishings	But it's a quality firm and low bid
Punchlist	Patience, patience
Relocation and Occupancy	Patience, patience
Project Close-Out	Patience, patience
Financial Closing	The CFO rigs the numbers
Post-Occupancy Evaluation	I can do this myself
Maintenance and Operations	Not enough money
Preventive Facility Management	Not enough money
Starting All Over	I knew we needed more space

Figure 1.10   Strategic plan viewpoints facilities management.

Finding the business card

I quickly found that a rotary card file was impossible to maintain. I started my own unique business card file in 1981, and it is still growing. I have a three-ring binder with 8½" × 11" clear plastic sheets. Each page holds 20 cards. I file cards alphabetically by name. An alternative is to maintain cards by business. I date-stamp the back of each card when it is received to recall when I first met the individual. When I get a card through the mail, I mark the back accordingly.

Every few years, I read through my file and cull out outdated cards or cards of no further interest to me. The binder sits on my bookshelf, takes up minimal space, and serves as a readily available telephone and reference book.

Finding the right action words to use

One of the frustrations that asset and facility managers face is coming up with the right words—in particular, with the words that best describe an activity in a short, succinct phrase. To save you time in the future, I have compiled almost every combination of words we use in Figure 1.11. By selecting a word at random from each column, you can create your own asset management jargon.

Responding to complaints and compliments

In a calendar that features a new fact or word each day, I discovered the astonishing truth regarding memoranda. The average memorandum takes 54 minutes to plan, write, and revise. In fact, it is actually rewritten 4.2 times before it's sent. And the memorandum costs over $65. The apparent message is: Do not bother to write memoranda.

	Column 1		Column 2		Column 3
A	SYSTEMIZED	A	TECHNOLOGY	A	GUIDELINES
B	PLANNED	B	SPACE	B	UTILIZATION
C	UNREALIZED	C	ADMINISTRATIVE	C	NEEDS
D	PHYSICAL	D	BUILDING	D	CONTROLS
E	SEGREGATED	E	LOCATION	E	REQUIREMENTS
F	FUNCTIONAL	F	DEMONSTRATIVE	F	CHARGES
G	BALANCED	G	OPERATIONAL	G	CRITERIA
H	PRE-DETERMINED	H	OCCUPANCY	H	ALLOCATIONS
I	DESIGNATED	I	AREA	I	STANDARDS
K	ALLOWABLE	K	DEFINITIVE	K	PROJECTIONS
L	CONCEPTUAL	L	EQUIVALENCY	L	DISPOSITION
M	DELINEATED	M	POTENTIAL	M	ACCESSIBILITY

INSTRUCTIONS:
1. SELECT ANY THREE LETTERS (A THROUGH M)
2. MATCH WORDS OPPOSITE LETTERS IN EACH COLUMN
3. YOU HAVE CREATED YOUR OWN JARGON
I.E., THIS CHART'S TITLE IS:

| A | A | A |
| SYSTEMIZED | TECHNOLOGY | GUIDELINES |

Figure 1.11 Systemized technology guidelines.

But everything you will find in this book confirms just the opposite. That is, you really do need to put things in writing: your strategic and tactical plans, agreements and contracts, and understandings reached between yourself and your client. Therefore, the answer is to reduce the time you spend (54 minutes) in preparing such memoranda. One solution is to use a stock of standard response letters, paragraphs, and clauses. Why reinvent the wheel each time?

One of my colleagues in another corporation has it down to a science. He gives instructions to his secretary in an acronym: STSORJ (Send The Same Old Response, Joanne). This is just one of several prepared responses designed to instantly turn down a vendor, job applicant, or real estate broker.

Of course, each strategic plan or project has variables that appear not to lend themselves to routine responses. Step back and try to analyze the root of the situation. I believe you will discover a constant theme. In most cases, misunderstandings are due to lack of communication: the failure to alert others to a change. Of course, you need to address the specifics of a complaint or compliment on a case-by-case basis.

The complaint or compliment arrives in any one of several different ways. In all cases, you should follow up with a written response. All too often, what you thought you said in response is not what your client heard. It's a matter of perspective, interpretation, and misunderstanding. And people tend to hear without listening.

The common denominator to a complaint or compliment is the client's feelings that prompted the inquiry. Whether you agree with the client or not, it is still important to respond. You need to acknowledge your receipt of a client's feedback. It is equally important that you examine what caused the complaint or compliment to be made.

You should establish a standard response time, regardless of the level from which the inquiry arrived. If the complaint is from the CEO, you may want to respond sooner. Remember, a standard is only the targeted time.

Client response standards

There are two basic inquiry types: formal and informal. Either type can be transmitted in three ways: written, verbal, and in person. Formal complaints and compliments arrive in a conventional manner. Informal inquiries arrive in a casual way that defies any format.

Figure 1.12 outlines suggested client response standards for formal inquires. Figure 1.13 outlines suggested client response standards for informal inquiries.

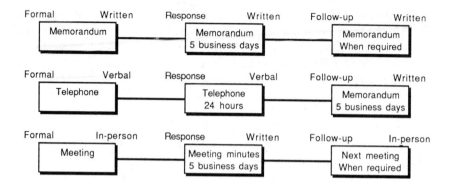

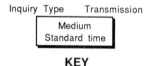

KEY

Figure 1.12   Client response standards formal complaints/compliments.

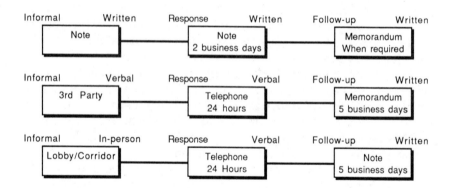

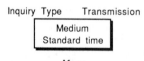

Key

Figure 1.13   Client response standards informal complaints/compliments.

The following sample responses and follow-up messages are designed to add a little variety to your routine correspondence. Rotating the opening, middle, and closing paragraphs will give you about 30 "standard response letters" to choose from.

Sample responses to complaints

Opening paragraphs

- Thank you for writing me regarding your frustration with ___-___ , and for allowing me the opportunity to respond to your inquiry.

- Thank you for taking the time to call our senior vice president, (name), regarding your problem with _____ . I was disappointed to learn of your problem but I am happy to write that it has been resolved.

- Please accept my apologies for the problems you had with _____ . I am pleased to inform you that we have resolved the matter.

Middle paragraphs

- I have researched your problem completely, and can report that we have resolved it as follows: _____ .

- Before I outline the problem's resolution, let me first assure you that it is completely resolved and procedures are in place to ensure it will never occur again.

Closing paragraphs

- I appreciate your bringing the matter to my attention. We pride ourselves on the best possible service. We didn't achieve it this time, but I assure you that truly exceptional service will occur in the months ahead.

- Please do not hesitate to contact me at (telephone number) or at the address indicated above if I can be of service to you again.

Sample responses to compliments

Opening paragraphs

- I appreciate your bringing to my attention the exceptional service which you received from (name). I'm delighted that (first name) handled your transaction in a timely and helpful manner.

- Thank you for the considerate note regarding (name).

- Thank you for taking the time to write your thoughtful letter.

Middle paragraphs

- I will be delighted to forward your kind words to (name).
- (Name)'s dedication is an example of the exceptional service that we strive to achieve.

Closing paragraphs

- Thank you for taking the time to write your thoughtful letter.
- Again, thank you for the considerate note about (name).

Sample follow-up responses

Opening paragraphs

- As a follow-up to my letter of (date), I'm pleased to inform you that we have resolved the matter.
- I wasn't aware of the complexity in resolving the matter when I last wrote you on (date).

Middle paragraphs

- I can now understand your concerns when you first brought the matter to my attention.
- Your apprehension regarding _____ has been satisfactorily resolved by (name) of our staff.

Closing paragraphs

- Thank you for your consideration; and I look forward to seeing you soon.
- Your comments are important to us. Thank you for taking the time to write to us.

2

Decision Taking

Introduction

Globalization (noun)   Making something worldwide in scope or application

Bombay, India

- Present in India's history and future
- Since 1902

Buenos Aires, Argentina

- Present in Argentina's history and future
- Since 1914
- Contributed to the construction of a 3013-square-foot health center in the country's poorest area

London, England

- First bank in Europe to establish an in-house art advisory service for individuals with an active interest in art

Nashville, Tennessee, United States

- $50,000 donated for the construction of an aviary at Grassmere Wildlife Park

São Paulo, Brazil

- Present in Brazil's history and future
- Since 1915

Tokyo, Japan

- Present in Japan's history and future
- Since 1902
- 40 new branches being added to the existing 9 branches
- Membership in a Japanese on-line cash-dispensing network with 20,000 automated teller machines (ATMs)

Worldwide

- In 90 countries
- 20 million customer accounts
- 2200 overseas offices
- 1100 domestic offices and buildings
- Ten percent of all Belgian households bank here
- Five percent of West Germans bank here
- Three percent of British households bank here
- Over 180 years young

What Is the common goal?

This financial institution is positioning itself in today's global marketplace. It is furthering its recognition and reputation as a global financial services company that has been satisfying customer needs since 1812. The scope of services required are enormous when viewed from the facility side.

As an employee of Yourco, your functional title probably is one of the following:

- Facility manager
- Operations manager
- Service manager
- Premises manager
- Real estate manager
- Some other "support-related" adjective

Your career, to date, has been filled with daily administrative tasks—all in the reactive mode:

- The desk drawer doesn't lock.

- The senior vice president's office is too hot.
- Why isn't the sheet-rocking completed?
- The furniture delivery is late.
- My plant is dying.
- Is it too late to change the floor plans?
- No one ever answers my telephone.
- Why don't people return my calls?
- Elevator number two is stuck—again.
- Cleaning got fouled up on the executive floor last night.
- The utility company announced a 6 percent increase, and we didn't budget for it.
- The computer is down.
- I thought you said the check was in the mail.
- I need an office larger than the standard 135 square feet.

With all of these mighty tasks, your days are filled running around. So here is your opportunity to stop. The 1990s are 20 percent over already!

- Time has come for you to be proactive.
- Time has come to transform yourself into an asset manager.
- Time has come to transform yourself into a resource manager.

Be a decision taker

You are the individual responsible for analyzing corporate changes and trends. You are the one who is financially responsible for the facility bottom line. And the facility world you manage is not limited to your building, to your campus/complex, or to your city or state. You are an asset manager in a global marketplace.

Embrace the challenge! Go for it.

As the 1990s approached, the chairman of the financial institution described above cited the corporation's goal: to become the world's first truly global financial institution. At any given time, the corporation's board of directors may include members from Europe, Asia, and the Americas. Shareholders may be from any country. Corporate managers will as likely hold degrees from the University of Turin or São Paulo as they will from Dartmouth or Wellesley.

The stock analysts' reaction to the corporate goal announcement was: "We do not need any more visions of globalization but good ol' nuts-and-bolts implementation."

As a member of the corporate team, I found myself faced with an increase in responsibilities: to track space and manage projects in 60 buildings in New York encompassing 7 million square feet; to review and approve all real estate decisions in North America covering 20 million square feet, with an eye on the balance of our other 2000-plus sites.

The new facility issues facing us—and any global financial institution—in the early 1990s were:

- Does your building in Hong Kong have the approval of the local Fung Shui?

- Do your space plans for Switzerland include mandated bomb shelters in the basement?

- Do your standards in the Middle East include space for prayers or orientation to Mecca?

When we recently introduced new worldwide space guidelines, we tested them first, not in New York, but in Paris. Our guidelines were in square feet and square meters. Next time, they may be in:

tsubo   about 3.3 square meters (used in Japan)

pyong   about 33 square feet (used in Korea)

ping   about 36 square feet (used in Taiwan)

Think globally

What can you expect in the years ahead when managing your corporation's globalization? Among the hot topics this decade is the reduction and, in some cases, the elimination of trade barriers among countries. Consider the following:

1988

- Elections in Canada center on the issue of the Canadian-American trade agreement, which wins overwhelming support from an enlightened voter base.

1989–90

- Eastern European (communist bloc) nations become our newest democracies and potential global markets.

1990

- Group of Seven (United States, Canada, Italy, England, France, Germany, and Japan) reaches an agreement on global trade barriers.
- United States–Japanese trade barriers are being reduced or eliminated.
- Iraq invades Kuwait and is sanctioned by the United Nations.
- United States and its allies send over 550,000 troops to force Iraq back within its own borders.
- France buys the Motel 6 chain.
- East and West Germany merge into one country.

1991

- Nationwide banking restrictions are eased in the United States.
- Does Quebec secede from Canada? (No.)
- The Commonwealth of Independent States is formed, virtually eliminating the old USSR and the Communist party. There are 11 republics, plus three independent Baltic nations and an independent Georgia.

1992

- European Economic Community issues standard measurements and currencies as the major marketplace.

A *Building, Design, and Construction* magazine article entitled "Building Better Is the Challenge of the 1990s" stated that

> the adversarial relationships among building team members have been cited as one reason why designers and contractors are losing work to foreign contractors. Japanese firms are successful due to their strong teamwork and flexibility, trust in other team members, attention to consumer satisfaction, and avoidance of litigation.

Your company will be facing competition from virtually everywhere and anywhere. Your organization must be able to supply its product on a very competitive basis.

What languages do you speak?

- English
- Spanish

- French

- Japanese

In 1990, I spoke at the Canadian Facility Management Conference. Afterward, I tried to use my bank's local automated teller machine. The ATM quickly rejected my card as not compatible with its system.

I have since discovered that within a short period of time, there will be worldwide ATM acceptance. Bank technology staff is working on the software to allow each ATM to "speak" the local language, give customers local currency anywhere, and debit their accounts in their respective countries. The facility staff is working on building the physical data centers to house this technology as well as the basic ATM infrastructure.

At the root of financial costs is the direct overhead for which you bear responsibility in your position. The global asset manager starts by reducing costs or by implementing cost-avoidance techniques. Your value-engineering skills are critical. This is not a question of turf. Your corporation cannot compete if all its services are duplicated.

Take decisions. Coordinate efforts and your company wins. Manage efforts and you win too.

A *New York Times* article (Op-Ed page, June 13, 1990) credits Gregory Staple and Mark Mullins, consultants to the International Institute of Communications in London, with devising a new statistic to measure global communications: MiTTs, or minutes of telecommunication traffic. This includes all voice, facsimile, and data publicly transmitted. Americans lead the way with over 5.3 billion MiTTs annually. However, when measured in MiTTs per 1,000 people, Americans drop to ninth, with about 22,000. Hong Kong leads the world with over 56,000. *The New York Times* states, "In an era of global economic competition, a communication link is an axis of influence."

In this world of instant communication, you must have today's technology in place or you'll never catch up with tomorrow's market. I suggest you start planning for the future through more flexible facilities.

Plan for the unknown

Add relatively inexpensive solutions now to accommodate future changes:

- Extra vertical shafts in that new building for future wiring, chilled water, et cetera

- Raised flooring for maximum flexibility of communications and electrical distribution

- Oversized ducts for heating, ventilation, and air-conditioning changes

- Chilled water availability for the unknown large data center
- Open-plan furniture that responds to changing demographic and ergonomic concerns
- Carpet tiles for quick replacement of soiled or damaged floor covering
- Easy-open ceilings for quick, clean accessibility
- Anything that makes your next churn project easier

In the past, your experience has probably been limited to a region or country. But expect your organization to really become a multi-domiciled set of companies. Managers from other countries will be transferred into your location and vice versa. They carry their local ideas and traditions.

Although the world appears to be moving toward an international language—most likely, English—this trend is not applicable in every location. When planning signage for your corporation's worldwide locations, know that only your logo transcends all languages. Examine all aspects of your management realm and work toward making them global in scope. Yes, your future may include these problems.

- The country head's office is too cold.
- You never answer my E-mail.
- The computer was delivered for the wrong voltage.
- Lift number one is stuck—again.
- Over here, floor one is on the second level.
- The furniture is impounded at the dock.
- I need an office larger than the standard four *pyongs*.

On the other hand the world is really at your desk. Don't wait until it's too late. Plan ahead. Use all your international contacts for information and review management styles and techniques, foreign trends and customs.

Find out about the Fung Shui now. Read all about it.

Time magazine in July 1991 ran an article on the inevitability of global banking. The article estimated that the financial institution described above has spent at least $1.3 billion on computer and telecommunications in the last five years. This expenditure has helped maintain the bank as the world's top dealer in foreign currencies.

Guess what? The bank's facility staff is one of its key resources. Facility managers are providing the hospitality to the staff: planning, designing, engineering, furniture and furnishing purchasing, constructing, scheduling, and moving.

Good ol' nuts-and-bolts implementation. You can leverage your facility management business too. The discounts on volume that you get for your current sphere of facility and asset management can be multiplied enormously when you pool your corporate global resources. Your new functional title probably will be asset manager or resource manager or even global project manager.

We *all* have to stop talking in FM jargon:

- Square feet
- Square yards
- 55 percent discount
- 500 work stations

We have to start talking in corporat-ese:

- Impact to the bottom line
- Return on investment
- Net present value
- Earnings per share
- Return on assets
- Payback period

And it may be in any of the following currencies:

Austral	Baht	Bolivar
CFA franc	Cruzeiro	Dinar
Dirham	Dollar	Drachma
Escudo	Franc	Gruzeiro
Guilder	Inti	Krona
Krone	Lira	Mark
Peseta	Peso	Pound
Punt	Rand	Ringgit
Rival	Rupee	Rupiah
Schilling	Shekel	Shilling
Sucre	Won	Yen

(See Appendix Table A.4 for conversion rates.)

Site Issues and Considerations

Senior management considerations

Whether Yourco will be building or leasing its space, senior managers are always interested in the bottom line impact of any new venture. Yet developers, real estate brokers, and other vendors try to sell senior management on everything else.

Yes, senior management will absolutely want the answers to these questions:

- How large will the parking lot be?
- Where will their parking spot be?
- How large will their new office be?
- What's the view?
- What will their new commute be?

A word to the wise developer (and Yourco facility manager): Think again. In addition to overall costs, the following types of questions need to be answered prior to selling the senior manager. This is what vendors will hear.

Senior management questions to developers

Stop

- Selling me; that's why I have a Yourco facility manager
- Calculating your fee on project size; evaluate it on your time and the value of your contribution
- To compare your costs to the finances of the project
- Making promises on services that you cannot possibly deliver
- Short-term relationship pricing

Look at

- How we operate; do your homework
- How your approach matches our operations
- My calendar—it is jammed; get to the point

- The time you've taken up; please feel free to leave (before being asked)
- Your competition: How do you measure up professionally?
- The reason you did not get the last project
- The size of this project compared with your capabilities

Listen to

- What we need
- What you are selling
- Your lack of research into the rationale for our need to change
- The hype of your sales pitch: Where are the details?
- Our need to communicate to our staff
- The door opening to show you out of my office

Answers

Yourco facility managers: It is your job to stop, look, and listen. You should screen all vendors. Do not let any vendor meet with senior management without satisfying yourself that the questions above have been met.

You cannot stop the vendors who somehow get to senior management directly. The selling point to senior management is that the firms you present have all been filtered. Senior managers will eventually realize that their time is best served by having you initially screen these vendors.

If a developer stops, looks, and listens to the questions above, then the last point senior managers will make to the developer is this: "Stop! Look and listen to the sound of the contract being signed."

Developer questions to facility managers

Stop

- Being evasive
- Giving us hypothetical information
- Being transactional: What about a long-term relationship?
- Making changes after our first meeting

Look at

- The level of individual we have to deal with prior to getting to senior management

- Your request for proposals versus what you are now requesting
- The lack of detail you are giving us

Listen to

- Your lack of conviction about the project actual proceeding
- My pleas to tell me your reasons for not selecting us
- All of our services, even though you may not need them initially

Answers

If Yourco facility managers stop, look, and listen to the questions above, then the last point developers will say to them is this: "Stop! Look and listen to the quality firm at excellent pricing Yourco gets when the contract is signed."

Asset management site considerations

While the business, marketing, and financial evaluations are under way, the facility manager will be deeply involved with evaluating essential site-specific concerns. The concerns are regulatory, geographic, environmental, and facility.

Regulatory concerns include:

- Approval process
- Buildable area allowable
- Building usage restrictions
- Covenants
- Easements
- Environmental impact statement requirements
- Fire and safety requirements
- Height restrictions
- Jurisdictions: federal, state, city, town
- Landmark designation
- Land use
- License and permit regulations
- Lighting restrictions
- Moratoriums on construction

- Nuclear evacuation plans
- Parking requirements and restrictions
- Satellite dish locations
- Sewage treatment requirements
- Signage restrictions
- Water and mineral rights
- Zoning regulations and restrictions

Environmental concerns include the approval process as well as issues involving toxicity. During the site survey, water quality should be checked and adjacent (surrounding) properties investigated. Toxic fumes and chemicals, contaminated materials, and noise pollution can be carried to your site. Specific checklist items include:

- Storage tanks for toxic waste, chemicals, fuels
- Manufacturing exhaust
- Weapons, nuclear plants
- Agricultural pesticides
- Aquifers and streams on property that runs through contaminated adjacent properties
- Shafts and mines underneath property
- Ground residue from previous usage
- Designated route for transportation of explosives and toxic materials

Geographic concerns are wide-ranging. Depending on the site, they may include:

Airport
- Radio transmissions
- Glide path
- Noise

Drywells
- Location
- Depth

Egress/loads
- Rail, air, and roadways

Food service
- Proximity, quality, costs

Future potential

- Anticipated zoning

Historic usage

- Archeological site
- Wildlife preservation
- Landfill sources (odors, gases)
- Storm and sanitary drainage systems
- Gas service

Locale

- Urban
- Suburban
- Rural
- Waterfront

Rail and road

- Proximity
- Loads
- Egress
- Vibrations
- Noise

Septic tanks

- Location
- Depth

Topography

- Soils testing
- Bearing capability
- Composition
- Suitable for foundation
- High-water tables
- Settlement or sinkhole
- Rock

Solar exposure

- Exposure

Water

- Supplies
- Site drainage

- Potability

Wildlife
- Hazards

Facility concerns include:

Approval
- Process

Floor
- Plate size
- Configuration and loads

Existing
- Structures
- Elevator capacity and number of cabs
- Heating, ventilation, and air-conditioning systems

Document
- Reviews required

Emergency
- Services available
- Location
- Response time

Lightning
- Protection requirement

Post office
- Location
- Address
- Size
- Capabilities

Site elevation
- Effect on height and other restrictions

Temperature
- Range (sunscreen, glazing, orientation, landscaping, mechanical systems)

Utilities
- Availability

- Type
- Fees
- Feeders
- Substation
- Rates

Miscellaneous
- Scenic views
- Parking
- Security
- Taxes

Site and environmental issues

In reviewing a site, historic usage will be absolutely critical in your decision to acquire or lease it. The past exposure to toxic materials must be audited.

In addition, the building orientation and physical footprint must be reviewed against a myriad of factors. These environmental factors will have negative and positive impacts upon your architectural plans.

The environmental impact checklist includes:

Earth

- Vegetation types and quality (trees, brush, ground)
- Insect types and density
- Wildlife types and migration pattern
- Soil conditions
- Hydrology
- Topography
- Hazards (earthquakes, flood area)
- Earthquakes (frequency, seismic ratings)
- Floods (location of flood plains, location of flood controls, frequency, storm high water level)

Wind

- Wind tunnels
- Contribution to acid rain
- Direction and speed

- Seasonal hazards (hurricanes)
- Air quality
- Windstorms: frequency and type (hurricanes, tornadoes, monsoons)

Fire

- Sunlight: angle, glare, cloud cover
- Orientation: heating and cooling cycles
- Relative humidity

Toxicity

- Asbestos
- Polychlorinated biphenyl (PCB)
- Radon gas

What is radon?   Radon is colorless, odorless, and tasteless. It is totally undetectable by human senses. The gas comes from the natural breakdown of uranium. Radon is found in rocks that contain uranium and in soils that have been contaminated by wastes from industrial dumping of uranium by-products. Radon is usually diluted in exterior spaces and is not considered lethal. However, the gas can accumulate and raise indoor levels to the danger zone. The greatest risk, according to government surveys, is lung cancer.

Detailed state profiles.   State economic development organizations will gladly supply Yourco with all pertinent information on any city or area in their state. Among the data readily available for Yourco consideration:

- Education and training available for Yourco staff
- Historical background of the state
- Listing of economic development councils for business and financial aid
- Names and addresses of all officials
- Statistics (population, age, unemployment, costs, home prices, office vacancy rate)
- Tax incentives and federal enterprise zones
- Utilities and energy

Review of the Americans with Disabilities Act (ADA)

The new Americans with Disabilities Act (effective January 26, 1992) will have a significant impact on the facility manager. A brief review is presented here. (I suggest you get a detailed copy of the law and analyze its impact on Yourco.)

Under the new ADA mandate:

> No individual person shall be discriminated against on the basis of disability in the full and equal enjoyment of the goods, services, facilities, privileges, advantages, or accommodations of any public accommodation by any person who owns, leases (or leases to) or operates a place of public accommodation.

Who is affected?

Employers. For all employers, protection of the disabled may mean changing existing facilities to provide equal access for all employees. Existing facilities must make those alterations that are "readily achievable." The ADA provides for tax deductions and other incentives to comply.

Effective July 1992, employers with 25 or more employees must meet ADA requirements. Effective July 1994, employers with 15 or more employees must comply.

Public and government facilities. Effective January 1992, all government facilities and all public transportation systems and buildings must be accessible to the disabled.

Public accommodations operated by private entities. Effective January 1992, all public accommodations must be accessible to the disabled. In addition, new construction must be fully accessible if initial occupancy is after January 1993.

Telecommunications. Effective July 1993, 24-hour access to telecommunications services equipment must be available for the disabled.

Priorities

If you are concerned about priorities in meeting the ADA guidelines, follow this order:

1. Provide access onto site and into building.

2. Provide access to rest rooms.

3. Provide access to any area within the building where goods or services are available.

4. Provide access to all other areas.

Enforcement

The Americans with Disabilities Act is not considered a building code. Therefore, it is not (yet) enforceable by any state or municipality. Legal suits by victims of nonconformance will be the methodology of enforcement. The U.S. Attorney General may levy a cash penalty up to $50,000 for the first offense.

Effective January 26, 1992, ADA lawsuits against public accommodations may be filed. Effective July 26, 1992, lawsuits may be filed against businesses with 25 or fewer employees and gross receipts of $1 million or less. Effective January 26, 1993, lawsuits may be filed against businesses with 15 or fewer employees and gross receipts of $500,000 or less.

Public accommodations defined

Here is a partial listing of public accommodations that are usually owned or operated by private entities.

Lodgings

- Hotels
- Inns
- Motels

Public display or gathering places

- Auditoriums
- Convention centers
- Galleries
- Libraries
- Museums
- Stadiums

Service and recreational establishments

- All establishments serving food or drink
- Amusement parks

- Banks
- Day care facilities
- Dry cleaners
- Fitness centers
- Funeral parlors
- Gas stations
- Health care centers
- Hospitals
- Parks
- Professional offices
- Shelters for the homeless
- Zoos

Developer Letters

Asset and facility managers are barraged daily by letters from developers. Just to spare you from reading too many (and me from typing them), I have included two sample letters.

Figure 2.1 represents the typical solicitation letter received by facility professionals. Figure 2.2 represents the typical testimonial letter. This format relates how satisfied another company is or how well an individual, like yourself, appreciates the new site. At the end of the letters, look for the discussion checkpoints.

Building Issues and Considerations

Space-planning woes

Modern methods of floor measurement call for a brief review of basic algebra. Let's begin with a few simple problems.

Problem 1. You have three dozen eggs. After one week you have used 12 eggs.

Question: How many dozen eggs do you have left?

Answer: Two dozen eggs.

Discussion. This problem requires knowledge that there are 12 eggs in a dozen. Subtract 12 from 36 (3 × 12 eggs) to get 24 eggs. Divide 24 by 12 to get the answer of two dozen eggs.

EXTERNAL COMPANY

456 Union Street Yourville, Yourstate

Yourco
123 Main Street
Yourville, Yourstate

Dear Executive:
Enclosed is a brochure on the recently constructed Management Place office building, which is now offering 250,000 square feet available for lease. This space can be easily divided to suit your company's needs.

This first class office building is located within minutes of the Yourville commuter train station with express service to downtown Yourville. Management Place also benefits by being just a few miles off two major freeways: the Yourstate Turnpike and the Overpay Freeway. These provide you with quick and easy access to all parts of the greater Yourville area.

Management Place, located in Yourburbs, has abundant parking, easy access to banks, restaurants and shops in the nearby Yourmall complex. Should your company have a need for offices in this area, we ask that you consider Management Place. We, the undersigned, are available to meet with you to discuss your real estate needs and to formally present Management Place to you.

Sincerely,

Discussion
√This is highly impersonal
√Rentable is usually a fixed number in the lease
√Just a form letter and a purchased mailing list
√These usually get ignored
√Marketeers should at least personalize the letter with your name and your corporation's name

Figure 2.1 Sample developer letter.

Problem 2.   You buy two pounds of shrimp from the store.

Question: How many ounces of shrimp did you buy?

Answer: 32 ounces.

Discussion.   This problem requires knowledge that there are 16 ounces in a pound. Multiply 2 (pounds) by 16 (ounces) to get the answer of 32 ounces.

EXTERNAL COMPANY

456 Union Street Yourville, Yourstate

Yourco
123 Main Street
Yourville, Yourstate

Dear Facility Manager:
Competitor Corporation's move to the new Management Place site in Yourburbs
marks a major milestone for this exciting project. It will become the anchor tenant
in our 250,000 square foot office building.

Management Place is the first phase of the entire Management Campus Project.
The project is planned for approximately 1 million square feet of low rise office
space, 1,000 residential units, retail space and abundant parking. Additionally, the Yourmall complex is nearby.

Management Place represents a unique opportunity for investors, developers and
space users. The economic advantages of the project include very competitive
rental rates, available equity (ownership) participation for major users and
significantly reduced state and local taxes.

Join Competitor Corporation in this economic development. If you would like
additional information or have any questions on the project, please call me.

Sincerely,

Discussion
√Letter is at least addressed to me. (Ever receive a form letter that has your name
and mailing address but the "Dear...." is not your name?)
√Do you want to be in the same building or campus as your competitor?
√What about rights to name the building or campus?
√Anchor tenant may have ability to have building or campus renamed
√These usually get ignored

Figure 2.2 Sample developer testimonial letter.

Problem 3. You rent 1 square foot from a landlord. The landlord
charges 1 cent per rentable square inch.

Question: What is your rent expense?

Answer: $1.88!

Discussion. You multiplied .01 (cents) by 144 (square foot = 12
inches × 12 inches) to get 144 cents, or $1.44. Why in the world did
you think that the answer was $1.44? Obviously, you haven't rented

space recently or renewed a lease in a building that has been remeasured. Landlords add on a factor of 25 percent and charge $1.88 (1.25 × $1.44) for the 144 square inches.

The world of the rubber ruler. The term *rubber ruler* has come into vogue in the world of real estate. Basically, landlords are permitted to remeasure the square footage with any factor (or multiplier) they wish. The only caveat is that they disclose their methodology, *if you ask*. This measurement technique is done prior to any new building being offered to let. Buildings are often remeasured and the new square footage implemented when a tenant renews a lease.

Definitions

Gross area. The gross area is the total space on a floor, window to window (inside face of exterior glass), including all core space, columns, and projections.

✔ This is the same old measurement method, but is frequently *less* than the rentable area!

Rentable area. According to the Real Estate Board of New York, Inc.: "Because of dissimilarities among buildings, calculations of rentable area may vary. If requested, owners should disclose to prospective tenants the loss factor used for spaces under consideration."

✔ Always request full disclosure of the calculation methodology.

✔ Always do your analysis of the ratio of usable to rentable square feet of space.

Usable area, sole tenancy. Measure the floor from the outside face of the glass or wall. Subtract from this calculation the area for multiple floor spaces—i.e., public stairs, elevator shafts, machine rooms, fire stairs, and courts (these spaces are located in the building core; see definition below). Do not subtract such spaces that serve only the floor being measured. Do not subtract columns and other building projections.

✔ This methodology includes washrooms as part of the usable area.

Usable area, multiple tenancy. Use the same initial measurement as that for sole tenancy. Subtract corridors, washrooms, and building storerooms on the floor. Measure the net usable area of each tenant. Prorate corridor calculation to each tenant. Do not subtract columns and other building projections.

Share and share alike.

Usable areas, below grade. Use the same calculation methodology as that for sole or multiple tenancy. Subtract any building support space—building office, equipment rooms, switch gear rooms, and so on. Do not subtract columns and other building projections.

✔ And the view is lousy.

✔ Negotiate a rate substantially lower than the above-grade rental rate.

Net usable (carpetable or assignable) area. Net usable space is the actual space that can be utilized by the tenant to house people and office furniture and equipment.

✔ This is the same old measurement method.

Core. The building core represents the area occupied by building support systems and spaces.

■ Building support: maintenance room, fan room, air-conditioning room

■ Closets: janitor, electric, telephone, technology

■ Elevator lobbies: passenger, service

■ Elevator shafts: passenger, service

■ Shafts/risers: mail, ducts

■ Structure: building structural beams, public and fire stairs

■ Washrooms: toilet rooms, slop sinks

Some of these areas are calculated in usable, some in rentable, as noted above.

Loss Factor. The loss factor represents the ratio of usable to rentable square feet and the resulting percentage of nonusable space. The lower the loss factor, the more efficient the space. Usually, a low loss factor will result in your requiring less rentable area.

To calculate the loss factor, subtract the usable square feet (USF) from the rentable square feet (RSF) and divide the result by the rentable area. For example:

$$50{,}000 \text{ RSF} - 40{,}000 \text{ USF} = 10{,}000 \text{ sq ft}$$

$$\frac{10{,}000}{50{,}000} = 20 \text{ percent loss}$$

To quickly calculate from usable to rentable if the loss factor is known:

- 15 percent loss percentage, multiply usable by 1.177
- 20 percent loss percentage, multiply usable by 1.250
- 25 percent loss percentage, multiply usable by 1.334
- 30 percent loss percentage, multiply usable by 1.429

Comparisons. In the calculation above, assume the rental rate is $40 per rentable square foot. Remember that 50,000 rentable square feet with a 20 percent loss factor equals 40,000 usable square feet. To calculate you "true" cost, multiply rentable area by rent expense and divide by actual usable area:

$$\frac{(50,000 \text{ RSF} \times \$40) = \$2,000,000}{40,000 \text{ USF}} = \$50 \text{ per usable square foot}$$

If you would take space under similar conditions, but in a building with a 10 percent loss factor, the comparable costs would be as follows:

$$\frac{(50,000 \text{ RSF} \times \$40) = \$2,000,000}{45,000 \text{ USF}} = \$44.44 \text{ per usable square foot}$$

If you would take space under similar conditions, but in a building with a 25 percent loss factor, the comparable costs would be as follows:

$$\frac{(50,000 \text{ RSF} \times \$40) = \$2,000,000}{37,500 \text{ USF}} = \$53.33 \text{ per usable square foot}$$

✔ In comparing similar facilities, calculate rental expense on the basis of cost per usable square foot. You can then equate buildings according to their varying loss factors. Now you understand the basics. You should actually compare buildings on the basis of net usable area. This requires a further study of the carpetable/assignable space on which you can physically place staff.

World's highest rents. Both the Associated Press and *The Wall Street Journal* have reported on the highest rents in the world as of October 1991. These are prices Yourco would pay if placing a branch or retail operation on these sites. The pricing is also indicative of the commercial office space value directly above these retail spots.

Retail space. The annual costs for 1 square foot of retail space at the top 10 rental sites are as follows:

1. The Ginza	Tokyo	$675
2. Nathan Road/Queens Road	Hong Kong	$575
3. East 57th Street	New York	$550
4. Fifth Avenue	New York	$500
5. Madison Avenue	New York	$400
6. Rodeo Drive	Beverly Hills	$275
7. Lexington Avenue	New York	$225
8. Bond Street	London	$200
9. Rue du Faubourg	Paris	$175
10. Orchard Road	Singapore	$175

Office Space.   The annual costs for 1 square foot of office space in the top 10 rental cities are as follows:

1. Tokyo*	$201
2. London	$101
3. Singapore	$ 68
4. Paris	$ 63
5. Hong Kong	$ 56
6. Madrid	$ 54
7. Toronto	$ 44
8. Glasgow	$ 43
9. Sydney	$ 42
10. Frankfurt	$ 41
Incidentally:	
70. Denver and Memphis (tied for last)	$ 13

*In addition, tenants are usually required to *pay* the landlord a deposit of 18 to 24 months' rent in a non-interest-bearing account.

Lease request for proposal

Depending on the situation, the site owner may be either the developer of a new facility or the landlord of an existing facility. In the example below, the term *landlord* is used to represent either circumstance.

You may find several buildings that meet Yourco's site, location, and image needs. You can have the prospective landlords respond to your other needs by writing a request for proposal (RFP).

Each landlord will respond in writing to each of the criteria listed in the RFP. This can help you enormously in comparing all aspects of one facility with those of another. The cost-per-square-foot method listed above is only one of several factors to consider. The sample leases presented later in this chapter will outline specific achievable terms with your landlord.

At this point in your relocation plan, you need somewhat specific answers to the actual workings of the building. The components of a typical RFP are described below. This RFP can also be used for developers who will build to suit Yourco's needs.

Components of an RFP. Figure 2.3 is a sample cover letter you may use to go along with your detailed RFP. Attached to the cover letter are all of the following requests that might pertain for your search for space.

Building requirements

- Provide an energy-efficient, full-service office building acceptable to Yourco.
- Provide evidence that the building complies with National Fire Protection Association codes.
- Supply an asbestos/toxic materials form stating the building's composition.
- Provide building standards for electrical and mechanical systems, vertical transportation, finishes, and all other general building requirements and building standards.
- Provide sample workletter allowance for physical work and cash allowance on a rentable-square-foot basis.
- Provide building ownership, financing, and management information.
- Provide three tenant references.

Exterior requirements

- Yourco requires five parking spaces per 1,000 rentable square feet of office space.
- There will be no extra charge for parking.
- Yourco may require roof/site space to erect a communications dish, with approximate space needs of 10 feet square, 9 feet high, and 450 pounds in weight. Please confirm that this requirement can be met.
- There will be no extra charge for the satellite dish space.

123 Main Street
Yourville, Yourstate

Building Owner (Landlord)
456 Union Street
Yourville, Yourstate

re: Building, Tenant, Floor

To Whom it May Concern:
Pursuant to our recent tour of your site, please find enclosed a request for proposal covering Yourco's business requirements in Yourville. Would you kindly review and respond to the attached request by (date, time).

Your response should be sealed, and marked (Building /Lease) Request For Proposal on the outside of the envelope. Please include any and all appropriate literature that highlights the site and amenities featured in your facility.

Please do not hesitate to contact me at (telephone number) if you have any questions.

Cordially,

(Your name and title)

Figure 2.3   Sample landlord request for proposal.

- Provide your ability to allow exterior signage displaying Yourco logo at landlord's cost.
- Provide your ability to name facility after Yourco.

Floor/space requirements

- Yourco requires floor plates with a minimum of 25,000 usable-square-feet.

- Yourco minimum initial requirement is 50,000 usable square feet.
- Yourco requires growth potential up to 125,000 usable square feet.
- Yourco actual needs may change by up to twenty (20) percent.
- Provide total building size, floor sizes, and specific floor(s) that will meet Yourco's current and future needs.
- Provide a typical floor plan of a proposed Yourco floor.
- Yourco requires a live load minimum of 100 pounds per square foot for people (80 pounds) and partitions (20 pounds).
- Provide your ability to offer Yourco first right of offer on any option space that becomes available.

Terms and conditions

- Rental term will be 10 years, with two 5-year renewals.
- Provide cost of buyout after 5 years.
- Occupancy is to commence October 1, 1993.
- Provide the length of months of free rent for tenant installations.
- Provide gross rent per rentable square foot.
- Provide how many rentable square feet are required to meet Yourco's usable-square-foot needs.
- Indicate your method of escalation of operating expenses.
- Yourco sample lease will be utilized (sample attached).
- Provide a list of all concessions.

Case work study: reviewing the RFP

Yourco information.   You sent out requests for proposals to three building landlords: Old Stain, B.C., and Cushion Realty. You received all three responses by the specified date. All buildings are in the vicinity of Yourville and meet the 50,000-rentable-square-foot minimum, as well as future needs.

All buildings also meet Yourco's basic requirements for image. All boast a loss factor of only 12 percent and are the same basic square with a center core. All the tenant installations and workletter allowances are close enough to consider them about the same.

RFP responses.   The only difference is in the rentable cost per square foot:

Old Stain	$43
B.C	$41
Cushion Realty	$45

Since your analysis is complete, you plan on recommending B.C.'s building as low bidder. The next day, Old Stain comes in with a new rental cost that is significantly lower than B.C.'s price.

Among the alternatives to be considered

- Accept the new bid, and sign a lease with Old Stain.
- Request that Old Stain withdraw the new bid, as the deadline had past.
- Request that B.C. and Cushion rebid to give them an equal chance to compete.

What is your recommendation?

Discussion. Why is life so difficult? Can't anyone follow directions? Now what do you plan to do with the new envelope and the new price?

Sign with Old Stain. With the new price in hand, Yourco stands to save a significant sum of money. Each additional square-foot dollar saves at least $50,000 a year, in addition to other lease costs that are based on the rental amount. You need only get another facility officer and your financial officer to co-sign the new bid and you'll be well regarded by senior management for the additional saving. Moreover, you can claim that you continued to negotiate with Old Stain.
On the downside: You run the risk of being found out.

- ✔ You also may violate the written or unwritten ethics of Yourco's bid procedures. But if Yourco's policy is to get the lowest price, when does your bidding end? Future bidders will never give their best price knowing Yourco continues to negotiate. You run the added risk that one of the bidders will call your senior executives about mismanagement of the bid process.

Ask Old Stain to withdraw the new bid. A deadline is a deadline. All bidders are given an equal opportunity to put their best price forward. If you don't ask Old Stain to withdraw, Yourco's reputation for endless bidding will spread quickly through the industry. What ethics do you live with if you accept the new bid and open the envelope?

- ✔ On the other hand, if Yourco's policy is to get the lowest price, have you served Yourco well?
- ✔ Should you look at the bid? If you do, go back to your first choice, B.C., and request a matching bid.

✔ Again, you run the risk of one of the bidders calling your senior executives about mismanagement of the bid process.

Have B.C. and Cushion rebid. You cannot believe what a wonderful new offer Old Stain made. You feel that Yourco will be best served by reopening bids—and you will be well thought of as getting even better prices than anticipated.

✔ If Yourco's policy is to get lowest price, you will definitely achieve that objective. Of course, Old Stain will be annoyed that you used the new price as leverage to invite the other two bidders back. And, once again, you run the risk of one of the bidders calling your senior executives about mismanagement of the bid process.

Analysis

Those who selected signing with Old Stain. You are correct if Yourco's policy allows late bids. Assuming you do not plan on bidding these firms in the future and your own ethics allow for this normally unacceptable bid procedure, you opened the Old Stain bid properly.

Those who selected asking Old Stain to withdraw the new bid. You are correct that all bidders had the same deadline. You should reject the new bid envelope, without knowing the new price. In so doing, you will have met all generally accepted bid procedures. Now you can live with yourself and with respect among your peers.

Those who selected having B.C. and Cushion rebid. You obviously opened the new bid envelope. Ethically, you should still reject it. After consulting with auditing on compliance with Yourco's policy, you may reopen the bidding. In this case, you should call each bidder and explain the circumstances, without revealing to B.C. and Cushion the amount of Old Stain's new bid. Request a quick turnaround and formal submission of a new bid from all three (some bidders may not change their price). Make your selection on the basis of the new bids.

And those who selected...? Other responses usually evolve around rejecting the new bid. Continue to negotiate with the low bidder, B.C. Seek rent reductions or other workletter, tenant, installation, or free rent concessions.

Strategic Lease Management

How does a real estate broker add value?

I was one of four professional realty executives asked to address an auditorium filled with real estate brokers. The occasion was a real estate seminar for the New America Network held on June 14, 1991.

First, I did some investigative reporting and found the following definitions from the dictionary:

Definitions

real estate (noun)   Property in buildings and land

broker (noun)   One who acts as an intermediary as an agent who arranges marriages; an agent who negotiates contracts of purchase and sale as of real estate, commodities, or securities

value (noun)   A fair return or equivalent in goods and services or money for something exchanged; the monetary worth of something: marketable price

As I addressed the members of the seminar, I outlined the following ways in which real estate brokers add value.

The broker's role.   A broker plays both a direct and an indirect role in lease negotiations.

Direct

- Broker is hired by landlord to market space.
- Broker is hired by tenant to find space offered by landlord.
- Broker isn't hired by anyone but calls everyone.

Indirect

- Landlord calls tenant to offer space.
- Tenant calls landlord to inquire if space is available.
- Broker calls anyone who will listen.

Providing clear definitions.   An important way brokers can add value is by supplying clear definitions of key leasing terms, particularly *rentable* and *vacant*.

Rentable square feet.   Rentable may be defined in several ways:

- Gross square feet less shafts and public stairs prorated by the shared building structures
- Gross square feet deducting shafts and prorating the corridor space on the floor to the tenants on the floor
- Usable space—that is, the carpetable area times a factor to be determined by a future lottery drawing
- Usable area (including washrooms) times the same factor mentioned above
- We don't know but as long as we fully disclose our method of calculation we will comply with the Real Estate Board of New York.

Vacant space.   Vacant, too, has a number of possible definitions.

- Space that is not under lease and is not occupied
- Space, over 10,000 square feet, unoccupied whether leased or not
- All space that is available
- Space that is available excluding five-year options
- Unoccupied space not under first right of refusal or first right of offer
- Unoccupied space in class A buildings only
- Space nobody is in

Providing verbal affirmation.   A broker's supportive, informative, and altruistic statements bring added value to any real estate deal. Here are some examples.

Supportive statements

- We understand your needs better than you; we have the perfect space.
- We wouldn't be showing you this building if we didn't think highly of it.
- That is not one of our buildings. However, it doesn't matter; it is not right for your company.
- I didn't want to call you back an hour after the last call, but this one is really *hot*.

Informative statements

- That broker is not on the up and up.
- Since Pat Dealer left that firm, it hasn't been the same.
- Our firm happened to make that big deal you mentioned.
- Our firm made the connection for the other firm to make that big deal you just mentioned.

Altruistic statements

- You are kind to deal with us; we don't deserve your account.
- This job is way too big for our firm. Here's a list of firms that could handle it, and no I don't want any commission.
- We are only in business to serve the industry.

Supplying factual information. Your brochures are filled with straightforward information on every deal you made during this millennium. You make sure the brochures are delivered to the client in a timely and straightforward manner. The client receives them at a meeting, from a landlord, through the mail, or through a third party such as an architect or a designer. Each brochure is glossier than the next, and the typographical errors are kept to a minimum.

Typically, your letters all have the following disclaimer:

> Although all information furnished regarding property for sale, rental, or financing is from sources deemed reliable, such information has not been verified, and no express representation is made nor is any to be implied as to the accuracy thereof, and it is submitted subject to errors, omissions, change of price, rental or other conditions, prior to sale, lease or financing or withdrawal without notice.

The best way for a broker to add value. Spend some time doing your homework. For example, if your potential client works for a bank, does that client have interest in branches? Analyze the needs. Maybe the client works for a financial institution. Don't know the difference? Do more homework. Try calling the client and asking for information. Do not use the call to sell. Do that next time. Add value by truly making a good, solid connection. Don't bother to impress your clients (both the landlord and the potential tenant) with volume. Focus on quality, not quantity.

Your time is valuable. Don't spend too much of it on needless calls when a letter or facsimile will do. You might also try customizing the brochure-type information to your prospective client. Most of all, have fun and try to enjoy your profession. Yes, profession. We are all professionals. Let's all act that way. That includes the parties on either end of that telephone call. Finally, do what you do best: Listen to the client's needs.

The lease

It is not unusual for a lease to be over 40 pages in length. The lease covers every conceivable event. The basic items are, of course, the rental rate and the term of the lease. In addition, a lease should provide for a good future working relationship once both sides agree to its terms. In general, the owner of the building is referred to as the landlord. Yourco, the firm that sublets the space, is the tenant.

A sample lease between the landlord and the tenant for commercial office space is presented below. The symbol § signifies the landlord's typical text. In some cases, there are comments to be aware of in accepting the terms of the clause. The clauses are arranged alphabetically for easy reference. They would not necessarily appear in that order in a lease. Generally, the "Demised Premises, Term, Rent" clause is first.

The symbol ✔ highlights realty and facility management terms that you want to achieve in negotiating Yourco's lease.

Sample lease between Owner (Landlord) and Yourco (Tenant).   This lease is dated as of October 1, 1993, between Building Owner Corporation, a Yourstate corporation, having its principal offices at 456 Union Street, Yourville, Yourstate (referred to as Landlord); and, Yourco, a Yourstate corporation, having its principal offices at 123 Main Street, Yourville, Yourstate (referred to as Tenant). Landlord and Tenant hereby covenant and agree as follows:

Access

§   Landlord and its agents shall have the rights in and about the demised premises to enter at all times to examine or inspect the use of the space.

✔ If Tenant shall notify Landlord that certain areas are used for storage of monies, securities, other valuables, or secured computer center, Landlord shall not exercise any right to enter these secured areas unless accompanied by an employee of Tenant.

✔ Landlord shall give Tenant 48 hours advance notification of entry.

✔ Tenant shall be entitled to utilize its prorata share of roof for special communications or heating, ventilation or air-conditioning equipment with no obligation for rent.

Alterations

§ Tenant shall not make or perform or permit the making of any alteration, installation, decoration, improvement, addition, and the like without Landlord's prior consent.

§ Landlord agrees not to unreasonably withhold its consent for nonstructural changes.

§ Tenant agrees to use trades from Landlord's list of approved contractors.

✔ Tenant requires that there shall be at least three contractors on each such list and the prices charged by the contractors shall be comparable to the generally prevailing prices charged by contractors in Yourville for similar work

✔ Tenant will receive one free repainting of facility during the initial lease term.

✔ Go for the gold: Tenant shall have the right to undertake any improvements with a contractor of its own choice.

Assignment/subletting

§ Tenant shall not assign, mortgage, encumber, or sublet the demised premises without Landlord's prior consent.

§ If Tenant's interest in this Lease is assigned, whether or not it is a violation of this Lease, Landlord may collect rent from the assignee.

✔ Supplementing the above provisions, as long as Tenant is not in default, Tenant shall have the right, without prior Landlord consent, to assign its interest in this Lease, for use permitted in this Lease, to any subsidiary or affiliate of Tenant provided that such assignee sign an instrument assuming the observance and performance of, and agree to be personally bound by, all of the terms, covenants, and conditions of this Lease.

✔ So long as Landlord shall maintain a directory in the lobby, Landlord shall make an assignment to Tenant a proportionate share of the space in the directory for the listing of Tenant's name and the names of any officers, employees, or departments.

✔ Building name shall be subject to Tenant's approval.

Compliance with laws

§ Tenant, at Tenant's sole cost, shall comply with all laws, orders, and regulations.

§ Tenant shall not do anything in or about demised premises which shall invalidate fire or other insurance policies or increase fire insurance rates.

✔ Tenant shall not be deemed to have caused any increase at any time unless such rates are increased and are necessitated or occasioned by the acts, omissions, or negligence of Tenant.

✔ A financial institution in New York installed a smoke detection system in compliance with a local law passed after the institution became a tenant. The Landlord quoted this clause and refused to pay. The New York State Supreme Court ruled that the law places the burden of compliance on the owner, who is responsible for the entire building, whether it is leased or vacant. The justices held that any shift to the Tenant must be "plainly discoverable" from the lease and the circumstances involved. In other words, a banking business would not have required smoke detection otherwise. So the court ruled that the Tenant could not be held liable for costs to comply with a regulation that is imposed on an entire building.

Demised premises, term, rent

§ Landlord hereby leases to Tenant and Tenant hires from Landlord the fifth floor hereinafter referred to as the demised premises in the building known as 789 Overpay Drive, hereinafter referred to as the "building."

§ The demised premises shall mean the space highlighted on the attached floor plans.

§ The demised premises are leased for a term to commence on October, 1, 1993, and to end on September 30, 2003, unless the demised term shall end sooner pursuant to other terms of this Lease.

§ The Tenant shall pay to the Landlord the sum of (amount) per annum, payable in equal monthly installments due on the first day of each month.

§ If Tenant shall fail to pay rent within 10 days when due, Tenant will be subject to a late charge at 2 percentage points above the current rate set by Yourbank or the maximum rate permitted by applicable law.

✔ Tenant has advised Landlord that Tenant requires certain alterations and Landlord has agreed that Tenant shall not be required to pay any portions of the fixed rent reserved in this Lease with respect to the period from the commencement date for 120 days following such commencement date.

✔ Tenant shall pay to Landlord, if Tenant shall fail to make payment within 10 days, 2 percent per annum above the then current prime rate set by Yourbank from the date such payment was due to and including the date of payment.

✓ Tenant shall have right to measure space and see the calculation of rentable square feet.

✓ If Landlord cannot deliver space by commencement date, then Landlord will be liable for any incremental rent expenses incurred by Tenant.

Destruction: fire or other casualty

§ If the demised premises are damaged by fire or other casualty and if Tenant gives prompt notice to Landlord, Landlord, at Landlord's expense, shall repair such damage but not replace Tenant's personal property.

✓ If prior to Lease end, the building shall be totally damaged or rendered wholly untenantable by fire or other casualty and there shall be at least two years remaining on the Lease, Landlord waives the right to terminate this Lease.

✓ Landlord shall have 9 months to restore such damage. If at the end of the restoration period, Landlord shall have failed to make full repair, Tenant shall have the next 10 days to terminate the Lease or renew the restoration period for a similar time and termination clause.

End of term

§ At the end of the lease, Tenant shall quit and surrender demised premises broom clean and in good order and condition, ordinary wear excepted.

§ Tenant shall repair all damage and remove all personal property and special installations.

✓ Landlord agrees to review special installations (e.g., kitchenettes, stairs) that are building enhancements for possible retention to reduce Tenant expenses at the end of Lease.

Escalation

§ The tax escalation year shall commence October 1 and end on the following September 30 (commensurate with lease).

§ Taxes shall include real property taxes and assessments of any type.

§ If taxes payable in any tax escalation increase, Tenant's fixed rent shall be increased by Tenant's proportionate share of such increase.

§ If energy costs increase or decrease from the base year (year in which lease commences—1993), Tenant rent shall be increased or decreased, accordingly, by a sum equal to Tenant's proportionate share.

✔ Tenant shall pay metered utilities costs. (Unfortunately, not all buildings have a meter per Tenant or floor.)

✔ Tenant (or its agent) shall have the right to examine those portions of Landlord's records which pertain to energy costs within 30 days of such energy change; otherwise, change is binding on Tenant.

✔ Tenant disputes with Landlord's increase or decrease shall be served in writing within 10 days of review and will be settled by arbitration in Yourville in accordance with the rules and regulations of the American Arbitration Association (or equivalent association).

✔ Exclude certain items from the definition of escalation; i.e., Landlord expenses of leasing space, costs of Tenant improvements, and special services to *other* tenants.

✔ Are Landlord calculations based on 100 percent occupancy? If this is not realistic in Yourville, negotiate down to 95 percent or lower.

Expansion (right of first offer or opportunity)

§ Not more than (number) months and not less than (number) months prior to the expiration of any lease in the building to a third party, Tenant shall be given notice of scheduled expiration and shall have the option to lease such space.

§ Tenant shall notify Landlord (number) months prior to such expiration of its election.

§ Such space shall be co-terminus with the then current term of the Lease.

§ Rental rate shall be (number) percent of fair market value.

✔ You need to maximize the time (months) prior to lease expiration and between notification and your election to lease space.

Force Majeure

§ Landlord obligations that are delayed by acts of God, strikes, riots, and the like shall not constitute a default by Landlord and shall be performed within a reasonable time.

✔ Define reasonable as: Tenant has right to terminate Lease if delays exceed 120 days.

Indemnity

§ If Tenant shall default in the observance or performance of any term within this Lease, Landlord may without notice remedy such default at Tenant's expense.

✔ Landlord shall give Tenant 10 days' written notice prior to proceeding with remedy to correct default.

Initial construction

§ Landlord agrees to perform all initial construction work for Tenant at Tenant's expense.

✔ Tenant agrees to allow Landlord to submit a proposal for Tenant consideration prior to letting out construction work.

Notices

§ Except as otherwise stated in this Lease, any bills, statements, or notices shall be given in writing, sent by registered or certified mail.

§ Landlord shall have the right to rename building upon notification to Tenant.

✔ Landlord's monthly bill and Tenant's payment can be made by regular mail.

✔ If building is renamed, Landlord shall be obligated to pay for cost of new stationery.

Occupancy

§ Tenant shall use and occupy the demised premises for the following purposes: executive, administrative, and clerical offices of Tenant.

✔ Tenant shall use and occupy premises for any purposes as provided by Yourville zoning.

Quiet enjoyment

§ Landlord covenants that upon Tenant paying the rent, Tenant may peaceably and quietly enjoy the demised premises.

✔ Tenant may withhold monthly rent if quiet enjoyment is not achieved but not without 10 days' written notice to Landlord.

Security deposit

§ Tenant shall provide a security deposit and it is hereby acknowledged as received by Landlord.

§ If Tenant does not meet its financial obligations at any time during the lease, Landlord may apply deposit accordingly.

✔ Get rid of this clause.

✔ If you cannot delete it, reduce the amount required through negotiation.

✔ If any deposit is required, make sure it is held in an interest-bearing account.

Subordination, attornment

§ This Lease and all rights of Tenant under this Lease are, and shall remain, subject and subordinate in all respects to all ground or underlying leases now or hereafter in effect, and to all mortgages which may now or hereafter affect such leases or the real property, et cetera.

✔ Landlord agrees, within a reasonable time, to request the then holders of mortgages to enter into an agreement to the effect that in the event of any foreclosure of said mortgage such holders will not make Tenant a party defendant to the foreclosure or disturb its possession under this Lease provided Tenant meets all other provisions of this Lease.

Waivers

§ No option in this Lease shall prevent Landlord from exercising any option or right granted to terminate this Lease. No option in this Lease to Tenant to renew shall be deemed to give Tenant any further option to renew.

§ Landlord and Tenant waive trial by jury in any action or counterclaim brought by either party in any matter arising out of the Lease.

✔ See "Destruction: Fire or Other Casualty" and "Escalation" for waiver rights.

Signing the lease

At the end of the lease is a signature page for Tenant and Landlord to sign their agreement to the document. It is not unusual to have Landlord request that your signature be notarized. As a reminder, once you sign, your leveraging and bargaining demands are reduced dramatically.

You should be attentive to Yourco's approval process as follows. Your approval on a 10-year lease of 50,000 rentable square feet at $40 per rentable square foot is a corporate commitment of at least $20 million over the life of the lease. In fact, the total commitment is 20 percent higher. Following the terms stated in the sample lease and the build-out assumptions outlined later in this chapter, the commitment will be over $24 million.

Sample lease analysis

Table 2.1 shows the assumptions underlying the sample lease between a landlord and Yourco. These assumptions are utilized to calculate the total costs that Yourco may expect over the life of the lease. The final cost calculations are shown in Table 2.2.

Are you authorized to sign for this level of expenditure? Your corporation will normally require that an authority for capital expenditure be approved prior to signing a lease. If so, follow the corporate rules, no matter what pressures you think you are under now.

Check again. Are *you* designated to sign on the form or is the client listed as the appropriate signee? Why do you want to sign the Lease? If your position includes this responsibility, then sign away. A prudent management view may be to have the business manager sign and you co-sign.

✔ Why not have the business take ownership of the commitment and the impact on its profit and loss statement?

Lease abstract

After the Lease is signed, a brief summary of its terms is prepared. This is called the *lease abstract*. In general, it lists the salient conditions (usually following the paragraph headings used in the lease) with a brief description of the terms.

TABLE 2.1   Lease analysis assumptions

Column	Assumptions	Values
1	Initial occupancy	
	Rentable Square Feet	50,000
	Usable Square feet	37,775
2	Base rent (gross)	
	10/01/93–9/30/98	$40.00
	10/01/98–9/30/03	$45.00
3	Operating escalation (Direct)	
	Base Amount per RSF	$4.00
	Base Year	1993
	Est. Annual Increase	5.00%
4	Real estate tax escalation	
	Base amount per RSF	$2.00
	Base Year	1993
	Est. Annual Increase	5.00%
5	Tenant electric (inclusion)	
	Estimated Cost	$2.00
	Est. Annual Increase	4.00%
6	Leasehold depreciation cost	
	Est. Construction Cost per RSF	$48.00
	Initial Landlord Workletter	($40.00)
	Net Cost to Yourco	$8.00
	Interest Rate	8.00%
7	Cost of funds	
	Discount Rate	10.18%

Sample Lease Abstract Headings

Assignment

§ Terms and conditions

After hours

§ Cost to heat/air-condition leased space after hours specified in lease

Base rent

§ Amounts (total and per rentable square foot)

Base year

§ Starting year for escalations, formulas, percentages

Cleaning

§ Charges (per rentable square foot)

Electric

§ Amount (per rentable square foot)

TABLE 2.2 Annual Costs for Yourco Lease

Term	Rental sq. ft. (RSF)	Base rent Rate	Base rent Extension	Operating escalations	R. E tax escalations	Tenant electric	Leasehold depreciation	Annual cost total	Annualized cost @ RSF
	Col. A	Col. B	Col. C	Col. D	Col. E	Col. F	Col. G	Cols. C + D + E + F + G = Col. H	Col. H ÷ A
1993	50,000	$40.00	$500,000	$0	$0	$ 25,000	$ 14,903	$ 539,903	$ 43.19
1994	50,000	$40.00	$2,000,000	$ 10,000	$ 5,000	$ 104,000	$ 59,612	$ 2,178,612	$ 43.57
1995	50,000	$40.00	$2,000,000	$ 20,500	$ 10,250	$ 108,160	$ 59,612	$ 2,198,522	$ 43.97
1996	50,000	$40.00	$2,000,000	$ 31,525	$ 15,763	$ 112,486	$ 59,612	$ 2,219,386	$ 44.39
1997	50,000	$40.00	$2,000,000	$ 43,101	$ 21,551	$ 116,986	$ 59,612	$ 2,241,250	$ 44.83
1998	50,000	$40/$45	$2,062,500	$ 55,256	$ 27,628	$ 121,665	$ 59,612	$ 2,326,661	$ 46.53
1999	50,000	$45.00	$2,250,000	$ 68,019	$ 34,010	$ 126,532	$ 59,612	$ 2,538,173	$ 50.76
2000	50,000	$45.00	$2,250,000	$ 81,420	$ 40,710	$ 131,593	$ 59,612	$ 2,563,335	$ 51.27
2001	50,000	$45.00	$2,250,000	$ 95,491	$ 47,746	$ 136,857	$ 59,612	$ 2,589,706	$ 51.79
2002	50,000	$45.00	$2,250,000	$110,266	$ 55,133	$ 142,331	$ 59,612	$ 2,617,342	$ 52.35
2003	50,000	$45.00	$1,687,500	$125,779	$ 62,889	$ 148,024	$ 44,709	$ 2,068,901	$ 55.17
Total			$21,250,000	$641,357	$320,680	$1,273,634	$596,120	$24,081,791	$481.64
Net Present Value @ 10.18			$13,100,800	$329,891	$164,946	$ 763,025	$372,724	$14,731,386	$294.63

SOURCE: CB Commercial, 437 Madison Avenue, New York City, Steven A. Swerdlow, Executive Vice President & Managing Officer.

Escalation

§ Percentage

Landlord pays

§ Free rent (abatement period), workletter allowance, broker fees

Options

§ Terms and timing to cancel, expand, renew

Parking

§ Number of spots included in lease/costs per extra spots

Parties

§ Landlord and Tenant, names and addresses

Restrictions

§ Covenants

Security

§ Deposit amount and due date

Size

§ Rentable and usable square feet leased

Terms

§ Lease commencement and termination dates

Sublet

In the event that Yourco, as Tenant, would ever sublet the space, then Yourco would be called the Sublandlord and Yourco's sublet tenant would be the Subtenant. Below are excerpts from a Sublandlord and Subtenant Agreement of Sublease. As most of the same terms and conditions apply from the sample lease above, only unique clauses are described below.

Sample Sublet Agreement Terms

Condition of the premises

§ Subtenant agrees to take possession of the premises "as is."

Indemnity

§ Subtenant shall indemnify Sublandlord for and shall hold it harmless from and against any and all losses, damages, penalties, liabilities, costs, and expenses including, without limitation, reasonable attorney's fees and disbursements which may be sustained by Sublandlord by reason of Subtenant's failure to keep, observe, or perform any of the terms, provisions, or covenants under the Lease.

Subleasing of Premises

§ Whereas, by Lease Agreement dated October 1, 1993, between Building Owner (Landlord) and Yourco (Sublandlord) as Tenant, Landlord leased to Sublandlord the fifth floor in the building known as 789 Overpay Drive, this agreement shall be deemed as a Sublease not an assignment

Term

✔ Same as sample lease above, but do not sublet for longer than you are legally allowed under the Lease.

Gross lease versus net lease.   You will pay for the space and its services one way or the other. There may be tax or other financial advantages for Yourco depending on the manner in which your lease is structured.

Landlord expenses

- Building and land depreciation cost
- Cost of funding the building and land cost (interest payments)
- Property taxes
- Building-specific utilities (water, gas, electric)
- Tenant-specific utilities
- Building management costs (insurance, maintenance, landscaping)
- Building support services (janitorial, repairs, miscellaneous)

Gross lease

- Landlord calculates cost per square foot based on the sum of all the costs listed above.
- Building costs are usually based on square footage to calculate your occupancy proportion.

✔ This simplifies your monthly payments: one check to the Landlord.

Net lease

- Landlord calculates cost per square foot based on building and land costs, as well as base building costs.
- Yourco is responsible for paying property taxes.
- Yourco arranges for its own services and payment for them.

✔ This requires monthly payments to several different entities (landlord, government, utilities, cleaning services).

There is no such thing as free rent

Well, maybe it is free to you in facilities. However, how does your financial controller treat the nonrental payment portion of your occupancy?

Landlords usually include several months' free rent to allow for construction of your facility. In harsher economic times, the landlord would rather extend the free rent period and not reduce the rental cost per square foot. It is more impressive and financially astute for a landlord to have tenants at the higher cost per square foot in the long run than to prorate the value of the free rent over the lease term and compute a lower cost per square foot. The lower rate may reduce the resale value of the building or even affect loan rates.

Simply put, a 10-year lease for 50,000 rentable square feet at $40 per square foot would cost Yourco $2 million per annum—and, in simple mathematics, $20 million over the entire lease. One year free rent would still cost Yourco $2 million per year—however, only for the last 9 years of the lease, or a total of $18 million. This equates to an average rental cost per square foot of only $36 when spread over the full 10-year period.

Such clauses can make for very creative accounting. Entrepreneurial managers who feel that they will be promoted to another position would opt to have no rental expense in the first year to make their profit and loss (bottom line) look very good. Financial controllers who operate under a fixed budget for the year (federal, state, and city agencies) may not get funding the following year if the entrepreneurial manager is in charge.

The generally accepted accounting principle for this phenomenon is to spread the full rental costs over the full period. Thus, in the case above, the tenant should budget for the $36 rental charge.

Trade journals often list other financially accepted, but devious ways to circumvent the even distribution method. A few of the better methods were described in *Expansion Management* by Joseph Viola, Jr., chief financial officer of Tanguay-Burke-Stratton, a real estate services firm in Chicago, Illinois. Two are worth noting.

Third-party lease. Under the third-party approach, the landlord leases to another tenant and the tenant, in turn, leases to Yourco. Yourco and the second tenant mutually agree to allow Yourco to pay the $40 rate. Rent payments start at the end of the free rent period (in the sample above, month 13).

Special accounts: Interest-bearing. Yourco makes regular monthly payments to an interest-bearing account. When the free rent period ends, money accumulated in the account is used toward paying the rent.

The workletter

In general, the landlord will offer Yourco a workletter as an incentive for a signed lease in the building. The workletter can be offered in two basic ways: cash or building allowance credits.

Cash. Cash is definitely the preferred way to go for facility managers with good construction abilities. The amount of cash offered is negotiable and related to the marketplace. The worse the economic depression or greater the competition, the higher the amount of cash that can be obtained.

An average goal might be the equivalent of the rental cost per rentable square foot. Therefore, if your rental rate is $40 per rentable square foot, you should be able to achieve a cash workletter of $40 per rentable square foot leased. If the average constructed office space is $60 per *usable* square foot, the workletter should provide a fair degree of the funding required.

Assume that Yourco leases 50,000 rentable square feet at $40; 50,000 rentable square feet equals 40,000 usable square feet.

Workletter cash: 50,000 × $40 = $2 million

Build-out cost: 40,000 × $60 = $2.4 million

Value engineering may achieve your build-out for the total value of the cash credit.

In some instances, the landlord will offer the cash against construction costs only. A point to achieve in negotiating is cash without any conditions. In this case, if your construction costs are lower, the cash can be utilized by Yourco to offset other facility costs, including design fees, furniture, and moving.

The cash credit, when achieved, will be offered against copies of invoices received. A point of your negotiating skills will be to receive as much of the cash credit as possible before construction. One reason is the possibility of a landlord's financial problems, takeovers, or sellouts interfering with future payments of the cash workletter credit.

Building allowance. Each landlord has its own construction firm that either built the new building or is the "resident" contractor. The landlord has arranged special pricing. The landlord is guaranteed lower pricing from the contractor owing to expected volume of build-outs. In some cases, the building allowance will offer the cash amount of a construction item, but at the landlord's cost. This may not be at the cost at which you could purchase a similar item on your own.

Consequently, the landlord has calculated these costs into the build-out allowance offered. While the build-out allowance generally has a lower cash value, there may be occasions when you would prefer this method. For example, if you plan only private offices or the majority of spaces are enclosed, the building allowance credit may be better.

Stated differently, if you are primarily a user of open planning, you may not fully utilize such items as partitions, doors, and hardware. You may not have the in-house expertise to run a major construction project and may prefer that the landlord provide this service. I strongly recommend that you still consider hiring external services to run your project to make sure you get your full construction value.

The landlord's workletter also includes the building construction standards. These hold for both sides. The landlord will build out to these standards. You must build out to these standards, as a minimum, if you opt for the cash credit.

Sample workletter

✔ When it is customary for a landlord to specify a particular vendor, the term *ABC* is used in the sample workletter below. When a level of product finish would be specified, the notation *123* is used.

Note that the standard measurement varies with the allowance. In some cases, the landlord's allowance is based on units, usable square feet, rentable square feet, linear feet, or yardage. This sample does not include every possible item in a workletter; rather, it outlines the general nature of offerings from the landlord.

Air conditioning

- Each floor will be provided with a self-contained water-cooled air-conditioning unit that serves only that floor and includes all necessary fans, compressors, and related controls.
- System is based on maintaining 78°F dry-bulb and 50 percent hu-

midity when outside conditions are not more than 95°F dry-bulb and 75°F wet-bulb and minimum temperature of 65° when the outside is 5°. (Typical for Northeastern, United States)

- System provides efficient ventilation with 100 percent fresh air when neither heat nor air conditioning is required.

Ceilings

- All ceilings shall be nondirectional 12" × 12" × ¾" beveled-edge mineral fiber acoustical tile on a concealed spline suspension system.
- Finishing trim is white with ¾" × ¾" revealed edge.
- Ceiling height shall be 8'6" and be throughout demised space.

Doors

- All doors will be full height (3'0" × 8'4½"), solid core, with prefinish white ash veneer, 1¾" thick.
- Door frames will be ceiling height, primed 16-gauge welded metal.
- Tenant will be entitled to one door for each 25 linear feet of interior partitions.
- Tenant is entitled to one entry door and door frame assembly (polished stainless steel and a 1'2"-wide full-height glass sidelight) but not less than one per floor.

Electric

- Landlord will provide electric service of bus duct risers sized at 6 watts per usable square foot.
- Landlord will provide one standard duplex wall outlet (120 volts, 15 amp) for every 150 square feet of rentable area.

Flooring

- Landlord will provide and install *ABC* carpet or *ABC* vinyl throughout the demised premises. Tenant may choose any available color.
- A continuous vinyl base of *ABC 123* or its equivalent. Tenant may choose from four finish schemes.

Floor load

- Building is designed to support a live load of 50 pounds per usable square foot and partition load of 20 pounds per usable square foot.
- Core spaces support a live load of 100 pounds per usable square foot.

Hardware

- Each entrance door will be fitted with two pairs of polished chrome ball-bearing butt hinges, *ABC* lever handle, chrome mortise lockset, and surface-mounted door closer.
- Each interior door will be fitted with two primed butt hinges, *ABC* lever handle, polished chrome mortise lockset, and a polished chrome coat hook.

Heating

- Each floor will be heated via steam-heated hot water circulated through convectors along the perimeter wall.

✔ This is most typical. Other buildings may offer all-electric heating.

- Capacity based on occupancy of one person per 100 usable square feet and a continuous electrical load of 2 watts per usable square foot and 1.2 watts per usable square foot power.

Lighting

- Lighting will be a 2′ × 2′ recessed fixture with twin-tube parabolic low-brightness fluorescent bulbs and an air return vent.
- Landlord will provide one fixture per 85 rentable square feet.
- Landlord will provide one single pole light switch for five standard fixtures and at least one switch for each private office.

Painting

- All wall surfaces shall receive two coats of *ABC 123* or its equivalent.
- All metal door frames within the premises shall receive two coats of semigloss enamel color.

Partitions

- Tenant will be entitled to 1 linear foot of dry-wall partitioning for each 15 square feet of rentable area.
- All partitions shall be 2½″ metal studs, 20-gauge on center, with one layer of ⅝″ gypsum board on each side.
- Partition will extend from floor and penetrate acoustic ceiling tile.
- Demising partition shall be the same as above except two layers of ⅝″ gypsum board on one side. The inside layer of the double-layer

side will extend from floor to underside of structure above and be acoustically insulated.

Security and life safety

- Landlord will provide for full life safety and security systems that meet the most stringent fire safety regulations and utilize state-of-the-art security controls throughout the building.
- Landlord will provide closed-circuit cameras as follows: elevators, elevator lobbies, building entrances, roof, stair towers at the first point of access to a tenant floor, loading dock.
- Landlord will provide a control center with six monitors which will be monitored 24 hours per day.
- Building is designed for 24-hour, 7-day-a-week access.

Sprinklers

- Building will be fully sprinklered.
- Landlord will provide sprinkler distribution system to include recessed concealed sprinkler head, finished white.
- Tenant will be entitled to one sprinkler head per 175 rentable square feet.

Telephone

- Landlord will provide one wall telephone outlet consisting of a junction box and conduit running inside the partition to the plenum above the ceiling.
- Tenant is entitled to one wall telephone outlet per 150 rentable square feet.

Water cooler

- Landlord will provide two *ABC* recessed wall-mounted stainless steel water coolers per floor.
- Floors under 10,000 rentable square feet will receive one water cooler.

Window treatment

- Landlord will provide white opaque polyvinyl chloride louver drape vertical blinds in a 15 percent open perforated pattern.
- Tenant window treatment will be on office side of building, standard blinds.

Alterations

Once you have moved into the building, you will be faced with the landlord's ongoing alteration standards. Rather than be surprised, you should request a copy of the standards during lease negotiations. You have the most leverage to change the wording of the landlord's standards prior to signing the lease. Guess who benefits from these standards? The landlord, of course.

The alteration standards consist of the following items:

1. Alteration request form
2. Rules for tenant alterations
3. Standards for drawings
4. Guidelines for engineers working in landlord's buildings
5. Standards for construction

1 Alteration request form. To commence alteration work in a landlord's building, Yourco must seek approval. Figure 2.4 is a sample letter format requesting such permission from the landlord.

2 Rules for tenant alterations

Drawings

- All drawings must be submitted to the landlord prior to commencement of work.
- A minimum of 4 weeks' review is required.

✔ Landlord will review drawings in a timely fashion.

Contractors

- Landlord will furnish a list of suggested subcontractors for tenant guidance.
- Certain alteration work will require the use of preapproved subcontractors.
- Advanced approval, prior to commencement of work, is required for plumbing, electrical, mechanical.
- Advanced approvals *before* Yourco bids are required for general contractors and construction management firms.

- No advance approvals required for: architect, interior designer.

Building Owner (Landlord)
456 Union Street
Yourville, Yourstate

re: Building, Tenant, Floor

To Whom it May Concern:
We wish to make an alteration in our premises in accordance with the provisions of our lease and request Landlord's consent. We acknowledge receipt of Rules for tenant alterations and agree that our alteration shall be made in accordance therewith and that owner shall have right to enter premises to inspect our alteration and to insure compliance with said lease.

We are enclosing with this letter the following items for your review and approval:
•Four copies of detailed final plans (all appropriate drawings)
•Detailed specifications of the alteration and of all materials
•All project team names addresses and affiliations
•Schedule including dates and hours of work. Project will commence not less than four weeks from this letter
•Freight elevator requirements
•Changes in plumbing, significant electrical usage changes
•Certificates of insurance, worker's compensation, etc.
•Indemnification clause from contractor holding landlord harmless from claims, etc.
•Permits from all applicable governmental and jurisdictional units

We request you sign your concurrence below.

Cordially,   Concur _____ _____
                                             Building Owner (Landlord)   Date

Yourco (name and title)

Figure 2.4   Sample alteration request letter.

✔ Landlord will not withhold its approval of Tenant contractors without reason.

Demolition

■ Demolition and other work which creates dirt and/or disturbing noise must be performed after 5:00 P.M., before 8:00 A.M., or on weekends.

✔ Tenant may seek approval of adjacent tenants in the building to proceed with such demolition during normal working hours.

Elevators

- Tenant shall comply with rules as to availability, etc.
- Tenant shall be required to pay for the contractor's use of elevators and the entire cost and expense for operator, including but *not* limited to wages, fringe benefits, insurance, etc.

✔ Savvy facility managers stay clear of dealing with the elevator operator. It is best left to the construction manager.

Filing

- Tenant's architect shall file all plans.

Inspections

- Tenant is responsible for all controlled inspection reports including submitting a copy to landlord.

Insurance

- Certificates of insurance are required prior to commencement of work.
- Landlord may specify limits of liability for personal injury, property damage, and bodily injury.

✔ Landlord limits of liability must be fair and reasonable and be commensurate with accepted industry norms at the time.

Jurisdiction

- Alterations shall comply with all rules and regulations of the city, state, and federal governments.

✔ Tenant is responsible for ensuring such compliance.

Protection

- Tenant is responsible for protection of all public areas and building equipment.

Standards

- Alterations shall comply with building standards.

Wood

- All wood must be of fireproof construction.

3   Standards for drawings

Floor plans

- All plans must be ¼" or ⅛" per foot scale.
- Indicate work to remain.
- Show work to be removed.
- Show new work.
- Provide key/legend of material covering all new and existing work.
- All new work must be fully dimensioned.
- Must use building column numbers.
- All spaces must have room numbers.

Finish plan

- Show manufacturer's name and model number for:
- Floor covering (vinyl, carpet, etc.)
- Base (wood, vinyl)
- Walls (paint, wall covering, wood panels, partitions)
- Ceiling (spline, plaster, tile, grilles, lights)

Stairs

- New convenience stair must be detailed by architect and structural engineer.

4   Guidelines for engineers working in landlord's buildings

Electric

- Existing riser and panel must be checked for new work.
- Empty conduits must be so indicated.
- Conduit work should be kept above the floor whenever possible to avoid disturbing the tenant below.
- New exits lights must be added to local panels.

Floor plans

- Basically same as architect's rules above.

Heating, ventilation, air conditioning

- All exhaust fans or equipment to be hung from the slab above must have weight indicated.
- Equipment weighing over 100 pounds must have proper handing detail established with structural engineer.
- Outside louvers, when approved, must match curtain wall color.
- Pipe and duct insulation must be clearly specified.
- All floor-mounted air-conditioning units will sit within a waterproof enclosure with floor drain and hose bib.

Plumbing

- All plumbing including water coolers must be shown.
- Demolition must be indicated.
- Plumbing risers must be shown.
- Pipe work should be kept above the floor whenever possible to avoid disturbing the tenant below.
- Sediment interceptor trap *ABC 123* must be provided on all sinks.
- All private toilets will receive a floor drain and required hose bib.

Structural

- Structural engineering drawings must be prepared for all miscellaneous iron work.
- Equipment over 100 pounds being hung from the slab above must be detailed in a drawing.
- Structural engineer will field check to determine if beam fireproofing can be used or if welding or bolting to the building steel is required.

5   Standards for construction

- Many of the construction standards are implicit from reading the workletter or from the standards for architects, engineers, drawings and alterations listed above. Some variations and new items are added below.

Demolition

- Landlord must be notified at least 48 hours before demolition is to start.

- Overtime security is at tenant expense.
- Standard blinds are to be removed prior to demolition.
- Electric power is to be cut off before removal of outlets.
- All public areas are to be protected.

Electric

- All work is to be performed according to local codes.
- Tenant is to provide for temporary light and power for the duration of work, including on electricians' holidays where other trade will be working.

Fire alarm and communications

- It is imperative that the building fire alarm and communications system wiring and related hardware be protected at all times during alterations.
- Landlord's electricians will make removals and reconnects and charge tenant for the cost of this work.
- ✔ Tenant's electricians shall make removals and reconnects in accordance with building engineer.

Heating, ventilation, air conditioning

- Systems shall be balanced at the end of work and report submitted to Landlord.
- All piping in hung ceiling which may cause condensation must be insulated.

Iron

- Floor loading and steel shop drawings subject to Landlord review.
- Fire watch shall be provided during welding and burning operations.
- No gasoline powered welding machines at any time.

Supervision

- General contractor will have a competent superintendent.
- Job will be kept clean and orderly.
- General contractor will protect all building units, equipment, and windows.

Window treatment

- New or refurbished blinds shall match existing blinds in color and style.
- All windows must have building-standard blinds next to the glass.

Wood

- All materials and installations shall conform with local codes.

Writing a "lease" for your own building

You are now well acquainted with the terms and conditions that an outside landlord would impose upon you when you move into a building. There are occasions that you will own your facility.

In this case, *you* are the landlord. Imposing rules and regulations on Yourco may seem like a punishment for your own staff. You can avoid endless complaints, arguments, discussions, and interpretations of what can and cannot be done in your own building.

✔ Develop an in-house lease.

✔ Your own 'Lease' should be called an agreement to avoid any legal issues when your municipality collects occupancy taxes on leased space.

Additionally, you should have a building lease abstract (space agreement), tenant alterations request form, and rules and regulations (Yourco Building Cleaning Provisions), workletter (if applicable), guidelines for drawings and engineering. A sample Space Agreement appears below. These other agreements are basically the same as the Landlord versions reflected earlier in this chapter.

- The Building Cleaning Provisions sample appears in Chapter 4.
- Remember that these departments work for the same company as you do.
- Terms and conditions need not be as harsh.
- Only you really know how devious your own in-house clients are.

✔ So write the terms accordingly.

Yourco space agreement.   Yourco department agrees to be charged on a cost per rentable square foot per annum in addition to electrical usage charges. Yourco department also agrees to the following terms and conditions while it is an occupant of 789 Overpay Drive:

Rate

- Rental rate for the year will be (amount) per rentable square foot.
- Rental rate shall include building depreciation expenses, cost of funds, real estate taxes, porter wages, etc.
- Rental rate will include an estimate for forecasted rate changes during the coming year.
- Actual tax and other rate changes during the calendar year will not be passed on to Yourco department.
- Electric and other utilities will be (metered, proportioned or surveyed).
- Occupancy changes will be adjusted on the last business day of the month.
- All new charges are effective the first of the month following the change.

Square feet

- Yourco facility management will maintain computer occupancy records that shall be updated on the last business day of the month.
- Department may not increase or decrease occupancy without Yourco facility management concurrence.

Term

- Commencement January 1, (year) and ends December 31, (same year).
- Any vacancy prior to term end date, Yourco department will be liable for no less than 3 months' rent expense unless another department is found to backfill space.

Usage

- Yourco department may utilize space for the following: (fill in appropriate space utilization: executive, general office, computer, storage, etc.).

Signing the agreement

- Agreement should be signed by you and senior-most manager of the occupying department.
- A key plan (8½" × 11") outlining the "demised" premises should be part of the agreement.
- Do not forget to date the agreement.

Tenant acknowledgment letter

Yourco should acknowledge that it has moved into the landlord's or its own building with an acknowledgment letter. For the outside lease, the letter should be on Yourco letterhead. For internal space, a memorandum will suffice.

✔ See Figure 2.5 for sample tenant acknowledgment letter.

Yourco

123 Main Street
Yourville, Yourstate

Building Owner (Landlord)
456 Union Street
Yourville, Yourstate

re: Building, Tenant, Floor

To Whom it May Concern:
This is to confirm that Yourco has accepted possession and occupied the subject space effective (date).

Our obligation is to pay (dollar amount) by the first of each month commencing (month, year).

We also accept that all Landlord obligations required in the Lease have been met to our satisfaction.

Furthermore, there are no outstanding rent credits or deductions required by either Yourco or the Landlord.

Cordially,

(Your name and title)

Figure 2.5   Sample tenant acknowledgment letter.

Realty Financing

Review of types of financing and loans offered

In Chapter 3 there are a series of charts that reflect the amount of money we spend on professional firms to design and build our facilities. Another way of looking at the information is: we, asset managers, control billions of dollars of corporate investment.

There is no question of your worth to Yourco. Your "save" on a project is income to your corporation. One of the ways you contribute to Yourco is by the best financing deal, and requesting the appropriate amount of capital required for the investment.

There are numerous ways to arrange the financing of an investment. As this is being written, the North American real estate market is in a great recession.

It is very difficult to get any deal without:

- The building being considered a class "A" investment
- The developer being considered free of risk
- The lender analyzing its own bad-debt portfolio first

The following are a few types of financing arrangements.

Start-up loans

Open-ended temporary loan

- Developer borrows money to build and to finance for 2 or 3 years after building is completed.
- Developer converts to permanent loan during first 3-year completion period.
- Permanent interest rate is based on the prevailing rate market at time of conversion.
- Lenders may require personal guarantees.

Joint venture loan

- Financial institution usually lends 100 percent of financing through a permanent loan (bullet loans are the normal course of financing).
- Developer manages entire project.
- Both partners share in the profits (if any, based on today's economy).
- Financial institutions prefer this investment with highly successful

developers of class "A" properties to ensure a return on their investment.

- Developers prefer this investment, as it secures all investment and guarantees long-term banking relationship.

Syndication loan

- Similar in most respects to a joint venture
- However, the financing comes from more than one financial institution or investor

Bridge loan

- Interim loan which funds project between start-up loan and permanent loan, usually at prevailing market rates based on United States Treasury index or L.I.B.O.R. (see definition below)

Permanent loans

Bullet loan

- Usually up to 15 years in length
- Fixed rate with larger (balloon) payments of principal at the end of the loan
- Usually no prepayment allowed by developer as lender is guaranteed steady state income
- Interest rate at 100 to 200 basis points above lender's cost

Convertible loan

- Lender has option around tenth year to
  - Convert loan to up to a 90 percent equity partnership
  - Buy out developer at prevailing market rate
  - Let the loan continue as is

- Due to conversion options, lenders generally will lend more funds than the bullet loan
- Interest rates generally lower than bullet loan

Participating loan

- Up to 20 years in length
- Lender receives balloon payment at end of loan (maturity)

- Lender participates in up to 50 percent of profits and property appreciation at end of loan, after debt service is subtracted
- Interest rates generally lower than bullet loan

Hybrid loan

- Developer obtains lower-cost interest rates but shares property's future increases in income and appreciation with investor via cash flow options or conversion options.
- A combination of the convertible and participating loan types.

Loan cycle

Figure 2.6 shows the typical cycle that a building loan goes through. Starting with the initial debt, a successful loan cycle will end up with

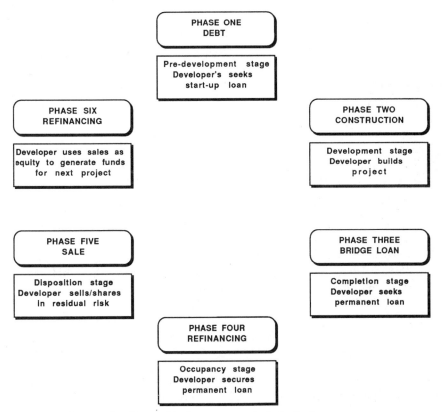

Figure 2.6   Loan cycle. (Start with phase one, read clockwise.)

the building sold and its proceeds used to finance another new building. The typical cycle could take 10 to 15 years to complete.

Typical loan terms listed and explained

Area
✔ See discussion on methods of measurement earlier in this chapter.

Gross square feet

- Total space measured from inside face of exterior glass to inside face of exterior glass

Rentable square feet

- Total space based on tenant-usable square feet multiplied by a factor (about 25 percent) that includes the building's mechanical, lobby, and other common areas

Usable square feet

- Total square feet within floor area less public access space on the floor (fire stairs, elevator lobby, and multiple-tenant accessible corridors)
- May include washrooms

Net usable square feet

- Total space that is physically occupiable, and includes any columns or projections within office area; also referred to as assignable or carpetable

Common square feet

- Total space of building specific functions: including, main lobby, elevator lobbies, mechanical and service rooms, and floor washrooms if not included in usable area measurement

Commitment

Temporary (Interim)

- Written commitment from lender to developer to fund construction with repayment at time of conversion to permanent loan
- Some lenders may require a deposit or fee from developer upon acceptance of commitment

Permanent

- Written commitment from lender to provide mortgage upon property's occupancy

Escrow

Completion

- Lender holds a fixed amount of the loan aside to cover any unfinished construction work.

Insurance

- Lender holds 1 month of insurance premium each month and pays taxes when due.

Retainage

- Lender holds 10 percent of loan until construction is completed, then disburses.

Tax

- Lender holds 1 month of realty taxes each month and pays taxes when due.

Other terms

Basis points

- 100 basis points equal 1 percent

L.I.B.O.R.

- London Interbank Offered Rate

Securitization

- Financing a commercial property with rated securities sold in domestic or foreign capital markets

Estimating construction costs

New building costs. What does it cost to build a building? Nobody knows until you estimate the costs based upon what the image, level of finish, amenities, and everything else you can think of; and, possibly anything else that you cannot.

Table 2.3 reflects a typical spread sheet of a new building. An explanation of some of the terms used is below.

TABLE 2.3 Yourco New Building Costs

(Based on One Million Rentable Square Feet; Shown in Costs per Rental Square Foot)

	Rate	Oct-93	1994	1995	1996	1997	1998	1999	2000	2001	2002
Capital costs											
Building depreciation	$170/RSF 50 Years	$0.88	$ 3.49	$ 3.49	$ 3.49	$ 3.49	$ 3.43	$ 3.43	$ 3.43	$ 3.43	$ 3.36
Funding rate	Variable	2.80	10.58	10.26	9.95	9.64	9.33	9.02	8.72	9.35	9.98
Subtotal capital		$3.68	$14.06	$13.75	$13.44	$13.13	$12.76	$12.45	$12.15	$12.78	$13.34
Operating costs											
Cleaning	5.00%	$0.31	$ 1.25	$ 1.31	$ 1.38	$ 1.45	$ 1.52	$ 1.60	$ 1.68	$ 1.76	$ 1.85
Repairs	5.00%	0.38	1.50	1.58	1.65	1.74	1.82	1.91	2.01	2.11	2.22
Maintenance	5.00%	0.01	0.03	0.04	0.04	0.04	0.04	0.04	0.05	0.05	0.05
Security	2.00%	0.09	0.34	0.35	0.35	0.36	0.37	0.38	0.38	0.39	0.40
Management	2.00%	0.17	0.67	0.68	0.69	0.71	0.72	0.74	0.75	0.77	0.78
Insurance	5.00%	0.15	0.59	0.62	0.65	0.68	0.72	0.75	0.79	0.83	0.87
Common areas	5.00%	0.02	0.07	0.07	0.08	0.08	0.08	0.09	0.09	0.10	0.10
Taxes	10.00%	0.03	1.52	1.67	1.84	2.02	2.23	2.45	2.69	2.96	3.26
Subtotal operating		$1.15	$ 5.97	$ 6.32	$ 6.69	$ 7.08	$ 7.50	$ 7.96	$ 8.44	$ 8.97	$ 9.53
Utilities											
Sewer/water	5.00%	$0.01	$ 0.03	$ 0.04	$ 0.40	$ 0.04	$ 0.04	$ 0.04	$ 0.05	$ 0.05	$ 0.05
Electric/gas	6.00%	0.33	1.70	1.80	1.91	2.03	2.15	2.28	2.41	2.56	2.71
Subtotal utilities		$0.34	$ 1.74	$ 1.84	$ 1.95	$ 2.07	$ 2.19	$ 2.32	$ 2.46	$ 2.61	$ 2.76
Grand total per rentable sq. ft.		$5.16	$21.77	$21.91	$22.07	$22.27	$22.46	$22.73	$23.05	$24.36	$25.53

- Attention financial wizards—all numbers in this chart are approximate.
- Note that Yourco moves into the building in October 1993.
- First *full* year expenses are shown in 1994.

Capital costs

Building depreciation

- Sum of all costs to purchase land, plan, design, and construct a 1 million-square-foot office building
- Building cost $170 million or $170 per rentable square foot
- Building is written-off or depreciated over its useful life
- Your call on how long useful is; in this case, it is 50 years
- Write-off is based on straight-line method
- Book value of the building is reduced by one-fiftieth each year

✔ This is not necessarily the cost in Yourville.

✔ I recommend R.S. Means and the Dodge Reports for typical construction costs in various locations around the United States.

Funding rate

- Rate at which Yourco borrows funds to cover the outstanding balance of the building cost
- Variable rate may float with any number of rates, i.e., Treasury bills, prime, prime plus a percentage
- Fixed rate based on a long-term pool rate; i.e., 10 percent for the next 10 years. Then, a new long-term rate would be established at the then prevailing rate

Operating costs

- All operating costs are calculated for the first year's operation.
- All costs are increased each subsequent year by the percentage that *you* feel is appropriate based on your location and experience.
- Total cost for each operating cost, for each year, is divided by the total rentable square feet for the entire building to arrive at a cost per RSF per year.

Cleaning

- Tenant cleaning costs are usually borne by the tenant directly.
- Cost to clean the base building only.
- Cost is divided by total square feet in building (not area actually cleaned).
- This service is normally outsourced.

- ✔ If this is a completely Yourco-occupied building, you may opt to include all cleaning in this line and charge it back as a rent product.
- ✔ Chapter 4 has typical cleaning contracts for both leased and owned buildings.

Repairs

- Estimate all building repairs.
- Look at life-cycle costing (see Chapter 3 for an explanation).
- Some repairs will be covered by warranties and guarantees.
- Compensate in the second year when Yourco will bear full expenses.
- Repairs may be made by Yourco building staff or be outsourced.

Maintenance

- Estimate items for the first year.
- Make sure you anticipate all four seasons if Yourco is located in such a climate.
- May be done by Yourco building staff or by an outsourced firm

Security

- Calculate all security needs, 24-hours a day, 7 days a week, for the first year.
- Yourco departments that require special security guards (i.e., branch bank, retail shop, employment office) should be "billed" directly for security costs over and above the base building security expenses.
- Service is usually outsourced but may be performed by Yourco security staff.

- ✔ If this is a completely Yourco-occupied building, you may opt to include all security in this line and charge it back as a rent product.

Management

- Costs for building office personnel (rent, electricity, salaries, and benefits).
- Service is equally performed by outsourced management firms or by in-house Yourco staff.

Insurance

- All costs to insure building against any and all liabilities and catastrophes

Common areas

- Spaces shared by all staff (lobbies, cafeteria, exhibit area, on-site park)
- Cost to heat, light, secure, et cetera, are calculated

Taxes

- Cost to pay all applicable building—not business—taxes, i.e., real estate taxes, municipality taxes
- Certain towns offer tax abatements
- Do not forget to increase tax amount to full rate in appropriate year after tax abatement ceases

Utilities

- All utility costs are calculated for the first year's operation.
- All costs are increased each subsequent year by the percentage that *you* feel is appropriate based on your location and experience.
- Total cost for each utility, for each year, is divided by the total rentable square feet in the building to arrive at a cost per RSF per year.
- Do not divide by the particular area that is applicable to the line item.
- Usually electricity will be submetered by each floor.
- Costs in this case reflect base building electric and gas only.

Sewer/water

- Calculate costs based on information received from local utility company for a building of this size.

Electric/gas

- Calculate costs based on information received from local utility company for a building of this size.

Grand total

- Cost in 1993 is not annualized.
- Annualized cost would be approximately $20.64 ($5.16 represents 3 months only, multiply by 4 for full year rate).
- Cost per rentable square foot represents what Yourco should pay in rent.
- Assumes there are no additional mark-ups on cost to run building.

Case work study: project financing— estimated preliminary costs

Yourco Information

- See Table 2.4 Case work study: project financing—estimated costs
- You have completed your cost estimate as reflected in the chart
- Each line item of your estimate includes a 10 percent contingency
- This a new start-up business
- Landlord workletter credit is given in cash
- Landlord requires a copy of paid invoice to process credit to you
- Senior management previously approved the lease
  - 125,000 rentable square feet
  - $42.00 per rentable square foot
  - 10-year lease, with two 5-year options

TABLE 2.4   Case Work Study: Project Financing Estimated Cost

| | | Cost per sq. ft. | | |
| | | Net usable | Usable | Rental |
	Total	91,743	100,000	125,000
Consulting	$ 712,860	$ 7.77	$ 7.13	$ 5.70
Furniture/furnishings	4,894,100	$ 53.35	$ 48.94	$ 39.15
Construction	9,701,000	$105.74	$ 97.01	$ 77.61
Technology	3,301,610	$ 35.99	$ 33.02	$ 26.41
Expenses	436,000	$ 4.75	$ 4.36	$ 3.49
Subtotal	$19,045,570	$207.60	$190.46	$152.36
Landlord workletter credit	($ 5,250,000)	($ 57.23)	($ 52.50)	($ 42.00)
Final cost	$13,795,570	$150	$138	$110

- Yourco accounting requires no overrun unless approved in advance prior to making commitment

✔ Your assignment: prepare a memorandum requesting approval for funding

✔ How much do you request?

✔ What do you emphasize?

Among the suggestions to be considered

- Emphasize costs per rentable square foot ($152.36/$110).
- Emphasize costs per usable square feet ($190.46/$138).
- Emphasize costs per net usable square feet ($207.60/$150).
- Yourco must 'lay-out' $19,045,570; request this amount.
- Yourco cost is estimated to be $13,795,570; request this amount.

✔ What is your recommendation to management?

Discussion

Emphasize rentable square feet

- Senior management will relate to rentable based on their having signed the lease which quotes costs per rentable square feet.

Emphasize usable square feet

- Estimated cost includes finishing lobbies and other nonoccupiable areas.
- This is a more accurate cost estimate and is in line with the quotes you received from contractors.
- Explain the difference between rentable and usable square feet to senior management in cover memorandum.

Emphasize net usable square feet

- "True" facility cost.
- Cost per square foot will be used by you to calculate costs to house each employee.
- Explain the difference between rentable and net usable square feet to senior management in cover memorandum.

- No reason to try to explain usable; it will only confuse "the seniors."

Request appropriation of $19,045,570

- Accounting will not permit any overrun expenditures.
- Project will require making payments prior to cash reimbursement from landlord.
- No sense being caught short of cash flow, especially during critical construction period.
- Provide a comfortable cushion for any unexpected surprises that the contingency will not cover.
- Will be a success when final costs come in around the estimated $13.8 million.
- Project will "save" the equivalent of the landlord cash contribution.

Request appropriation of $13,795,570

- Rely on accounting to promptly process bills.
- Rely on accounting to follow up on landlord reimbursements.
- Should not overstate the true cost to Yourco; after all, funding rate is based on cash required by Yourco.
- Based on phasing and timing, bill payments and reimbursements should provide sufficient time so as to not make a commitment beyond approved amount.

Analysis

Emphasize rentable square feet.

Emphasize usable square feet.

Emphasize net usable square feet.

The most selected answer is rentable square feet based on:

- Senior management familiarity with costs quoted on rentable square feet.
- Unit costs are the lowest and therefore "look" better.

- Relates to landlord's workletter cash credit, which is always based on rentable square feet.

✔ I suggest using at least rentable and net usable square feet, and, when appropriate, all three cost rates.

✔ This appropriation request is not only for senior management's use.

✔ You need to include measurements that are of practical use for you for this project and for future historical reference needs.

Request appropriation of $19,045,570

- Notwithstanding accounting purists: give me a break.

- Never try to ask for the moon; it can come back to haunt you.

- For further discussion on this topic, see next section.

- Part two of this case work study appears in the next section:

✔ What happens when you have sold management on $19,045,570 and the final costs come in at a surprisingly different amount?

Request appropriation of $13,795,570

- This is correct solution
- Unit costs for this line amount is what you should include in your appropriation request for information purposes
  - $110 per rentable square foot
  - $138 per usable square foot
  - $150 per net usable square foot

And those that selected...?

- Of course there are other solutions.
- The most obvious is to attach Table 2.4 to the appropriation request.
- You are all in the same company, why not share the complete picture?
- You will need to explain the difference in measurements.

✔ Better suggestion, give each senior manager a copy of this book.

Selling Management

Preparing for the senior management presentation

D & B Software, an Atlanta, Georgia software firm, surveyed 300 management information systems (MIS) directors as to the leading hurdles to implementing a client/server computing model in their respective organizations. As you might suspect:

- Number one hurdle is the cost of implementation.
- Number two hurdle was selling senior management on the need for the client/server computer structure.*

Selling senior management on computers, strategic plans, tactical plans, or whatever is always viewed as a headache. The MIS directors should follow your lead (once you finish reading this book).

First, we need to develop the common language that senior managers expect to hear. As stated in this chapter's introduction, it is not square feet or number of chairs purchased or bytes or nanoseconds.

When square feet are used, they are used as a measurement of income or assets. When Donald Trump was having financial woes in the early 1990s, the newspapers focused on his individual businesses. It was particularly interesting to see the generic words that were utilized in describing his financial position. It was heartening for the asset and facility managers to see the details of Mr. Trump's Atlantic City casinos listed as follows:

- Promotional allowances (millions of dollars)
- Operating expenses (millions of dollars)
- Operating income (percent of net revenues)
- Revenues (per square foot of casino space)
- Number of rooms (percent of the total available in the city)
- Meeting and exhibition space (percent of the total available in the city)
- Maintenance for his 282-foot yacht (dollars)

- ✔ This last point is included as a reference, since this is roughly the same length as a 21-story building is tall

---

*Source: *U.S. Banker Magazine,* August 1991.

Requesting project funding

Internal project funding.   You will recall the case work study in the pre-vious section requested either $19,045,570 or $13,795,570. The past practices of asset and facility managers have been to request the higher amount. This is clearly wrong from all perspectives. Most im-portant, it is not good corporate practice to be known for requesting far more than necessary.

Let's take that case work study to the next step. See Figure 2.4 to refresh your memory as to the cost estimates. A standard request to senior management would outline the essential rationale for the project. The one-page memorandum would include the following:

- Purpose of the project
- Project description, including cost and size
- Financial summary, highlighting benefits and net impact
- Rationale

Purpose.   A paragraph that describes the business purpose, not the facility solution. The business manager should be responsible for sup-plying the input for this paragraph. The mission statement for the business would be appropriate for incorporation into this paragraph.

Project description.   This is your paragraph to describe succinctly what the facility solution is to meet the business needs. The projected bottom-line cost is included as well as the project size in square feet.

✔ Okay, you figure it out—rentable, usable, or net usable square feet?

Financial summary.   Figure 2.4 is not sufficient to include as a back-up to senior management. Among the essential financial costs that Yourco management needs to review are project costs (construction, furnishings, and technology); income stream (a new business venture must project its revenue); pay-back time (income should pass start-up investment within 2 to 4 years).

Companies usually have a "form" that captures this information. My colleagues have funding forms with such titles as:

- Appropriation Request Form
- Authority for Expenditure
- Capital Authorization Proposal
- Capital Expenditure Proposal
- Financial Appropriation Request
- Major Expenditure Proposal

- Management Capital Request
- Request for Funding

The forms all include a signature page. This page includes a sign-off line for any and all appropriate divisions of Yourco to approve their particular specialty. Problem-seeking techniques can lead to a "bad" solution when you handle more complex projects that require additional signatures:

More funds requested	means more signatures required
More signatures	means more questions to answer
More questions	means more time to get approval
More time required	means project start-up delayed
Delayed start-up time	means costs rise due to inflation
Inflated costs	means a cost overrun is required
An overrun request	means a lack of project control
Lack of control	means more reviews next request

Management's acceptance: their signature. Each company has its own level of signing authority. There is no one correct solution. It is whatever Yourco's policy is. You must understand the procedures as well as anyone else if you expect to steer your project requests through management.

In general, on a significant size investment project (many millions of dollars) you can expect these departments and/or individuals to review and sign off on the signature page:

1. Asset/facility manager (you)
2. Supervisor of asset/facility manager
3. Realty manager
4. Corporate strategic planner
5. Division head of facilities
6. Technology department head
7. Corporate accounting officer
8. Audit officer
9. Business financial controller
10. Business manager's chief-of-staff
11. Business manager
12. Division head's chief-of-staff
13. Division head
14. Group executive's financial controller

15. Group executive

16. Yourco's financial controller

17. President's chief-of-staff

18. President

19. Chief executive officer's chief-of-staff

20. Chief executive officer

21. Board of directors

■ And then it comes back to you to proceed with the project

✔ Does your project schedule include sufficient timing for this process?

In *Corporate Facility Planning,* the "deadly" overrun was discussed. This simply means your project costs come in higher than the funds you initially requested. After 21 signatures, you now need more money. Most companies require that no commitment be made for extra funds without first seeking the necessary approvals.

In most cases, the extra funds, themselves, are not what determines the level of signature. The new, total expenditure is what dictates the level of authority required.

For example, assume your original project required approval through signature number 15, group executive. With an overrun, it is possible that the new total expenditure will require the next level of approval, from the president. That means another round of signatures, but this time 18 signatures will be required.

While this would make you think to include sufficient funds, it can haunt you if you ask for too much. Consider the case work study at the end of this chapter as part two of the project financing sample used in the previous section.

Sample rationale. A sample memorandum from the division head of the credit division to the senior manager has an extensive set of supporting documents. The final package that goes through all the requisite signatures will be enough to fill a three-ring binder.

Selling management with a capital appropriation request

Summaries

■ Cover memorandum (Figure 2.7)

■ Financial summary analysis (usually a spreadsheet for 10 years)

Yourco

123 Main Street
Yourville, Yourstate

Memorandum to: Senior Manager
From: Credit Division Head
Re: Capital Appropriation Request
Date: October 1992

This capital appropriation request (CAR) documents the funding the relocation and consolidation of the Credit Division of the Commercial Group to 789 Overpay Drive. The 125,000 rentable square feet will consolidate approximately 400 people from four different facilities onto five contiguous floors of the new Yourco tower. The ability to locate staff offices in one building will improve management control, work flow, staff synergies, and quality of intra-divisional communications.

Credit Division implemented a strategic plan in October 1991 to realign certain businesses and to right size (reduce) staff through this planned centralization. This relocation, scheduled for August 1993 completes our strategic plan.

This CAR shows a rental reduction over ten years due to the favorable rent expense at Overpay drive as well as our ability to reduce our overall occupancy by 35,000 square feet. Current rental expense is $7.5 MM per annum. At Overpay Drive, our new annual rent expense will be $5.25MM. A reduction of $22.5 million over the next ten years.

The total capital outlay for this relocation and consolidation is $13,795,570. Financial summaries and detailed strategic and tactical plans are attached. Your concurrence to the capital is requested.

_____   _____
Concur: Senior Manager   Date

Figure 2.7 Sample capital request memorandum.

Net Impact of Investment

- Beginning investment
- Subsequent investment

Income Statement

- Net customer revenue
- Rental income from sublet

Operating expenses

- Write-off of old facilities
- Depreciation
- Rent expense
- Utilities
- Salaries/fringes
- Technology depreciation

Summary of earnings

- Net operating income
- Funding rate
- Cost of funding the investment
- Earnings before taxes
- Income taxes
- Earnings after taxes

Summary of investment

- Required return on assets to cover the cost of equity investment
- Earnings less return on assets
- Impact of investment on operating expenses
- Net investment at year-end

Selling management with facility investment detail.   Each item listed below would be supported with as much detail as you feel is appropriate to delineate all costs and rationale for spending.

✔ Put in too much detail, only the detail doesn't get read.

✔ Put in too little detail, the whole package will be rejected for being incomplete.

Capital expenditures.   These items are usually depreciated over their useful life, as determined by Yourco accounting policy. Shown in parenthesis are the typical write-off periods in number of years. A complete depreciation schedule would support the summary page.

- Consultation fees (10)
- Construction costs (10)
- Furniture, furnishings (10)

- Office support equipment (7)
- Technology (5)
- Security systems (5)
- Telecommunications (5)
- Art work, signage, graphics (10)
- Contingency (10)
- Work letter credit (10)
- Net capital expenditures

Direct expenses. These items are not depreciated and are included as expenses in the year of initial occupancy.

- Communications
- Desk, office accessories
- Furniture, furnishings inventory
- Rental expenses for equipment
- Relocation/moving for staff
- Furniture disassembly/reassembly
- Leased equipment buy-outs
- Employee severance expenses
- Horticultural expenses
- Contingency
- Total direct expenses

Approvals

Signature page

- Each person or department name listed under the appropriate line where their signature is to be signed

✔ Always have a line for the senior manager(s) concurrence

Selling management with a capital divestiture request. The same format as a capital appropriation request is followed. However, in this instance you are requesting senior management to accept your rationale to divest of an existing owned facility. Your financial impact analysis would include:

Credit/assets

- Sales price

Debits/costs

- Broker's commission
- Closing costs
- Real estate taxes
- Title insurance
- Transfer taxes, et cetera

The balance of the above would result in net proceeds. Against this subtotal, subtract the book value of the building to obtain net profit on the transaction. The net amount is subject to capital gains taxes.

One of the credits you may consider is the subsequent operating costs that Yourco will avoid by not having the facility. It is possible to take a financial loss on the sale yet still save Yourco money through less expensive operating expenses in your new facility.

Selling management with a facility analysis.   In the rationale that supports why the building is being sold, asset and facility managers would write the various alternatives they considered before recommending the sale. Sample reasons are reflected below.

1 Restack

- Inefficient floor plates.
- Building is too large for the remaining functions.
- Building is too small for new consolidated operations.
- Major expenditures are required to meet the Americans with Disabilities Act.
- Building infrastructure is beyond normal preventive maintenance expenditures.
- Parking lot is insufficient.

2 Sublet

- Real estate market is depressed.
- No inquiries were expressed during last 12 months.
- Professional brokers forecast less than 50 cents on the dollar for income not enough to cover our out-of-pocket costs.

3 Reuse with another department

- Yourco space planning analyzed possible units to backfill, none would easily fit
- Costs to retrofit building for any unit would be prohibitive
- No other units have expiring leases—would result in sublease loss reserves

4 Demolish/rebuild

- Cost to demolish is more than purchasing an empty building in the same industrial park.
- Timing would be extensive.
- Would require a temporary camp-out of the existing units during the entire process.
- Write-offs of the building's book value would be prohibitive.

5 Do nothing at all

- Very speculative to assume a turnaround in real estate market.
- May be required to mark down building to market value which would result in a substantial write-off.
- On-going taxes and minimal operating expenses would still be necessary.

6 Sell

- Despite depressed market, buyer with exact needs of our facility has been found.
- Sales price is equal to net book value.
- Sale is "as is."
- Yourco has 15 months to relocate units.
- Move to 789 Overpay Drive is already under way, and will be completed within 12 months.
- No structural or other repairs are required as a condition of the sale.

Case work study: project financing—final costs

Yourco information

- See Table 2.5.
- You wisely requested the final cost estimate of $13,795,570.

TABLE 2.5   Case Study: Project Financing Final Costs

		Cost per sq. ft.		
	Total	Net usable 91,743	Usable 100,000	Rentable 125,000
Consulting				
Estimate	$ 712,860	$ 7.77	$ 7.13	$ 5.70
Actual	637,650	6.95	6.38	5.10
Furniture/Furnishings				
Estimate	4,894,100	53.35	48.94	39.15
Actual	3,909,830	42.62	39.10	31.28
Construction				
Estimate	9,701,000	105.74	97.01	77.61
Actual	6,813,590	74.27	68.14	54.51
Technology				
Estimate	3,301,610	35.99	33.02	26.41
Actual	2,037,210	22.21	20.37	16.30
Expenses				
Estimate	436,000	4.75	4.36	3.49
Actual	408,750	4.46	4.09	3.27
Subtotal				
Estimate	$19,045,570	$207.60	$190.46	$152.36
Actual	$13,807,030	$150.50	$138.07	$110.46
Landlord Workletter Credit				
Estimate	($ 5,250,000)	($ 57.23)	($ 52.50)	($ 42.00)
Actual	($ 5,250,000)	($ 57.23)	($ 52.50)	($ 42.00)
Final cost				
Estimate	$13,795,570	$150	$138	$110
Actual	$ 8,557,030	$ 93	$ 86	$ 68
Actual Better than Estimate	$ 5,238,540	$ 57	$ 52	$ 42

- Yourco chief executive officer (signature #20) approved the $13,795,570.

- Surprisingly, you actual costs are significantly lower—only $8,557,030.

- Yourco requires a written report to all signers comparing the original appropriation request to final (actual) costs.

- You had included 10 percent contingency in each line item estimate (except for the workletter credit).

Among the suggestions to be considered

- Outline how your staff (and your) superlative value engineering techniques were responsible for bringing the project in at about 62 percent of the original estimate.

✔ Value engineering definition is found in Chapter 3.

■ No more projects based on incomplete plans. You have explained to senior management the need to spend money "upfront" to get drawings completed before getting estimates. That is why your original appropriation request was 161 percent higher than actual costs.

■ You blew it.

✔ What is your recommendation?

Discussion.   What happened?

■ You have been caught short too often.

■ You keep getting costs from your staff or colleagues.

■ Everyone adds contingency on top of contingency—including you.

■ Everyone has covered themselves.

■ This is the one job that gets done within your original design and cost parameters.

✔ Voilà, for the first time no overrun, but an underrun—a save.

✔ How do you convince senior management that your next estimate will be accurate if this one was so far off the mark?

Outline your staff (and your) superlative value engineering techniques

■ Projects always come in close to your estimates.

■ Your past value engineering has kept those projects from actually costing more than the appropriation amount requested.

■ This project was the ultimate save for Yourco.

■ Costs reductions without loss of quality were secured by your staff in virtually all aspects of the project.

No more projects based on incomplete plans

■ Absolutely requested more money than required.

■ The senior management pressure to know costs up front causes facility staff to estimate on the very high side of the ledger.

■ Usually only 10 percent of design is complete (about $64,000 in this case) and estimates are required.

- The ratio of design fee to project total should warrant a larger investment up front.

- Getting quality contract documents will allow for very accurate estimates.

- Memorandum will outline the need to change policy on appropriations.

You blew it

- Project was a success, but Yourco set aside funds 161 percent higher than required ($5,238,540 too much).

- Cost of money is almost 10 percent—money Yourco could have invested elsewhere for a higher return.

- Allowing each discipline to estimate their own project costs reflects your minimal project leadership.

- Action plan or next steps to change this practice will be included in the memorandum.

Analysis

Those who selected outline your staff (and your) superlative value engineering techniques

- Yes, your value engineering contributed to the actual cost being significantly lower than your original budget.

- Can you face senior management with taking credit for a 62 percent save?

✔ This is correct if you succeed at liar's poker

Those who selected no more projects based on incomplete plans

- Of course, this is an opportunity to display the rational thinking of spend a few dollars more up front to save big dollars later in the project.

- However, what does that have to do with the fact your budget was way off from the actual?

✔ This is correct for those that elected not to switch to Door #2 from your choice of Door #1 when shown the goat is behind Door #3 (Let's Make a Deal)

✔ If you switched to "You blew it," 67 percent of the time your switching will result in the correct decision; and, the car

✔ And for those reading this book, switching may mean continuous employment

Those who selected you blew it

■ Yes, we all blew it.

■ However, the secret to this is to figure out a logical explanation for senior management.

✔ Memorandum to senior management would be a great exercise for you to try on your own.

Selling management with a financial impact and cash flow analyses

To "graduate" with honors in selling management, you should be familiar with the preparation and explanation of a cash flow analysis. This combines your best skills in realty financing and selling.

Table 2.6 reflects the *Pre-tax financial impact and the cash flow analyses* for the Yourco relocation to 789 Overpay Drive.

How to read Table 2.6

Capital investment

■ Total construction investment in the year it will be made (1994)

■ Total furniture investment in the year it will be made (part in 1993, part in 1994)

■ Total equipment investment in the year it will be made (1994)

Expense base

Depreciation

■ Construction depreciation begins in 1994, straight-life, 10-year write-off period and ends in 2003.

TABLE 2.6 Pretax Financial Impact and Cash Flow Analyses

Yourco Relocation to 789 Overpay Drive (Thousands of Dollars)

	Notes	1993	1994	1995	1996	1997	1998	1999	2000	2001	2002	2003	Total
Capital investment													
Construction	10 yr		$22,940										$22,940
Furniture	10 yr	$2,700	$2,700										5,400
Equipment	7 yr		$15,597										15,597
Subtotal capital investment		$2,700	$41,237										$43,937
Expense base-depreciation													
Construction	'94 Start		$2,294	$2,294	$2,294	$2,294	$2,294	$2,294	$2,294	$2,294	$2,294	$2,294	$22,940
Furniture	'93 Start	270	540	540	540	540	540	540	540	540	540	270	5,400
Equipment	'94 Start		2228	2228	2228	2228	2228	2228	2228				15,597
Subtotal depreciation		$270	$5,062	$5,062	$5,062	$5,062	$5,062	$5,062	$5,062	$2,834	$2,834	$2,564	$43,937
Other expenses													
Annual rent cost (Table 2.2)	Part '93	$540	$2,179	$2,199	$2,219	$2,241	$2,327	$2,538	$2,563	$2,590	$2,617	$2,069	$24,082
Moving	'93/'94	225	225										450
Legal		175											175
Write-offs		4,500											4,500
Sublet income	Part '93	(225)	(900)	(900)	(900)	(900)	(900)	(900)	(900)	(900)	(900)	(900)	(9,225)
Cost of funds			2,504	2,614	2,307	2,285	1,933	1,779	1,384	1,098	659	220	16,784
Subtotal other expenses		$5,215	$4,008	$3,913	$3,626	$3,626	$3,360	$3,417	$3,047	$2,788	$2,376	$1,389	$36,766
Total expenses		$5,485	$9,071	$8,975	$8,688	$8,688	$8,422	$8,480	$8,109	$5,622	$5,210	$3,953	$80,703
NPV of expenses	9%	$51,450											$51,450
Cash flow													
Capital investment		($2,700)	($41,237)										($43,937)
Expense base		(5,485)	(9,071)	(8,975)	(8,688)	(8,688)	(8,422)	(8,480)	(8,109)	(5,622)	(5,210)	(3,953)	(80,703)
Add back:													
Depreciation		270	5,062	5,062	5,062	5,062	5,062	5,062	5,062	2,834	2,834	2,564	43,937
Write-offs		4,500											4,500
Net cash flow in/(out)		($3,415)	($45,245)	($3,913)	($3,626)	($3,626)	($3,360)	($3,417)	($3,047)	($2,788)	($2,376)	($1,389)	($76,203)
NPV cash flow in/(out)	9%	($57,390)											($57,390)
Cost of funds	Variable		6%	7%	7%	8%	8%	9%	9%	10%	10%	10%	
Beginning asset value	Straight-Line		$43,937	$39,543	$35,150	$30,756	$26,362	$21,969	$17,575	$13,181	$8,787	$4,394	
Ending asset value			$39,543	$35,150	$30,756	$26,362	$21,969	$17,575	$13,181	$8,787	$4,394	$0	
Average			$41,740	$37,346	$32,953	$28,559	$24,165	$19,772	$15,378	$10,984	$6,591	$2,197	

- Furniture bought in 1993 ($2,700) begins depreciation in 1993 with a 10-year write-off and ends in 2002.
- Furniture bought in 1994 ($2,700) begins depreciation in 1994 with a 10-year write-off and ends in 2003.
- Equipment bought in 1994 ($15,597) begins depreciation in 1994 with a 7-year write-off and ends in 2000.

Other expenses.   These must be shown in the year the expense is incurred.

Rent

- Shown for part of 1993 at new location (one-fourth of year)
- Other years include all expenses shown in Table 2.2.

Moving

- For moves in 1993, expenses are shown in that year
- For moves in 1994, expenses are shown in that year

Legal

- Show expenses to cover estimated legal expenses for lease negotiations and any other legal costs.

Write-offs

- Balance of undepreciated assets from old facility must be written off in the year that the facility is abandoned.

Cost of funds

- Cost to Yourco to set aside the money to purchase the full capital investment.
- Calculation is at bottom of Table 2.6.
- Starting balance of total capital investment ($43,937,000) is shown in first full year of project closing (1994).
- Straight-line depreciation is set for 10 years, or $4,393,700 per year.
- Annual depreciation is subtracted from the year's beginning asset value to arrive at year-end asset value.

- The beginning and ending balance are added together and divided by 2 to arrive at an average depreciation balance for the year.
- Rate is obtained from Yourco treasurer for each of the next 10 years.
- Rate is multiplied times average asset value and "posted" on cost of funds line under expenses.

Net present value (NPV) of total expenses

- Add up all expenses for each year:
    - Subtotal depreciation
    - Subtotal other expenses

- Total for the entire period is $80,703,000.
- NPV rate is obtained from Yourco treasurer.
- NPV represents the 1993 cost to Yourco of all the funds it will pay over the entire project life.

- ✔ In other words, $51,450,000 in 1993 dollars is equivalent to $80,703,000 paid out over the entire period

- The yearly expenses are discounted by 9 percent each year working back until 1993

- ✔ This is where a computer becomes a necessity

Cash Flow

Yourco also needs to know exactly how much cash will flow out of the corporation each year.

Cash out

Capital Investment

- Same amount as capital investment line from first set of numbers
    - 1993: $2,700,000
    - 1994: $41,237,000

Expense base

- Same amount as total expenses line: $80,703,000

Cash in

Depreciation

- Amount is a credit of annual depreciation against the original capital investment
- Same line as subtotal depreciation expense line from above

Write-offs

- Amount is a credit of any write-offs taken from old facility
- Same amount as write-offs from above (only amount appears in 1993)

NPV total cash flow in/(out)

- The net amount of cash in and out is figured.
- Total cash out is shown as a negative ($76,203,000).
- Again, Yourco needs to know the 1993 value of its total cash outlay.
- Same NPV formula is applied to arrive at 1993 value: $57,390,000.

3

Managing Implementation

Introduction

The story continues

In *Corporate Facility Planning,* I recalled my earliest jobs as a produce clerk for a major food chain and a stock clerk for a major department store chain. What happened after I left the world of stock clerks? How did I get to manage implementation?

While I was studying engineering at City College of New York, I discovered the more beneficial life of the fraternity. Fraternity life beat Calculus 101. However, it also beat my grades and I transferred to business after two years. My Mom and Dad were very kind about the change from a "free" college to one that costs money!

"Stephen, who's going to pay for this?" Me, of course. So, I sought to parlay my abilities—achieved as a produce clerk and stock clerk—into the world of big business. (Anyone see *How to Succeed in Business Without Really Trying?*)

Job seeking

I was a natural at space planning, stacking, and inventory of produce and stock items. So, I carefully calculated my strategic plan of action to seek a job. My plan:

- Buy the Sunday paper.
- Check off every interesting job that could use my obvious talents.
- Map out my job interview route. (In those days, the New York City subway cost 15 cents, and we lived in a two-fare zone.)
- Pick out my best (and only) suit.
- Wait until the next day, since it was still Sunday.

The first subway stop on the F train into Manhattan from Queens is at Lexington Avenue and 53rd Street—the site of my first checked-off interview:

Firm	First National City Bank (now Citibank)
Job	Teller
Pay	A whopping $59 per 35-hour week
Talent	I could count pennies, and neatly stack them
Experience	Counting melons as a produce clerk
	Stacking toothpaste as a stock clerk

The personnel officer at the open-plan desk on the main floor explained the company's aptitude test requirement. Applicant versus time as measured by accuracy. At the completion of the test, I was told to proceed to the twenty-sixth floor. Already I was climbing up the corporate ladder. Apparently, within the allotted time I had answered more questions than any other candidate—and with 100 percent accuracy.

They said, "Kid (I was 20 years old), your talents as produce clerk and stock clerk could be better utilized by us as a signature control legal clerk." Although the personnel officer was talking about the job's importance in contract negotiations, corporate check signing, and corporate borrowing, I was numb. The conversation was prefaced with the starting salary of $99 per week! I had already received my first $40 raise and I wouldn't start until the following week.

From October 5, 1966, until April 1, 1968 (an appropriate day), I read virtually every corporate contract issued to Citibank by every company and financial institution that had a banking relationship with it. I was required to evaluate the lengthy and wordy documents for signing and borrowing authority as approved by the board of directors. And, when I didn't agree, as a $99-a-week clerk, I wrote directly to the corporate treasurer with my comments.

Even then, Citibank encouraged the entrepreneurial spirit. If you were responsible, you did it. This generates a feeling and attitude toward your company that are hard to convey in writing.

After the first 12 months, I received a lousy 5 percent raise (to $104 per week). I was approaching the end of my undergraduate schooling in business (major in marketing, minor in history). I walked down that long vinyl-asbestos-tiled corridor from my double-pedestal, gray metal desk to Mr. Fred La Chance's double-pedestal, gray metal desk on a patch of carpet. In my normal, straightforward fashion (a trait I maintain today), I said, "I quit."

Fred, convinced that I was a talent worth saving, asked what my interests were. I replied: "Major in marketing, like to draw and draft."

He said, "I don't think Citibank should lose a kid with your talent." He said there were three departments that could use my talents:

Graphic arts

Advertising and marketing

Premises (huh?)

"You know," Fred said, "the people who plan premises, branch layouts, and the like."

Interview 3 was my first (and only). The premises manager said, "Kid, your one year of architectural drafting, plus your one year of art, plus the fact that we are short one staff member make you perfect."

Up the corporate ladder

I was transferred in April 1968 after finding, interviewing, and training my replacement. Up the corporate ladder from the sixth floor (and $104 per week at grade level 8) to the thirty-third floor (and $115 per week with a promotion to grade 12). My first assignment was to plan, design, construct, and move a data center of 6,000 square feet. It almost went well. I thought that once you asked what the user wanted, that was it. No one told me about user changes.

My second assignment was to redesign our brand new 24-story, 885,000-square-foot operations center. A new breed of managers had taken over the day-to-day operations and wanted changes, as we were to move into the facility. My regular business contacts have since moved up the corporate ladder to chairman, vice chairman, corporate secretary, and group executive—among the top executives at Citibank. Their philosophies and mine were the same: Get it done as soon as possible, and make it flexible because we will change it as soon as you're done.

I did and they did.

I was involved with every aspect of business planning, space planning, design, construction, furniture, and moving. I was expected to understand the business inside out, and I felt I could sit at my desk and process the work at that position.

Four years later, in 1972, lightning finally struck when our chairman of the board discovered that the operations building was out of space. The chairman couldn't understand why no one had forecast the occupancy growth accurately. They retired my big boss early. They fired the consultants. They asked my immediate supervisor to handle the planning. (Seniority ruled in those days.) Having done virtually no work at the building, my supervisor floundered. They gave him furniture purchasing. They had no one left to try a hand at space planning. They gave it to the kid. (OK, no more kid. I was 26.)

Ninety days later, in the last months of 1972, without a single day off, I became the first in-house employee to complete a space plan for Citibank. I was asked to make the presentation to the group executive, who has since become chairman. At the end of the presentation, I was impressed with his intellect and ability to absorb all information, assimilate it, and ask fairly detailed questions that tested and acknowledged my rational thinking and logic in formulating the plan.

I was promoted and given the assignment of corporate space planner in 1973. Despite additional assignments and duties, I have held this position ever since. In those days, the corporate space plan and strategy was to maximize our 1.3 million rentable square feet in midtown Manhattan and 1 million square feet in downtown Manhattan.

In 1982, my colleague Neville Lewis asked me to speak to a "small" crowd at NEOCON (National Exposition of Contract Furniture) in Chicago. My assignment was to introduce the new professional—the facility manager. I spoke to the cozy gathering of over 950 designers on the role that facility managers would have in controlling their fates.

I survived the speech and they survived the facility managers.

I picked up other responsibilities as the years passed. Among the responsibilities were project management, furniture management, art management, and corporate space allocations.

I have also been on the speaking circuit ever since. I had the honor of introducing facility management to my European colleagues in a multilingual conference in Paris in 1988. I served on the International Facility Management Association's board of directors as treasurer and regional vice president (two years each) and as president of its New York chapter (three years). I have moved on from IFMA to the executive committee of the International Society for Facility Executives. This cerebral organization stems out of the Massachusetts Institute of Technology in Cambridge.

My most recent promotion, in early 1991, was to director of corporate space and occupancy management. We have over 18 million square feet of office space and 3 million square feet of branches—and that's only in North America. There are another 14 million square feet in another 93 countries. In asset terms, this means over $1.2 billion in facility expenses per annum. And my supervisor's boss is one of my original users from the operations building. His boss is the chairman of the board.

There you have it. Twenty-five years of strategic and tactical planning, taking decisions, managing implementation, and managing beyond occupancy. And so much more to learn.

The Facility Management Role

Management of the facility process is essential for one's initial success, continued success, and continuous employment in the field. The facility manager must deal with corporate politics and fiscal restraints while managing various professional disciplines to accomplish assigned project tasks.

The interior design phases of a project are shown in Figure 3.1. It deals with a logical, practical, actually tested, successful methodology of managing and coping with the corporate facilities management functions. The professional facility manager is only as good as the last successful project.

Sic transit gloria mundi. How quickly fame fades.

1 Space: The first frontier

The facility manager must attempt to be absolutely neutral in evaluating space requests and in taking decisions. The space plan, done in advance and updated regularly, should be the living document for space assignments.

Space decisions, when made, should take into consideration:

Sound thinking

Corporate goals and philosophy

Economics of the project and the times

Consideration for the master space plan

The facility manager can and must communicate. Do not sit back and wait. Do not be reactive. You will never catch up with the changes.

2 Standards: Setting and selling

Corporations use standards as a management tool, but end users look toward the standards as design tools in solving their special needs. The facility manager serves as the important link between corporate management's goals as to standards and the rest of the corporation's desire to be individualistic.

The facility management profession was born—or born again, if you prefer—out of corporate necessity and desperation to control the process. Management wanted an insider who could understand the needs

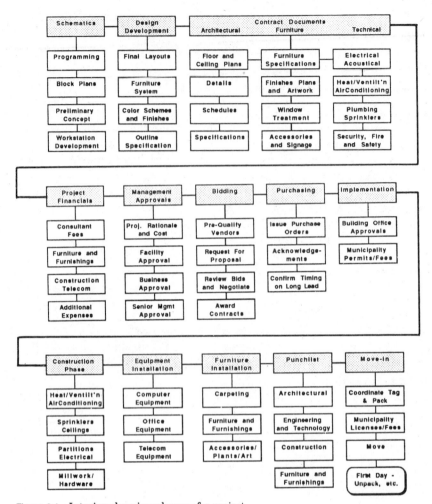

Figure 3.1 Interior planning phases of a project.

of the company yet could "talk" architecture, engineering, construction, and furniture.

3 Project management: An approach

The job requirement or position description for the facility manager should include (but doesn't) the following essential ingredients: ability to listen, common sense, logic, management experience, personality, sense of humor, stamina, tact, and understanding of corporate politics.

The role of the facility manager in the corporation requires an individual with special abilities. It is important to have the qualities listed because the larger the corporation, the more unusual the circumstances that the manager must contend with in resolving facility and corporate political issues. While balancing these issues, the facility manager must bring the project in under budget and on schedule. See Table 3.1 for the corresponding milestone schedule to accomplish the phases shown in Figure 3.1.

While one career path grows within the facility department, another can lead to line responsibilities that include other than facility operations. On the other hand, if the pressures of the job get to be too much, try another career. Hard work, attention to details, and awareness of oneself within the corporate environment can lead either up or nowhere!

Positive leaders get positive results.

4 Project feasibility

In 1949 or so, Parker Brothers introduced one of the first games devoted to project feasibility. This portion of a project requires the facility manager to answer some basic questions: who? where? how? You might recognize these three questions from the now-famous game *Clue*. During project feasibility, facility managers seek the answers to these same three questions as follows:

Who? Facility managers are required to perform a program or needs analysis of the proposed relocating units.

Where? Proper financial forecasting, rational thinking, and accurate budgeting will show management the best solution for the money.

How? Produce a project schedule outlining all the various steps, events, and critical items that must occur in a timely manner.

5 Interior design

Proper planning, skillful purchasing, and timely staff involvement will lead to the successful start of an in-house CAD (computer-aided design) system. It takes plenty of time and effort to get to this point. It takes even more time and patience to have day-to-day success with the system. In addition, a commonsense approach helps you get the most of the system and your staff.

If the analysis reflects that a computer-aided system is not to be, or senior management turns down the purchase requests, it's OK. Make the best of existing staff and external consultants. You can revisit the purchase issue at a future date. Management attitudes and financial conditions change.

TABLE 3.1   Interior Planning Schedule

Name	Earliest start	Latest finish
Schematics	4/29/93	6/24/93
Programming	4/29/93	5/29/93
Block plans	5/12/93	6/17/93
Preliminary concept	5/19/93	6/24/93
Workstation development	5/29/93	6/24/93
Design development	6/24/93	7/14/93
Final layouts	6/24/93	7/14/93
Furniture system selection	6/10/93	7/14/93
Color schemes and finishes	6/24/93	7/14/93
Outline specification	7/14/93	7/21/93
Contract document	7/21/93	8/26/93
Floor and ceiling plans	7/28/93	8/26/93
Details	7/28/93	8/26/93
Schedules	8/5/93	8/26/93
Specifications	7/21/93	8/26/93
Furniture specifications	7/21/93	8/12/93
Finishes plans and artwork	7/21/93	8/12/93
Window treatment	8/5/93	8/12/93
Accessories and signage	8/5/93	8/12/93
Electrical acoustical	7/21/93	8/26/93
Heat/ventilation/air conditioning	7/21/93	8/26/93
Plumbing sprinklers	7/21/93	8/26/93
Security, fire, and safety	7/21/93	8/5/93
Project financials	6/24/93	8/19/93
Consultant fees	6/24/93	6/30/93
Furniture and furnishings costs	8/5/93	8/19/93
Construction telecom	7/21/93	8/5/93
Additional expenses	8/5/93	8/19/93
Management approvals	6/24/93	9/16/93
Proj. rationale and cost report	6/24/93	8/19/93
Facility approval	8/26/93	9/2/93
Business approval	9/2/93	9/9/93
Senior mgmt. approval	9/9/93	9/16/93
Bidding	7/28/93	9/23/93
Prequalify vendors	7/28/93	8/12/93
Request for proposal	8/12/93	9/9/93
Review bids and negotiate	9/9/93	9/16/93
Award contracts	9/16/93	9/23/93
Purchasing	9/23/93	11/6/93
Issue purchase orders	9/23/93	9/30/93
Issue acknowledgments	10/13/93	10/27/93
Confirm timing on long lead items	10/27/93	11/6/93
Implementation	8/26/93	9/16/93
Building office approvals	8/26/93	9/16/93
Municipality permits/fees	8/26/93	9/16/93
Construction phase	9/16/93	12/10/93
Heat/ventilation/air conditioning	9/16/93	12/10/93
Sprinklers/ceilings	9/16/93	12/10/93
Partitions/electrical	10/6/93	12/10/93
Millwork/hardware	11/13/93	12/10/93

TABLE 3.1   *(Continued)*

Name	Earliest start	Latest finish
Equipment installation	11/13/93	1/6/94
Computer equipment	11/13/93	1/6/94
Office equipment	11/13/93	1/6/94
Telecom equipment	11/13/93	1/6/94
Furniture installation	12/10/93	1/15/94
Carpeting	12/10/93	12/24/93
Furniture and furnishings	12/24/93	1/8/94
Accessories/plants/art	1/8/94	1/15/94
Punchlist	12/10/93	1/15/94
Architectural	12/10/93	12/24/93
Engineering and technology	12/10/93	12/24/93
Construction	12/10/93	1/8/94
Furniture and furnishings	12/24/93	1/15/94
Move-in	1/2/94	1/29/94
Coordinate tag & pack	1/8/94	1/15/94
Municipality licenses/fees	1/2/94	1/8/94
Move	1/15/94	1/29/94
First day—unpack, etc.	2/1/94	2/1/94

If the facility manager and the design firm have CAD systems that interface, the relationship is further enhanced through on-line updates between systems. External architectural, interior and engineering design consultants are extensions of the in-house facility team. The possibility of electronic connections serves to help you respond faster and more accurately to senior management requests.

6 Furniture management

The national furniture purchasing contract has great advantages for the facility manager: good pricing, better service, reliability of product lines and finishes, and elimination of bidding each and every furniture purchase.

The argument that a standard furniture selection leads to stale space gets too little credit from facility managers. Buying one type of furniture in one color or finish can be deadly, but furniture manufacturers have moved far beyond this stage. Larger manufacturers have now purchased smaller manufacturers—to the facility manager's delight, for the following reasons:

- Offers one-stop shopping.
- Reduces dealing with multiple vendors on a single project.

■ Makes negotiating for a family discount from the combined manufacturer's product line possible.

■ Offers the opportunity to get exact matches on colors and finishes.

■ Affords reliability on the continuance of products.

7 Construction management approach

A construction manager's role is mainly with the GC (general contractor) and trades in the field. The contact with the corporation is basically limited to project meetings. It is probably safe to estimate that the construction manager spends 37 to 40 hours a workweek without contact with the users. This is by plan, not by chance. You are the principal liaison with the user.

This means you are responsible for all political negotiations, constant communications, and overall budget control. The facility manager is always *on*. Construction managers seem to have limited interest in the other aspects of the project. Facility managers seem determined to retain the full project responsibilities.

The successful facility manager recognizes that project management is a team effort. A productive team wins the game every time. Facility managers need not flaunt their leadership. Smart facility managers make the most of their talented resources and don't abuse them.

8 The "dumb" facility versus "smart" facility manager

A 1985 study found that 68 percent of managers responsible for arranging corporate moves were either *demoted* or *fired* after the move because of foul-ups during the move or reduced job performance resulting from the stressful experience.

Now, facility managers are far more educated and trained to handle the shortfalls and other situations that arise. Builders will provide you with smart buildings. You will guarantee that staff are better wired, more comfortable, and more productive through built-ins, including smarter and cheaper telecommunications systems, wire and wireless technologies, energy and building management systems, and access flooring for maximum flexibility and instant accessibility to wiring.

Your future is brightened by the fact that total flexibility will soon be achievable and within the worker's individual control. Today's smart facility managers embrace technology and avoid tomorrow's dumb problems.

9 Perceptions of a marketed facility manager

Rather than continually refer to our marketing friends as agents, representatives, or staffs, I'll use a term that I fondly call them: *marketeers* (in memory of the Mickey Mouse Club). Many college students study principles of marketing. The coursebook for "Marketing 101" lists the essential methods utilized to market a firm's talents, including an open letter. See Fig. 3.2 for my open letter.

Hiring the Professional Team

External consultants

Peter F. Drucker, the well-known management specialist, states that when criticized for doing a poor job, a manager is likely to go out and hire more staff. If you are utilizing a consultant to improve quality and cut costs, a poor job results in the consultant's replacement and maybe yours, too. This philosophy is prevalent in major corporations in the 1990s. In-house staffs are being whittled down, and the utilization of external consultants is increasing dramatically.

There are a few corporations that have or plan to hire staff to encompass all the specialties required for a major building or relocation project. The building project may be so complex that you will utilize as many specialty consultants as you have floors in the building.

✔ Pay attention to corporate consultant leverage lists.

Incidentally, when seeking a consultant or contract, pay attention to any Yourco directive against or in favor of certain firms. A New York City agency hired a contractor that had been previously stricken from the city's approved list because of "alleged Mafia connections."

Another example: A Yourco realty manager commissioned an external realty broker in Toronto to seek new office space. A month earlier, the *Yourco News* (in-house organ) announced that Yourco had 51 percent ownership of a different realty broker in Toronto.

Another source of help is the temporary employment agency. Traditionally, these agencies have been known for supplying secretarial or clerical workers. However, there are agencies that supply technical-

Dear Marketeers:

Do yourself and the facility manager a favor before you call, write that letter, lick the envelope, start videotaping, fold the brochure, or build the booth: Do your homework. Learn the customer's needs.

Facility managers need you to update them on your firm's or product's availability, innovation, and cost. You need facility managers to update you on current market demands and future market needs as well.

Remember, think ahead.

When you, the marketeer, respect the facility manager's rights and time, you will receive this respect back in terms of orders that will become future studies in the next printing of "Marketing 101."

Cordially,

Facility Manager

Figure 3.2   An open letter to marketeers.

professionals as well. In 1988, over 1 million workers were provided by some 9,600 temporary agencies, with total revenues in excess of $13 billion. *Modern Office Technology* magazine forecasts that by 1995 revenues will be $16 billion.

Consultants defined

Yourco may require consultants in any of the following fields (and there are many more than listed) for your next facility project:

Accounting	Alarms
Acoustics	Architecture
Advertising	Art
Aerial surveying	Asbestos removal
Air cleaning and purifying	Audiovisual
	Auditing
Barrier-free compliance	Business
Building maintenance	

Cable management
Civil engineering
Cleaning
Code compliance
Communications

Computer technology
Concrete
Construction
Conveyance
Cost estimating

Data processing
Demographics

Developer
Display

Ecology
Economics
Electrical engineering
Electronic communications
Elevator/escalators

Energy management
Environmental
Ergonomics
Executive recruiters/search firms
(headhunters)

Financial
Fire protection
Floor covering
Food
Fung Shui

Furniture installers
Furniture manufacturers
Furniture performance verifiers
Furniture procurers

Garbage
Geological

Glass
Graphic arts

Heating, ventilation, and air conditioning

Hoisting
Housing

Industrial planning and scheduling
Insulation

Insurance
Interior design

Janitorial

Keys (door, lock, machine)

Landscape
Legal
Life safety

Lighting
Lightning
Locksmith

Management
Marketing
Market research

Materials handling (human and vehicular)
Mechanical engineering
Messenger

Noise control

Office equipment (new, used, rentals)

Parking
Payroll
Photography
Plumbing
Politics

Programming
Project management
Psychology
Public relations

Quality control

Radiation shielding
Real estate
Relocation
Renderings

Reprographics
Roofing
Rubbish

Safety
Sanitation
Scheduling
Sociology
Soils and foundations

Space planning
Specifications
Strategic planning
Structural engineering

Tax
Telecommunications
Teleconferencing

Training
Transportation and traffic
Travel

Utilities

Vacuum cleaning

Wall (covering, curtain)   Water treatment
Waste handling   Window cleaning
Waterproofing

X-ray inspection

Zoning

Consultant letter

See Figure 3.3 for a letter I received from a professional firm seeking to be hired. As usual, the names have been changed to avoid embarrassment. As humorous as it may appear, it is an actual letter.

Professional contracts

Contracts defined. Once you have determined the right combination of external professionals required for your project, it is imperative that you and your consultants agree to a mutually satisfying contract.

Wait a minute, this sounds impossible.

Remember you are about to enter a working relationship that will last anywhere from 6 months to 3 years. If both sides can become "one" side, then the ensuing months of project-intensified work will be a win-win situation. Yourco expects you to use a Yourco contract. And the consultants will expect to use their own contract. The following sample contracts are definitely Yourco-oriented. After all, this book is written from the facility professional's point of view.

However, consultants do consider these terms and clauses to be among the fairest in use today. Architectural firms will prefer to utilize the standard American Institute of Architects (AIA) contract. While this is also a fair contract, you "sign" away some rights that really should belong to the client. The AIA contracts are also briefly reviewed.

Most contracts are two-party agreements between Yourco and the external consultants. The possibility that a third professional in the same field will be required can be handled in two ways:

EXTERNAL COMPANY

456 Union Street Yourville, Yourstate

Yourco
123 Main Street
Yourville, Yourstate

Dear Facility Manager:
I enjoyed our brief conversation regarding your company's facilities management program and was pleased to know that you prefer to work with firms familiar with local situations and operating conditions.

We work all over the Southeast and utilize state-of-the-art computer assisted drafting and design (CADD) hardware and software.

Attached is some information on our firm and our qualifications to work with you the next opportunity you have to do something in this part of the country.

In the meantime, we wish you all the luck in moving into your new building and hope that it's not a 737 from LaGuardia Airport that christens the building.

Sincerely,

Firm Partner

Figure 3.3   Sample consultant letter.

- Yourco signs a direct two-party agreement with the third firm.
- Yourco's primary contract provides for the first firm to hire other firms, with certain liability, confidentiality, and approval rights as part of the initial contract.

Contract terms.   Remember, the contract is a legal document committing each side to the terms and financial and professional liabilities stated within it. The generic contracts shown below require changes in tone or style pursuant to your company. As usual, check with Yourco's auditing department for the appropriate signing level required.

Contracts covered

Yourco version: Architectural firm (core and shell services)

AIA version: Architectural firm (core and shell services)

Design agreement (interior design services)

Engineering firm (core and shell or interior design)

Design-build firm (complete services)

Art consultant

Contract format

1. Boilerplate
2. Outline of Services
3. Terms of remuneration
4. Personnel vitae
5. Exhibits

Repetition

- Boilerplate is shown only once, since it is basically the same for all contracts covered.
- Subsequent contract sections show only those additional legal clauses that may be required.
- Choose any and all clauses that fit your situation.

Contract section headings

1. Boilerplate
    - Recitals
    - Personnel
    - Confidentiality
    - Compliance
    - Financial
    - Legal
    - Authorization

2. Outline of Services
    - Consultant-specific tasks

- Yourco-specific tasks

3. Terms of Remuneration
   - Compensation methodology
   - Yourco-specific tasks

4. Personnel Vitae
   - Consultant staff: qualifications, background, compensation
   - Yourco-specific tasks

5. Exhibits
   - Various attachments to the contract

Boilerplate

Recitals

Acceptance. All work products shall be subject to mutually agreed-upon acceptance criteria.

Performance. Consultant agrees to perform services in "Outline of Services" section, and to be paid as outlined in "Terms of Remuneration" section, with staff outlined in "Personnel Vitae" section.

Purpose. Yourco is engaging consultant to provide services outlined.

Personnel

Computer. Consultant may use its computer-aided design equipment without any increase in its fees.

Staffing. Consultant appoints project director acceptable to Yourco and replaceable only at Yourco's discretion.

Substances. Consultant agrees to Yourco-controlled substance abuse policies, including testing of employees when requested.

Work policy. Consultants shall follow business hours, rules, and holiday schedule of Yourco.

Confidentiality

Advertising. Consultant shall not advertise relationship without Yourco's approval.

Proprietary information. Consultant agrees that all tangible and intangible information developed, revealed, or obtained is both confidential and proprietary, and will not be disclosed without Yourco's approval.

Copyrights. Copyrights and patent works that arise out of the project belong to Yourco. In addition, consultant shall defend, at its expense, any claim that arises out of alleged infringements on a patent, copyright, and so on.

Ethics. No illicit payments are allowed.

Ownership. All information, studies, source codes, flowcharts, contracts, and specifications, excluding the license stamp of consultant, belong to Yourco.

Standards. Consultant shall abide by applicable Yourco standards.

Subcontractors. Consultant will have agents and/or subcontractors sign a separate confidentiality agreement.

Compliance

Laws. Consultant will comply with local, state, and federal laws and regulations. Yourco state law is the governing law.

Notices. All notices and other communications shall be in writing to persons and addresses listed.

Toxicity. Consultant is responsible to immediately notify Yourco if unanticipated toxic materials (such as asbestos, PCBs, and radon gas) are discovered. Yourco is responsible for the prompt removal or treatment of such materials.

Vendor. In the event that Yourco maintains a preferred vendor program for special services (i.e., reprographics, travel, overnight delivery, messenger services, long distance telephone), consultant will be required to use such vendor.

Financial

Audit. Consultant maintains records of time and expense to generally accepted accounting principles (GAAP). Records are subject to Yourco's or its representative's review at any time up to 5 years after project closing (2 years for interior design, 5 years for core and shell).

Errors. Consultant will maintain omissions and/or errors liability insurance (amount commensurate with project size). Certificate is to be part of contract.

Insurance. Worker's compensation, property damage, public liability, and the like are consultant expenses and must be a minimum of (amount commensurate with project size). In addition, consultant indemnifies Yourco against any claim or lawsuit that results from negligence of any employee of consultant. Suggested amounts of liability are:

- Architectural: bodily injury/property damage
    - Each occurrence and aggregate
    - $1,000,000
    - Excess liability (combined)
    - $5,000,000

- Interior design (professional liability)
- $1,000,000
- Engineering (professional liability)
- $1,000,000
- Worker's compensation (statutory)
    - Each accident
    - $100,000
    - Disease—aggregate
    - $500,000
    - Disease—employee
    - $100,000

Taxes. Consultant shall pay all sales/services taxes and be reimbursed by Yourco. Moreover, Yourco shall have no liability for taxes based on net income or gross receipts.

Tax status. Consultant performs as an independent contractor and not as an affiliate or partner of Yourco.

Value papers. Consultant shall maintain value papers insurance in the amount of $50,000 to cover costs of Yourco to engage consultant to replace lost or damaged originals of drawings or other documents.

Legal

Arbitration. All claims or disputes arising out of the agreement shall be decided by arbitration in Yourco's city and state in accordance with Construction Industry Arbitration Rules of the American Arbitration Association.

Force majeure. Neither party is at fault for acts of God, war, civil disobedience, rebellions, and so on.

Headings. Section headings are for convenience only.

Labor acts. Consultant will comply with all federal equal employment opportunity and labor acts.

Modification. No modification, waiver, or the like shall be effective unless put in writing and signed by both parties.

Severability. If any provision is deemed invalid by a court, remaining terms are unimpaired.

Subsidiary. Agreement extends to Yourco subsidiaries and affiliates.

Term. Agreement shall commence on (date) and terminate on or before (date), and may be renewed, extended, or modified in writing signed by both parties.

Termination. Either party can terminate upon 7 to 30 days' written notice. The exact length should be commensurate with project complexities.

Authorization

Signatures. Agreement is executed on the date signed below by duly authorized representative from Yourco and consultant (include for each company: lines for name, title, company name, address and date).

Outline of Services

Yourco version: Architectural firm (core and shell services)

Consultant-specific tasks

Additional work. Any work not specifically stated in the agreement is considered additional work, and will not be provided without written authorization from Yourco.

Authorization. Consultant shall be authorized to reject work which does not conform to contract documents. Consultant will give prompt written notice to Yourco.

Extras. Consultant may be requested to prepare an environmental impact study for submission to governing regulatory agencies at an additional compensation to be mutually agreed upon between consultant and Yourco.

Interpreter. Consultant shall be the interpreter of the requirements of the contract documents and the impartial judge of the performance thereunder by Yourco and construction firm.

Meetings. Consultant shall attend regularly scheduled project meetings, and visit the site as appropriate.

✔ Never limit your consultant to an upset number of visits or meetings.

Performance. Consultant shall perform all services as expeditiously as is consistent with professional skill and care and the orderly progress of the project.

Work phases. Work will be carried out in accordance with the attached schedule of designated services. Each of the phases should have as complete a list of services as required.

- *Phase 1.* Predesign
- *Phase 2.* Site analysis
- *Phase 3.* Schematic design
- *Phase 4.* Design development
- *Phase 5.* Contract documents
- *Phase 6.* Bidding/negotiations
- *Phase 7.* Construction administration
- *Phase 8.* Postconstruction
- *Phase 9.* Closing/supplemental services

✔ Note that the work to be accomplished is basically the same from project to project.

✔ The number of phases doesn't make a difference, as long as you have covered all expected activities.

Yourco rep. Consultant shall be a representative of Yourco during the construction and shall advise and consult with Yourco.

Yourco-specific tasks

Yourco tasks. Provide full information regarding project requirements. Provide a reasonable budget of expenses and timing. Designate a facility manager as the project's representative. Hire a construction firm. Furnish the legal certificates or deeds to property rights.

AIA version: Architectural firm (core and shell services)

The American Institute of Architects publishes a series of documents relating to the nature of the work relationship between the architect and the owner (Yourco) and other professionals. AIA document B162, "Scope of Designated Services," is briefly quoted below.

The complete document should be referenced prior to its usage. The AIA states that document B162 "has important legal consequences; consultation with an attorney is encouraged with respect to its completion or modification."

This is excellent advice.

The AIA document covers the following section headings for Phase 1. Detailed listings for the programming are included.

Consultant-specific tasks

Predesign. Predesign includes project administration, disciplines coordination and document checking, agency consulting (including review and approval), owner-supplied data coordination, and programming. The programming task covers:

- Design objectives, limitations, and criteria
- Space requirements and space relations
- Number and functional responsibilities of personnel
- Flexibility and expansibility
- Special equipment and systems
- Site requirements
- Space schematics/flow diagrams
- Existing facilities surveys
- Marketing studies
- Economic feasibility studies
- Project financing
- Project development scheduling
- Project budgeting
- Presentations

Design agreement (interior design services)

Consultant-specific tasks

Phase 1   Pre-occupancy evaluation, feasibility, programming, block allocations, preliminary layouts, schematic design, presentations as
required

Phase 2   Design development, specifications, furniture and art inventory,
moderate amount of revisions, presentations

Phase 3   Contract documents, moderate amount of revisions, filing (usually an additional service)

Phase 4   Bidding/negotiations

Phase 5   Contract administration, field observation, project meetings, shop
drawings, change orders, furniture delivery and installation, punchlist, move-in

Phase 6   Financial closing, postoccupancy evaluation

Engineering firm (core and shell or interior design)

Consultant-specific tasks

Definitions. The following tasks are required: Audiovisual, alarm systems, data link systems, telephone wiring, motor controls, lighting, light
and power distribution, building management systems, temperature controls, sprinklers, plumbing, and heating, ventilation, and air conditioning.

Services. Consultant shall provide Yourco with structural, mechanical/
electrical, and heating, ventilation, and air-conditioning services.

Scope. The project consists of new facilities or retrofit:

- Site: (number) acres
- Square feet: office/computer/landscape/parking/etc.

Spaces. Included under spaces are office space, reception areas, toilets, dining areas, mailroom, circulation space, file rooms, and other
interior spaces.

Design-build firm (complete services)

Consultant-specific tasks

Performance. Consultant shall, as part of the work:

- Meet with Yourco, construction lenders, etc.
- Provide timely and relevant information

- Provide architectural, landscape, interior design, and other services
- Meet with local authorities (building department, design review board, planning commission, public works, etc.)
- Prepare all plans and specifications
- Provide written progress reports
- Provide written cost reports
- Perform all site surveys
- Take all reasonable steps to reduce and limit costs
- Supervise and manage the performance of the work
- Hold job meetings

✔ And as many other items as Yourco requires.

Qualifications. Consultant represents (1) that it is fully qualified to perform the work specified, (2) that the site will not prevent timely completion, and (3) that it has all appropriate licenses, permits, and insurance.

Work. Work consists of the full, timely, and proper design and construction of a first-class building in accordance with Yourco criteria and achieved in a professional manner. In addition, work includes, but is not limited to (list or attach all services expected).

Art consultant

Consultant-specific tasks

Performance. Consultant shall as part of the work:

- Meet with Yourco project manager as directed
- Adhere to all Yourco guidelines and standards
- Adhere to predetermined vendors, galleries, art framers, movers, installers, and other suppliers
- Survey space, review floor plans, and inspect the facility
- Prepare and present proposal of concept, budget, location, and delivery schedule
- Understand that each artwork will include artist's name, biography, title, list and discount price, source, size, medium, and other pertinent information
- Obtain certificate of authenticity where applicable

- Supervise framing, storage, handling, delivery, and installation of selected pieces
- Obtain necessary licenses and permits when required
- Document and photograph final installation

Terms of Remuneration

Yourco version: Architectural firm (core and shell services)

Compensation methodology

Compensation. A lump sum of $500,000 (used as an example) shall be the form of compensation, broken down as follows:

Schematic design phase—20 percent	$100,000
Design development—20 percent	$100,000
Contract documents—40 percent	$200,000
Construction—20 percent	$100,000

Deletions. In the event of deletions, the phase fee will be readjusted and payment reduced.

Direct personnel expense. Direct personnel expense (DPE) usually includes salaries of professionals and technical staff (not clerical) and customary benefits such as insurance, sick leave, holidays, vacations, and pensions but excludes bonuses and profit-sharing allocations. (This is about 1.3 times base salary.)

✔ If you agree to DPE, you will pay base salary plus benefits (1.3) times DPE (2.5), which equals 3.25 times actual salary.

Extras. Consultant's employees' hourly rate is attached and will be billed at 2.5 times direct personnel expense (DPE) or lump sum at Yourco's option.

✔ You may opt for 3.25 times actual salary. It depends on the benefits in DPE.

Payments. Payments shall be made monthly per drawdown schedule.

✔ See discussion below under "Exhibits."
✔ See design fees schedule for alternate payment method.

✔ Usually, Yourco need not make an initial payment prior to starting work.

Reimbursables. Consultant is to bill reimbursables monthly at cost (no mark-up). These include:

- Transportation other than local at economy class
- Reproduction, postage, and handling charges
- Renderings, models, and photography
- Expense of liability insurance in excess of normal amount carried
- Computer time only if required under "Additions"

Yourco-specific tasks. Yourco is to pay all invoices within 30 to 45 days of receipt. If completion is delayed more than 90 days by Yourco, and at no fault of consultant, billing under "Additions" applies.

AIA version: Architectural firm (core and shell services)
Compensation methodology

Compensation. A different compensation methodology is available for virtually every service listed in each phase.

✔ In practice, a set method is agreed upon and prevails for all similar services.

✔ Another method may apply to different services in the same contract.

✔ The most common is the multiple of direct salary expense and reimbursables at cost toward a stipulated sum based on cost per usable square feet.

✔ Special services may also require a separate authorization and compensation methodology.

Methods. Compensation methods include the following:

- Multiple of direct salary (actual) expense
- Multiple of direct personnel expense (DPE)
- Professional fee plus expenses
- Percentage of construction costs
- Stipulated sum
- Hourly billing rates

- Multiple of amounts billed to architect

Rates and multiples shall be annually adjusted in accordance with normal salary review practices.

Payments. Consultant requests an initial payment prior to work beginning.

Yourco-specific tasks. The number of days to make payment after invoice receipt is negotiable. The following apply to these contracts:

- Design agreement (interior design services)
- Engineering firm (core and shell or interior design)
- Art consultant

Invoice. In addition to amount due, the invoice should reflect:

- Description of work produced
- Summary of total fee, amount expended, and percentage completed
- Phases and estimated fee to complete

Methods. Included under methods are:

- Cost per usable square foot (upset fee) by phase
- Multiple of direct salary (actual) expense
- Multiple of direct personnel expense (DPE)
- Professional fee pus expenses
- Percentage of construction costs
- Stipulated sum/lump sum
- Hourly billing rates
- Multiple of amounts billed to architect
- Principal to be billed at fixed rate

Rates and multiples shall be annually adjusted in accordance with normal salary review practices.

Payments. There is usually no advance payment, with monthly billing only. Depending on the method, the invoice will reflect:

- Employee timecard times multiple toward upset
- Percentage of phase
- Even amount (total fee divided by project months)

▪ Hours times multiple per technical employee

Yourco-specific tasks.   The number of days to make payment after invoice receipt is negotiable.

Design-build firm (complete services)

Compensation methodology

Caveats. The maximum fee may be subject to adjustments based upon revisions to the final plans/specifications, or delays resulting from acts of God or changes in the schedule requested by Yourco.

In the event that costs of performing work and consultant obligations exceed the guaranteed maximum, after caveats, consultant shall pay any and all amounts as they fall due to complete the work and to meet the obligations of the agreement.

Compensation. A number of different methodologies are available.

▪ Multiple of direct salary (actual expense)
▪ Multiple of direct personnel expense (DPE)
▪ Professional fee plus expenses
▪ Percentage of construction costs
▪ Stipulated sum
▪ Hourly billing rates
▪ Multiple of amounts billed to architect

✔ In practice, a set method is agreed upon and prevails for the project.

Guaranteed max. Yourco pays a consultant fee of (amount) based on full, timely, and proper performance within project budget of (amount). Such fee shall be allocated at (amount or percentage) toward design work fee and (amount or percentage) toward construction work fee.

Invoice. In addition to amount due, the invoice should reflect:

▪ Description of work produced
▪ Summary of total fee, amount expended, percentage completed by phases, and estimated fee to complete

Lien free. Consultant shall provide all labor, professional services, appliances, equipment free of chattel mortgages, liens, claims, and conditional agreements.

Methods. Guaranteed maximum is the most common method. Others include lump sum and percentage of construction costs.

Payments. Monthly billing is the established procedure, with advance payment negotiable.

✔ It is suggested that a payment maximum by phase be established to ensure that billing is commensurate with work.

✔ The payment section should state that the project guaranteed maximum has not been exceeded at the completion of each phase, as follows:

Schematic design	20 percent
Basic plans and specifications	20 percent
Final plans and specifications	20 percent
At 50 percent of construction	20 percent
At 100 percent of construction	20 percent

Reimbursables. Many construction-related items are covered under reimbursables, including:

- All tools and equipment purchased for work, at prevailing discounted prices
- Cost of site utilities
- Providing necessary field offices and sheds

Yourco-specific tasks. The number of days to make payment after invoice receipt is negotiable (30 days is the normal time). Except for termination or adjustments, consultant fee shall not be reduced.

Final payment. Final payment shall be in two installments:

1. Final amount due less two times the value of all incomplete work and unperformed obligations
2. Final payment consisting of total balance due based on final acceptance and completion of all obligations

Retainer. Yourco will withhold 10 percent of each payment as retainer until final acceptance and completion.

Personnel vitae

These terms will apply to all agreements.

Consultant staff: qualifications, background, compensation

Continuity. Consultant shall, to its best ability, maintain key personnel assignments unchanged on the project.

Qualifications. All personnel assigned by consultant shall be full-time employees and be fully qualified to perform tasks assigned.

Pay scale. Consultant will supply Yourco with actual salary rate for each employee assigned or pay scale range for each level of technical staff assigned.

Screening. Consultant shall supply Yourco with complete personnel vitae on any employee to be assigned.

Yourco-specific tasks

Refusal rights. Yourco may refuse to accept any employee within 5 days without bearing any liability or upon 20 days' written notice at any time during project.

Exhibits

Depending on the type of contract, various versions of the attachments listed below may be appended to any of the various agreements.

Attachments

Affidavits. Included under affidavits are partial payment, waiver of lien, indemnification, and subcontractor's warranty certificate.

Confidentiality. A separate rider is provided for use by consultant subcontractor.

✔ This provision is similar in nature to the clause in the boilerplate.

✔ Confidential information is extended to include nondisclosure and copyright assignment.

Insurance. A certificate of insurance and certificate of professional liability policy are required.

Monthly reports. Both a cost report and a drawdown schedule are required monthly.

✔ The cost report (see Table 3.2) captures original budget, scope changes to original budget, status of contract and field changes, and a comparison of anticipated costs to revised budget.

✔ The example in Table 3.2 reflects a running rate of $111,000 over budget.

TABLE 3.2 Monthly Cost Report

(Thousands of Dollars, Numbers May Not "Box" due to Computer Rounding)

Trade	Sub-contractor	G MAX budget Col. A	G MAX scope changes Col. B	G MAX revised budget Col. A + B = C	Contract amount Col. D	Scope change Col. E	Other change Col. F	Adjusted contract Col. D + E + F = Column G	Pending changes Col. H	Anticipated changes Col. G + H = I	G MAX better/(worse) anticipated Col. C − I = J
Site prep	ABC Diggers	$ 126	$5	$ 131	$ 130	$0	$ 0	$ 130	$3	$ 133	($1)
Site utilities	DEF Electric	245	(8)	237	235	15	0	250	3	253	(16)
Foundations	GHI Base	785	15	800	800	(5)	0	795	(6)	789	11
Slabs	JKL Decks	705	0	705	700	0	0	700	(10)	690	15
Roof	MNO Tops	398	12	410	400	0	0	400	9	409	2
Interior finishes	PQR Insiders	1,345	(45)	1,300	1,350	0	0	1,350	0	1,350	(50)
Electrical	STU Lights	2,456	33	2,489	2,500	(20)	0	2,480	(2)	2,478	11
Switchboards	VWX Wiring	876	(42)	834	900	11	0	911	5	915	(81)
UPS	YZ Power	1,750	(25)	1,725	1,725	0	0	1,725	8	1,733	(8)
Cost of work		8,686	(55)	8,631	8,740	1	0	8,741	9	8,749	(118)
Gen'l conditions		869	(5)	863	869	0	0	869	0	869	(5)
Subtotal		$ 9,554	($60)	$ 9,494	$ 9,609	$1	$ 0	$ 9,609	$9	$ 9,618	($124)
Design fee		1,000	50	1,050	1,000	25	10	1,035	0	1,035	15
Construction fee		900	0	900	900	0	3	903	0	903	(3)
Project G MAX		$11,454	($10)	$11,444	$11,509	$26	$13	$11,547	$9	$11,555	($111)

The drawdown schedule (see Table 3.3) is a schedule of forecasted months for each design phase, along with the estimated fees required each month.

Plans. Among the numerous plans required are:

- Architectural plans (floor, details, door and frame, partition schedule, building elevations, roof details)
- Civil (site plans, grading, and drainage)
- Electrical (lighting, fixtures, power, systems, panel boards, security, smoke detectors)
- Heating, ventilation, and air-conditioning
- Landscape (landscape, planting, fountains)
- Plumbing (all plumbing and fire protection plans)
- Structural (foundation, bracing, columns, steel)

Property description. A legal description of property is required.

✔ The legal phrasing usually reads:

That certain real property in Yourville, Yourstate, being all of Lot 2 as shown in final map of said Corporate Park recorded in Book 4 of maps on pages 56–60, Yourville County records, and described as follows: Beginning at the northeasterly corner of said Lot 2 and continuing northerly along right-of-way for 239.29 feet, thence continuing westerly.

Schedule. A project schedule must be provided.

Standards. A copy of applicable Yourco standards should be supplied, including:

- Space allocation and office guidelines
- Fire and life safety standards
- Technical standards for computer areas
- Corporate audit standards
- Corporate security
- Construction standards

Vendors. A list of approved vendors in all applicable fields should be supplied.

General conditions. All conditions are a flat percentage of the total costs. The comprehensive list below applies to a major new building site.

Items to be included with construction contracts are listed in the fol-

TABLE 3.3 Consultant Fee Drawdown Schedule
(Thousands of Dollars)

Phase	Per-cent	Fee	09/92	10/92	11/92	12/92	01/93	02/93	03/93	04/93	05/93	06/93	07/93	08/93	TO-TAL
Schematic design	20	$ 200	$70	$ 70	$ 60										$ 200
Design development	30	300		80	80	80	60								300
Contract documents	20	200			20	40	50	50	40						200
Construction	30	300						48	48	48	48	48	48	12	300
Totals	100	$1,000	$70	$150	$160	$120	$110	$98	$88	$48	$48	$48	$48	$12	$1,000

lowing section. Each item is listed with its unit of measure and estimated cost per measure.

✔ See Table 3.4 for sample listing and the following for more complete listing.

Building work

- Special scaffolding
- Temporary heating system
- Temporary light and power
- Temporary plumbing and water
- Testing: soils, concrete, structural, fire and safety

Egress

- Temporary ramps and stairs
- Temporary roads and parking

Expense

- Reproduction costs
- Permits and licenses
- Surveys

Equipment

- Rental cost for equipment, cars, and trucks
- Transportation and trucking expenses (gasoline, repairs)
- Hoists—materials, personnel, waste chute (erection and demolition)

TABLE 3.4   General Conditions Budget

Description	Measure	Quantity	Unit Cost	Total
Telephones	Lump sum	1	$3,000	$ 3,000
Trailer—office	Months	12	1,000	12,000
Trailer—storage	Months	11	200	2,200
Toilets	Months	8	500	4,000
Labor cleanup	Weeks	48	1,200	57,600
Final cleanup	Sq ft	200,000	0.25	50,000
Travel	Each	7	1,500	10,500
Bottled water	Months	12	150	1,800
Grand total				$141,100

- Crane rentals
- Temporary elevators

Insurance and bonds

- Worker's compensation
- General liability
- Automobile liability
- Crime insurance
- Excess general liability
- Hold harmless liability
- Protective liability
- Professional liability
- Performance and payment bond
- Bid bonds

Office space

- Field office (rental, purchase)
- Setup costs
- Utilities for office
- Office for Yourco, its staff and consultants
- Shanties for work staff
- Toilet facilities
- Temporary sheds and shacks
- Office equipment
- Telephone and facsimile

Site work

- Temporary drainage
- Temporary fire protection
- Temporary barricades, entrances, and security
- Seasonal cleanup (snow, leaves, dust)
- Rubbish removal
- General cleaning

- Signs
- First-aid facility
- Pest control

Tools and supplies

- Small tools
- Supplies for the tools

Union

- Standby master mechanic
- Standby teamster
- Watch person
- Traffic control
- Fire watch
- Payroll protection
- Topping-off party
- Staffing (accounts, schedulers, timekeepers, expediters)
- Equal opportunity officer
- Fringe benefits (union holidays, retirement funds)
- Taxes (social security, unemployment insurance, personal property, gross receipts, sales, real estate, utility)

Case work study: Hiring the professional consultant

Yourco information

- A request for proposal for architectural services has been sent out by you.

- The project size is 50,000 rentable square feet, 37,775 usable square feet.

- The preliminary budget is $2,500,000 (based on historical data, no drawings).

- Three firms, which you prequalified, have submitted their proposals.

- All the services appear to be about equal.

- Yourco audit requires low bid to be assigned to the project unless there is substantive rationale for different selection.
- Your immediate supervisor is of the opinion: "You get what you pay for. Go with the highest for the best quality."
- Your own budget of $2,500,000 includes $110,000 for architectural services.
- You have been burned in the past with another firm that "low-balled" its prices to get work with Yourco.

RFP responses

Gensbaum and Associates	$2.23 per rentable square foot lump sum
	10 percent reimbursables billed at cost
H.I.J., Inc.	4.3 percent of final costs
	reimbursables billed at cost
SeeAre Architects	$2.90 per usable square foot lump sum
	10 percent reimbursables billed 1.1

Among the suggestions to be considered:

- Select Gensbaum with a low price
- Select H.I.J. with a fixed percentage
- Select SeeAre with costs based on usable square feet

✔ What is your recommendation?

Discussion. You cannot compare the proposals as submitted, since they are based on different information. They must all be converted to a bottom line cost prior to making a final decision. In addition, you obviously failed to specify in which format you wanted prices submitted back to you!

✔ Prepare a bid summary spreadsheet as shown in Table 3.5.
✔ This bid summary sheet is incomplete.
✔ What is missing? (Answers are given below.)

Gensbaum

- Base bid converts to $111,500.

TABLE 3.5   Case Work Study: Bid Summary Sheet

	Gensbaum	H.I.J.	SeeAre
Bid price	$2.23/rentable lump sum	4.3% final costs	$2.90/usable lump sum
Reimbursables	10 percent (no markup)	At cost (assume 10 percent)	10 percent (10% markup)
Adjustments	50,000 rentable × 2.23	$2,500,000 estimate × 0.043 (assume accurate estimate)	37,775 usable × 2.90
Conversion			
Bid	$111,500	$107,500	$109,548
Reimbursables	$111,500 × 0.10	$107,500 × 0.10	$109,548 × 0.10 × 1.1
	$11,150	$10,750	$12,050
Total bid	$122,650	$118,250	$121,598

- Reimbursables convert to $11,150.
- Total bid converts to $122,650.

✔ All prices are lump sum and relatively stable.

✔ You can control some of the bid price by managing scope changes.

✔ You can control reimbursables by leveraging support vendors.

✔ If the price is based on rentable square feet, what happens if the measurement formula changes?

H.I.J.

- Base bid converts to $107,500.
- Reimbursables convert to $10,750.
- Total bid converts to $118,250.

✔ Price appears to be lowest.

✔ How certain are you of the $2,500,000 estimate?

✔ If the project estimate is off by just 3 percent ($75,000), your cost would become $2,575,000.

✔ H.I.J.'s new fee would then become:

$$\$2,575,000 \times 0.043 = \$110,725 \text{ (bid)}$$
$$\$110,725 \times 0.10 = \$11,073 \text{ (reimbursables)}$$

✔ The total of $121,798 would place H.I.J. in the middle of the three bidders.

SeeAre

- Base bid converts to $109,548.
- Reimbursables convert to $12,050.
- Total bid converts to $121,598.

- ✔ Price is based on usable square feet, which is perhaps a more reliable measurement.
- ✔ Reimbursable markup is somewhat standard for firms, but since the other bidders did not include it, try to negotiate this away.
- ✔ Offer to pay reimbursables directly, after reviewed by SeeAre, to alleviate the firm from 10 percent handling markup.

Analysis

Those who selected Gensbaum

- Rentable is usually a fixed number in the lease.
- Did you field-verify measurements?
- Usable is based on a measurement from a blueprint that can shrink.

- ✔ If this project's size is off by just 1.3 percent (500 usable square feet, for a total of 38,266 square feet), review for low bidder again.
- ✔ SeeAre's new fee would then become:

$$38{,}266 \text{ sq ft} \times 2.90 = \$110{,}971 \text{ (bid)}$$
$$\$110{,}971 \times 0.10 \times 1.1 = \$12{,}207 \text{ (reimbursables)}$$

- ✔ SeeAre's new total bid of $123,176 is not as good as Gensbaum's, which is fixed on rentable square feet.
- ✔ Gensbaum also had no markup on reimbursables.
- ✔ Go with Gensbaum.

Those who selected H.I.J.

- If the low bid requirement is absolute, select H.I.J.
- Yourco will depend on you to manage the project as close to budget as possible.
- If there is a scope change that requires the extra 3 percent change, then the H.I.J. increase of $3,548 is a minimal amount.

- ✔ Go with H.I.J.

Those who selected SeeAre

- If you are not sure of your cost estimate's veracity, select SeeAre.
- Guarantee Yourco a fixed price.

✔ Go with SeeAre.

And the missing bid summary information?

✔ Project name, location, and control number
✔ Date summary completed
✔ Signature lines for at least three individuals
✔ Usually signed by project manager, financial analyst, and another official from Yourco facility management

Managing Implementation

Construction management review

In *Corporate Facility Planning,* I noted that "interior design is a big business. While the facility manager is concentrating on negotiating fees to be under $3 per usable square foot, interior design firms are totaling their income in the millions." I also stated, "I wait for the top 100 or 200 firms list to see who's 'hot' and who's 'not.'"

Now, we can concentrate on the top construction consultants and design-build firms. The July 1991 issue of *Building Design & Construction* listed firms from those with the highest billings to those with the least billings. Therefore, the number 1 firm had the highest income. This is not necessarily a measure of the firms with the highest profit.

✔ An argument can be made that their billing rate would also be the highest.
✔ However, I don't think in light of the economics of the marketplace that this would be the case.
✔ Nonetheless, it is an indication of a firm's stability, continuity, and popularity in the marketplace.

Table 3.6 shows the top two firms, by name, and the total billings of the next eight highest firms for the following categories of consultants: architectural, architect/engineer, engineer/architect, and

TABLE 3.6 1990 Top Billing Architectural and Engineering Firms

		1990 (millions)	Totals (millions)
	Architectural		
1	Gensler & Associates, Architects	$ 68.0	
2	NBBJ	38.2	
3–10	The next eight firms	188.6	
	Total top ten:		$ 294.8
	Architect/Engineer		
1	Hellmuth, Obata & Kassabaum, Inc.	$ 77.2	
2	Ellerbe Becket, Inc.	68.7	
3–10	The next eight firms	360.5	
	Total top ten:		$ 506.4
	Engineer/Architect		
1	CRSS, Inc.	$392.5	
2	Sverdrup Corp.	208.2	
3–10	The next eight firms	709.2	
	Total top ten:		$1,309.9
	Engineering		
1	Fluor Daniel, Inc.	$477.0	
2	United Engineers & Constructors	364.0	
3–10	The next eight firms	463.8	
	Total top ten:		$1,304.8
	Grand totals		$3,415.9

SOURCE: *Building, Design & Construction,* A Cahners Publication, July 1991 Issue.

engineering. In 1990, the total earnings for the top ten firms in all four categories of consultants was $3,416 *million.*

Table 3.7 shows the top two firms, by name, and the total billings of the next eight highest firms for the following categories of builders: design/builders, construction managers, general contractors, and specialty contractors. In 1990, the total earnings for the top ten firms in all four categories of builders was $29,605 *million.*

✔ As facility and asset managers, we have enormous buying power with these firms.

✔ Use your leverage and do well by Yourco.

Another innovative way to measure success is the method utilized by *Facilities Design and Management Magazine.* This list measures success, not by dollar volume, but by the number of square feet of office projects being handled by the firm. The list also reflects all square feet handled by the firm for any type of project.

Facilities Design and Management's survey form includes the fol-

TABLE 3.7   1990 Top Billing Design/Build/Construction Firms

		1900 (millions)	Totals (millions)
	Design/Builders		
1	The Austin Co.	$1,566.0	
2	Fluor Daniel	1,313.9	
3–10	The next eight firms	2,512.6	
	Total top ten:		$ 5,392.5
	Construction Managers		
1	CRSS, Inc.	$4,750.2	
2	Daniel, Mann, Johnson & Mendenhall	1,375.0	
3–10	The next eight firms	5,749.8	
	Total top ten:		$11,875.0
	General Contractors		
1	The Turner Corp.	$3,003.2	
2	The Clark Construction Group, Inc.	1,070.6	
3–10	The next eight firms	5,846.5	
	Total top ten:		$ 9,920.3
	Specialty Contractors		
1	JWP, Inc.	$1,023.0	
2	Harmon Contract	303.9	
3–10	The next eight firms	1,090.0	
	Total top ten:		$ 2,416.9
	Grand totals		$29,604.7

SOURCE: *Building, Design & Construction,* A Cahners Publication, July 1991 Issue.

lowing instructions for design professionals to list for projects that they have under contract.

Interior design (office)

Full-scope projects. Included in this group are programming, design, construction, procurement specs/documents, and field supervision. Residential projects are not included.

Partial-scope projects. These types of projects involve some of the above mentioned tasks, along with "spec" layouts and/or building improvement work (such as lobbies) for landlords and developers. Again, residential projects are not included.

Architecture/engineering (all other work).

This type of work does not include land use, site, landscape, or residential projects. If a project has significant mixed uses, subdivide total size by use to determine applicable square feet.

The *Facilities Design and Management* 1991 list for top firms revealed a major change from 1990. Gensler & Associates dropped to number 2. Hellmuth, Obata & Kassabaum (HOK) purchased PHH Environments to edge past Gensler & Associates.

Anne Fallucchi, editor-in-chief, points out that the office square footage is relatively close for the top two (500,000 square feet apart). However, when you look at the total volume of all work, HOK has nearly double the volume of Gensler & Associates.

As usual, the lesson for the asset and facility manager is the volume of square footage being renovated or built. See Table 3.8 for the listing of the top ten *busiest* interior design firms and the amount of work facility managers are letting out to their consultants.

Managing the construction budget.   While the construction manager is the most instrumental team member to oversee construction costs, all members of the team participate. There are numerous methods available for extra charges to be passed onto Yourco from a contractor. Intentional or unintentional, these costs still must be found.

The construction manager is constantly watching the quality of the installation while monitoring units, quantities, change orders, approved overtime work, and the number of laborers. These concerns may be divided into mathematical and contractual. Excluded from the listing below are the extras that Yourco causes through revisions, reorganizations, and restructuring.

Mathematical

- Mathematical or accounting errors
- Invoice previously paid (double billing)
- Incorrect labor rates charged for straight or overtime
- Incorrect rates charged for supplies or services
- Incorrect markup on reimbursables
- Incorrect add-on percentage for general conditions, fee, profit
- Change order higher than actual change
- Contractor claim higher than actual
- Number of hours to complete task higher than actual
- Retainage not deducted from monthly invoice
- Interest charges applied incorrectly
- Subcontractor bills incorrect for any of the above reasons

TABLE 3.8 Busiest Interior Design Firms July 1990–June 1991

1989–1990	1990–1991	Firm	Headquarters	Rentable sq ft (000's)	
				Office only	All work
2	1	Hellmuth, Obata, & Kassabaum, Inc.	St. Louis	18,394	85,743
1	2	Gensler & Associates/Architects	San Francisco	17,906	46,999
3	3	Leo A. Daly	Omaha	15,490	83,370
7	4	CRSS Inc.	Houston	7,447	20,457
5	5	ISD Incorporated	New York	6,969	9,949
-	6	Sverdrup Corp.	St. Louis	6,940	24,515
8	7	Architectural Interiors Inc./Interior Design Inc.	Chicago/Los Angeles	6,040	8,590
6	8	Interior Architects, Inc.	San Francisco	5,899	6,994
11	9	Perkins & Will Group, Inc.	Chicago	5,850	29,880
29	10	Swanke Hayden Connell Ltd.	New York	5,585	10,635
		Grand Total, Top Ten Firms		96,520	327,132

SOURCE: *Facilities Design & Management Magazine* (Gralla Publications), "The Top 100 Design Firms," October 1991.

Contractual

- Labor, supplies, or services not delivered or installed
- Lower insurance, bond, or liability coverage
- Invoiced change order owing to error by contractor (not an extra)
- Item already included in general conditions (double billing)
- No proof of competitive bidding
- Billing for nonbillable person or service
- Interest charges applied too soon
- Total billing too high
- Subcontractor not on approved list
- Invoice that reflects nonapplicable union increase to labor rate

Construction team hiring techniques

What do you look for in hiring the right construction team?

1. *Pricing.*   Some of my colleagues argue strictly on pricing.
2. *Experience.*   Other facility managers state that pricing is indeed important. But what experience does the firm have on this type of project? This means requesting and checking a firm's references.
3. *Previous working relationship.*   Still other experienced practitioners state that the best selection is a firm that you have had a previous working relationship with and whose work you trust. (This would evidently rule out ever trying a new firm.)
4. *Value engineering.*   Still others look for the value engineering techniques a firm brings to the project.
5. *Other hiring criteria.*   Invariably, you will use all of these factors in making your decision—and sometimes a different reason as well.

Pricing

"You get what you pay for."   As already seen in this chapter's case work study, pricing can be deceiving. Firms bid low, high, or somewhere in the middle. What does it all mean?

Does a low bid really mean that Yourco will get the same product for less money? Does a middle-of-the-road bid mean that the firm is more honest than the other bidders? Does a high bid mean that the firm is of such a caliber that the end product will be superior? Here are some items that facility managers have learned from such bids.

Low-bid firms. Low bidders feel they can "break even" on the first job with Yourco—underbidding is a way to get a foot in the door—and that they will make their profit through the normal change orders. Such firms may be using different labor pools (union versus nonunion), may have lower overhead add-on costs, and occasionally omit an item from the bid or total the invoice incorrectly. Or such firms really can deliver the end product for less!

Medium-bid firms. Medium bidders often were high previously and did not get the job; were low, got the job, and lost money; actually bid on everything accurately; only took a moderate profit level; or occasionally totaled the invoice incorrectly. Typically such firms have experienced managers managing workers with less experience.

High-bid firms. High bidders feel they are worth the difference, have more experienced personnel earning higher salaries, feel you get what you pay for, and feel they are entitled to their fair profit each and every time. Typically such firms have extensive and/or expensive overhead expenses, really watch your expenses and minimize your extras, and occasionally add too many items, total the invoice incorrectly, or increase the specification level (and cost) of an item.

Experience

"The longer a firm is in business, the better it must be." Maybe. Do newer firms try harder? Do older firms rest on their laurels? How do new firms get references if they haven't done much? Here are some items that facility managers have learned by listening to the experience of firms.

New firms

- Usually get work for smaller projects and build on their performance
- Rely on aggressive pricing to get noticed
- Utilize the testimonial approach for one project manager to tell another
- Usually are started by experienced employees from another company
- Can afford to make less profit as a way to "buy" working experience

Old firms

- Obviously were new firms once and must be doing something right
- Offer incentives to better staff performers to stay on with the firm
- Sometimes offer Yourco their best performers but "pull them" from the job later
- Have such standard routines that the overhead expenses can be minimized

Previous working relationship

"We only use firms that we have worked with before."   But how did you pick the first firm?

- Doesn't pay to use a new firm, it takes too long to train them on how we work at Yourco.

Firms with a previous working relationship with Yourco

- Were never tried by Yourco before the first time they were used
- Continue to get used because they learned how Yourco operates
- Are only as good as their last job (which was good)
- Assign personnel who have the correct "chemistry" with Yourco staff
- Deliver quality work at negotiated volume pricing

Firms with no previous working relationship with Yourco

- There has to be a first time
- Came to your attention because of good work at another company
- Are only as good as their last job (which was good, but not with Yourco)
- Are willing to go the extra step to show their responsiveness
- Will match any pricing to get into the door

Value engineering

"We want more for less."   In other words, you are looking for the consultant who can reduce your costs on initial installation without sacrificing the quality of the end project. For the project manager, hearing that a consultant can show substantial cost reductions without loss of workmanship is usually very persuasive. However, there are those external consultants who may serve you better by analyzing the life-cycle value engineering on your project.

On a new building, there are many items that can be substituted initially to save money without loss of quality of operation. However, if the full life-cycle maintenance and repair costs are factored in, these same items may not be truly cost effective. A simple formula for calculating the life-cycle cost is to add the fixed costs to the variable costs and divide this total by the number of years in service for the item. The answer is the annual life-cycle cost.

$$\text{Life cycle cost} = \frac{\text{fixed costs} + \text{variable costs}}{\text{service years}}$$

✔ This formula has been well received by my own company as well as by many facility-related magazines, including *Building Operations Management* (July 1991).

✔ It is imperative that all team members participate during the design phase of a project. Otherwise, the architect cannot complete the plans and turn them over to an engineer to work on; similarly, the contractor will be left in the dark by engineering. Each construction team member contributes from a special expertise vantage point.

Other hiring criteria

"A variety of factors lead me to select a particular consultant." While some or all of the above criteria may come into play, in the end many professionals decide on a firm for intangible reasons, or for some of the factors listed below.

- Adequate personnel to handle project
- Education of firm's principals and staff
- Firm's office facility
- Firm's financial stability
- Integrity
- Project management approach utilized
- Proximity to the project
- Visual inspection of the firm's accomplishments
- Because!

Sample request for proposal

Whether you are seeking competitive pricing for professional services, furniture, telecommunications, or construction, you need to inform the prospective bidders of your needs. The more specific you are in describing the services or furniture you require, the closer the bidders will be to providing you with reasonably close estimates. This process is called an invitation to bid and done with a request for proposal.

In the simplest version of this process, you merely send out a set of floor plans and request construction of furniture estimates from the appropriate consultant. However, the time you spend now detailing your requirements will save you time and money later on during the project. The chances of a wrong item being delivered or, more important, the estimates being understated are greatly diminished.

In 1968, on my first renovation project, I asked the construction manager when was he going out for bids. (I didn't know the term RFP at the time.) The response was something like, "Bids? We don't do bids. We tell the contractors to forget about the drawings and 'hammer to fit' and 'paint to match.'"

I suggest you follow the longer, wiser RFP method outlined below. This particular sample request for proposal is for furniture. The same types of clauses and phrases can be utilized for any other RFP you may be required to write.

Components of the request for proposal. The length of the RFP can vary from a few to over 25 pages. The basic components are the invitation to bid cover letter, bid forms, instructions to bidders, and contractual items.

Invitation to bid cover letter. The cover letter should be typed on Yourco letterhead, mailed or hand-delivered to all bidders simultaneously, and sent per your project schedule. It should allow you sufficient time:

- To send out the RFP (and for firms to work on the RFP)
- To receive bids back and to analyze them
- To follow up on missing items or unclear pricing
- To negotiate with your selection

See Figure 3.4 for a sample cover letter.

Bid forms. The RFP should include a form letter addressed to you with blank spaces for:

- Base bid list prices
- Discount percentage
- Labor rates (straight time, time and one-half, double time)
- Prevailing unions and applicable trades
- Location of storage facility
- Months of free storage costs
- Names and references for all key project members
- Final cost to Yourco

Here is a sample opening paragraph:

> In accordance with your request for proposal (dated), we submit our final bid to furnish and install all products and materials. This bid meets all

123 Main Street
Yourville, Yourstate

Bidder
456 Union Street
Yourville, Yourstate

Re: Yourco Project #93-1115
      789 Overpay Drive

Dear Bidder:
You are invited to submit your bid for furniture for the subject project in accordance with the attached plans (dated). Your proposal must comply with the attached project schedule.

Your bid is to be submitted on the forms attached. Your sealed bid should be submitted by 5 p.m., (date) to (address in the letterhead). Mark the outside of the envelope with the bid: Furniture Bid for Overpay Drive.

Three weeks later on (date), Yourco will announce the successful bidder. All bidders will be notified of the outcome.

Please respond by mail, within seven (7) days from date of this letter, of your intention to participate in the bidding.

Yourco has the right to accept or reject any or all bids or any alternates. Yourco is not obligated to take the low bidder.

On behalf of Yourco, thank you for participating in this project.

Cordially,

(Your name and title)

Figure 3.4   Sample furniture request for proposal cover letter.

items specified in your plans and specifications given to us with the original request for proposal.

The letter should be signed (notarized if you prefer) and dated.

Instructions to bidders

Pricing

■ Shall be at list price per unit reflected in a dated price list catalog

- Shall include all freight, handling, delivery and installation (straight time), insurance, fees, profit, and overhead
- Shall be discounted by a stated percentage in the bid that is to be deducted from the list price
- Shall be effective for up to 90 days after the announced bid opening unless the date is mutually extended by successful bidder and Yourco

Bids

- Shall be signed
- May be rejected if they are incomplete
- Must be submitted on forms identical to those attached hereto

In addition, alternates that increase or decrease base bid are acceptable only when the RFP requests alternates. Bidders shall notify Yourco of any inconsistencies in the RFP. A meeting shall be scheduled with all bidders to discuss any items that require clarification, to correct any discrepancies, or to decide which substitute products will be rejected. All changes or erasures on the bid must be initialed by the signer.

Submission of bid

- Means that bidder understands all aspects of the RFP
- Means that bidder accepts the conditions of the site and can perform all required tasks at the site
- Means that bidder understands that Yourco may increase or decrease final order by 20 percent at same pricing
- Is considered final and no changes may be made by bidder

Contractual items. If you are sending the RFP to your prequalified firms, you need only reference the terms and conditions of your national corporate contract. If you are sending the RFP to a firm that is not on your preferred vendor list, you should reexamine why it is not listed or why you are including the firm in the RFP.

Attach a sample contract with the new firm's RFP as an example of the contract that the firm would be required to sign if it were to become the successful bidder. In all cases, Yourco national furniture contract should be referenced in the RFP.

National contract terms. *Corporate Facility Planning* includes a complete sample national furniture contract. Here are some highlights:

- Agreement term
- Purchasing definitions
- Invoicing terms
- Shipping terms
- Delivery and installation procedures and terms
- Acceptance and inspection
- Title and claims
- Account representation
- Warranties and indemnities
- Legal and regulatory terms
- Pricing definitions and terms (this bid will most likely lower the terms)
- Authorized dealers

Look for the union label

Not much more than a century ago laborer classifications and rates appear to be rather reasonable by today's economics. The rates were not in the $40-plus-per-hour range; rather, they were $1.25 to $5.00 per 10-hour day.

✔ See Table 3.9 for a look back to labor rates in 1870.

Construction costs. A word about pricing. As noted in the previous chapter, the recommended workletter option is for the cash credit. However you decide to proceed, you will need some idea on what construction pricing should be. There are many fine guides out to assist you, including R.S. Means Company, Inc., Dodge Reports Inc./McGraw-Hill, and Black's Guide. In addition, many construction estimating firms will assist in pricing your project.

Table 3.10 is a listing of composite prices in metropolitan New York for items most utilized in construction in 1992. Note that the quotes are for New York City, one of the more expensive markets in the nation. The prices should be considered budget estimates only and will increase or decrease according to quantity.

✔ Usually, the more you buy, the lower the unit cost.

TABLE 3.9   Labor Rates (circa 1870)

Classification	Per 10-Hour Workday	
	Apprentice	Experienced
Blacksmith	$2.50	$ 3.00
Blacksmith's helper	1.50	1.50
Bookkeeper	3.00	4.00
Carpenter	2.25	2.70
Coal passer	1.50	1.50
Driver	1.25	2.00
Driver with team	4.00	4.50
Foreman	3.00	4.00
Hammerman	1.75	1.75
Hoisting engineer	2.25	2.50
Labor—common	1.15	1.50
Labor—intelligent	1.50	1.60
Machinist	2.50	3.00
Pipe fitter	2.00	2.00
Rigger	1.50	1.75
Stone cutter	2.50	3.00
Stone mason	2.50	3.50
Stone mason's helper	1.50	1.75
Superintendent	6.00	10.00
Timekeeper	2.00	2.00
Watchman	1.50	1.50
Water boy	1.25	1.25

In addition, the prices will vary with the overhead of the firm and with the competitiveness of the marketplace. Today's prices will be higher, of course, owing to inflation.

Managing corporate security

security (noun)   Defense, protection, safety, strength, cer-
                                   tainty, confidence, sureness

Security planning is not a last-minute decision. Just like any other aspect of your strategic and tactical plan, security requires consideration early in the project. In the case of a new building, security concerns require decision making well before drawings for the base building begin.

Security measures fall into one of two categories of protection: physical or electronic. Obviously, some points of entry into your facility will have both types of protection. Listed below is a discussion of some of the ways to protect Yourco's two types of assets: people (the most important) and property. These measures will provide security protec-

TABLE 3.10   Construction Costs (circa 1992)

Classification	Specification	Unit	Cost
Ceiling tile, acoustical	Concealed spline	Square foot	$ 6
Ceiling tile, acoustical	Exposed spline	Square foot	5
Closet, interior	Shelf/hang rod	Linear foot	55
Demolition	General	Square foot	3.25
Door, closer	Surface mounted	Each	225
Door, flush walnut	No hardware	Each	1450
Door, hollow metal	Standard	Each	660
Flooring, raised	2 feet square, metal	Square foot	22
Flooring, vinyl	Composition	Square foot	3.25
Flooring, vinyl	Solid	Square foot	12.50
Flooring, wood	Standard	Square foot	16.50
Kitchen unit	Wet column within 5 feet	Each	7000
Lavatory	20" square (approx.)	Each	900
Light fixture	2 feet square	Each	225
Light fixture	2 feet by 4 feet	Each	250
Light switch	Single	Each	125
Light switch	Three way	Each	175
Lockset	Standard	Each	135
Outlet, duplex-electrical	Concrete floor slab	Each	250
Outlet, duplex-electrical	Wall	Each	150
Outlet, telephone	Concrete floor slab	Each	250
Outlet, telephone	Wall	Each	125
Paint, color breaks	Standard	Each	110
Paint, wall surfaces	Standard	Square foot	0.55
Paint, wall surfaces	3 coats	Square foot	0.85
Sheetrock w/steel studs	2 ply to ceiling	Linear foot	48
Sheetrock w/steel studs	2 ply to slab	Linear foot	58
Window venetian blinds	Standard slats	Per 4-foot width	135

tion and monitoring for the most common type of attack: unauthorized entry.

In all cases, security measures must comply with federal, state, city, local, and Yourco fire and safety standards and codes. All the security protection measures are applicable for a new building. Occupancy within a landlord's building should have this level of protection for you as the tenant. Additional security, including direct link to an external security company, must also be planned in advance.

New building

Physical protection

- Security film, .004 thick, on inside surface of innermost glass on first three floors of building (approximately 40 feet in height)
- Dead-bolt lock sets on all building-specific rooms (equipment, environmental, building and security offices)

- Audible alarms on doors that lead from fire stairwells to work space
- Glass vision panel on loading dock doors for afterhours visibility
- A well-lit exterior for the entire facility perimeter
- Public access space (branch bank, retail shop, airline reservation office, art gallery) that can be segregated from main lobby
- Physical entry into staff elevators designed so as to pass a single point of entry that can be monitored by security officer or electronic card entry
- Creation of a separate receiving room for messengers, overnight packages, and other deliveries
- Design of after-hours access that can close off all but one point of entry

Electronic protection. A Yourco proprietary alarm system should be provided for all essential building rooms and egress points:

- Building, receiving, and security offices
- Building equipment rooms
- Environmental support rooms (HVAC, generators)
- All perimeter doors (street level, loading dock, roof)
- Special tenant installations (data centers, vaults, public access areas, medical department, employment department)
- Emergency assistance (panic) alarms for other tenant locations, when required

Yourco closed circuit television (CCTV) should be provided for all public-accessed spaces:

- Building, receiving, and security offices
- Freight elevators
- Loading dock dispatcher office
- Key stairwells
- Lobby
- Branch, retail, and other public assembly areas
- Key exterior locations (entries, loading dock, sitting areas)

Security office. The centralized functions are to monitor, communicate (visually and orally), and control all security systems and subsystems from one secure location. The building security office is that central control room. A new building will require:

- A 24-hour control room (near or within one floor of lobby)
- On-building emergency lighting
- An uninterrupted power system battery backup lasting 24 hours if possible
- Bullet-resistant glass where applicable
- Dual control people-trap entry with CCTV
- All graphic display panels for electronic monitoring
- Communications network within building and to local police and fire departments
- Fire extinguisher

Access to premises.   During the installation and move-in to a facility, the security guards need a letter or memorandum of authorization that permits Yourco approved consultants access to the premises. Within a Yourco-owned facility, your corporate identification card will allow access. However, in a leased facility, always include the names of all in-house staff who will access the facility, including yourself. Figure 3.5 shows a sample security clearance letter.

Managing signage

Signage is a very important item that occasionally gets overlooked until late in the project implementation phase. Too late? All too often the signage will arrive after occupancy—and sometimes after the first reorganization.

Site and building signage should be of uniform style, design, fonts, and shape. The placement of signage should be consistent and accurate. The interior signage should have all the same characteristics, as well as flexibility. Is it really necessary to etch or paint names on a glass office wall? I suggest signage that is metallic or allows you to easily slip in a new name when changes occur. Here are the most typical building signs.

Exterior signage

Site

- Advertising

123 Main Street
Yourville, Yourstate

Building Owner (Landlord)
456 Union Street
Yourville, Yourstate
re: Building, Tenant, Floor

To Whom it May Concern:
I am the designated representative and project manager for Yourco's relocation to the subject space. I am authorizing security clearance for the following staff of Gensbaum, Architectural Firm to be admitted to the subject location after hours during the installation period of (date):

> Name
> Name
> Name
> Name

The following Yourco employees are authorized for free access at any time during the project:

> Your Name
> Name
> Name
> Name

If there are any questions, please do not hesitate to call me at (Telephone number).

Cordially,

(Your name and title)

cc: To individuals listed above: please carry a copy of this authorization letter
       with you when accessing the facility.

Figure 3.5   Sample security clearance letter.

- Billboards
- General information
- Parking restrictions
- Pedestrian traffic
- Site identification
- Street identification
- Vehicular traffic

Building

- Advertising
- Building identification
- Dedication plaques
- Entrance identification
- Graphics
- Service entrance identification

Interior signage

Base building

- Code required signage
- Floor directories
- Lobby directory
- Public telephones
- Rest rooms

Offices

- Code-required signage
- Company identification
- Departmental identification
- Glass distraction identification
- Maintenance labels and restriction signs
- Room identification
- Specialty signage (cafeteria, fitness center, and other areas)
- Work station identification

Relocation Management

Everything is movable

It is amazing that when a company is preparing for a major move, the business managers expect to discard old furniture and equipment. Why? What changed with the new location that prompted the decision to buy all-new everything?

Everything that got moved into the current location can usually be moved to the new location. One of my favorite *Far Side* cartoons (by Gary Larson) shows somebody with a suitcase standing in front of the Pearly Gates. Taped to the Pearly Gates is a sign that states, "We've moved to (with the address shown)."

There are discussion points on both sides of the issue. The biggest point against buying new is financial. Not only must you budget and receive approval for the cost of all new furniture and equipment; you must also account for the write-off of any undepreciated funds.

Depreciation.   Each corporation usually has a policy to depreciate the value of new purchases over a distinct period of time. The manner of how depreciation works is best explained by your financial wizard.

Basically, under the straight-life method, the value is reduced by even increments of the useful life. In other words, a desk that cost $1,000 with a 10-year life, is depreciated by $100 each year. After seven years, the desk still has a value of $300. Therefore, if that desk were to be discarded, the project cost would be increased by $300 to account for writing off the undepreciated balance of the desk.

- Construction is usually depreciated no more than 10 years or the length of the lease (whichever is shorter).

- Furniture is usually depreciated 10 years. Since furniture is movable, it need not be depreciated over the length of a shorter-than-10-year lease.

- Office-type equipment is usually depreciated over the equipment's useful life (generally, 3 to 5 years).

Personnel considerations

Personnel moving costs.   What about the cost to move an employee with a spouse and two children? It is estimated that the cost in 1993 will be about $55,000. Among the costs borne by Yourco will be:

- Trips to new hometown
- Time and costs to look for home
- Bridge mortgage to cover new home expenses prior to old home being sold
- Interest cost difference between old and new mortgages
- Fees to sell old home
- Physical move of household
- Incidental costs incurred during the move
- Temporary living expenses, if any

Relocation firms. Relocation specialists are consultants who will help organize the entire move with you. Their niche is experience in the physical relocation of large numbers of corporations of all sizes. These firms manage a well-coordinated communications project to keep the project move on schedule and all participants well informed.

These firms also cost a fair degree of money—often $350–$400 per employee to be moved. Therefore, a move of 500 employees might easily cost $175,000. This cost may be well worth the investment if it relieves you of the day-to-day responsibility of handling the relocation aspect of the project.

Sample relocation tasks. You may expect the following services when hiring a relocation firm. The projected fees included with each service are based on the following assumptions:

- Headquarters space contains operational staff.
- Some 1,000 employees in operations will be relocated from one city to another (25 miles apart).
- Headquarters staff will remain.
- Project start to finish will take 18 months.

Communications plan (see below for sample plan)

- Relocation planning, scheduling, and budgeting
- Communications plan, including slides, photographs, scripts

  $6,750 plus reimbursables (photographer, travel, printing)

Formal announcement

- Executive communiqué to all staff outlining decision and rationale to move
- Development of newsletter/memorandum to be issued every other month until relocation is completed
- Reinforcement of Yourco commitment for a first-class office facility with minimal disruption to the staff

  $24,500

Demographic survey (see Table 3.11)

- Survey sent to each employee involved in the move to identify real and perceived concerns

TABLE 3.11 Demographic Survey-Commutation Questions (Move to Suburban Yourville)

	Downtown Yourville	Northern Yourville	Eastern Yourville	Western Yourville	Southern Yourville	Out of Yourstate	
1. Where do you live?	Walked entirely	Metro/subway to nearest station	Local city bus	Express bus	Taxicab	Private car: (D)rop-off (G)araged (C)arpool	Commuter Railroad
2. How did you travel to work yesterday? (If more than one transportation means was used, number them in sequence from your home to work)							
3. How did you travel back home yesterday? (If more than one transportation means was used, number them in sequence from your work to home)							
4. If you have to commute to Overpay Drive, how would you get there? (If more than one transportation means was used, number them in sequence from your work to home)							
5. At what time did you arrive at work yesterday?	A.M. --:-- P.M. --:--	P.M. --:-- A.M. --:--					
6. At what time did you leave work yesterday?							
7. Did you receive any visitors yesterday? How many?	Yes	No	Number				
8. About how many days a year are you away from the office for…?	Business travel	Vacation	Sick days	Personal days	Other		

- Nature of survey: psychological attitudes, commutation routes, facility questions, site and city amenities, and other issues
- Commutation questions are route-specific

$19,250 (includes reproduction costs)

Newsletter

- Development of a four-page newsletter featuring project status, area information (shopping, arts and entertainment, city services)
- Assume a total of nine newsletters (every other month)

$125,000 plus reimbursables (reproduction costs)

Focus groups

- Meetings with staff to show videos, slides, or photographs of new site
- Review of survey concerns and responses
- Question-and-answer period to respond to concerns

$75,000

Yourco directory

- Development and distribution of a formal information directory of essential services available to employees in the new building and in the new city
- Building: general building information, floor plans, and building amenities (dining, fitness, shops, area map, phone directory)
- City: shops, services, hospitals, government agencies, schools, and transportation

$50,000 plus reimbursables (printing and production costs)

First-day activities

- Welcoming letters and mementos
- Free coffee/breakfast
- Local area merchants' welcome coupons
- Information desk (directions, information, general help)

$5,500

Extras

- Employee tours of new facility, city (time and materials)
- Billing rates:
    - Senior manager $250/hour
    - Director $200
    - Project manager $175
    - Senior adviser $150
    - Adviser $125
    - Associate $100
    - Support staff $ 70

- Managing the physical move (lump sum)
- Administrative costs at 5 percent add-on to above fees
- Administrative costs shall include: postage, handling, reproduction costs, reimbursables
- Reimbursables shall include: long-distance telephone, messenger and overnight delivery services, transportation expenses and other miscellaneous out-of-pocket expenses
- Any services that are bid out (video, photography, printing, etc.) shall be by competitive bids plus 19 percent charge for coordination

✔ Negotiate, negotiate, negotiate.

✔ Totaled up the amount? It's over $300,000 without the reimbursables and extras.

✔ Ninety percent of a corporation's costs are said to be in its employees.

✔ Relocation firms estimate that they save Yourco up to 10 percent of the cost to move each and every employee. (See above for employee moving costs.)

✔ Expensive.

✔ Necessary.

✔ The decision is yours.

Sample communications plan.   Another strategic plan in action.
    Remember the S · S · S · S · S · S · Strategic Plan:

Statement Strategies Suppositions Specifics Strengths Standbys Stengel

Statement

- To create a communications program to educate and champion a positive attitude among Yourco staff relocating to Overpay Drive and to further the good relations with local community groups and politicians.

Strategy

- Coordinate all staff communications for consistency.
- Create communications materials to make staff comfortable with move.
- Publish a newsletter to create a timely and accurate means to communicate to staff.

Suppositions

- Moves will occur as scheduled.
- Staff moving is not optional.
- Overpay Drive will be a showplace facility.

Specifics

- Develop staff feelings to accept transition as their own.
- Promote a sense of pride with new facility.
- Reduce anxiety with small tour groups of new facility.

Strengths

- Overpay is a first-class office building.
- New facility will house divisions that have been previously split between several locations.
- Transportation to new facility is better according to staff demographics studies.

Standbys

- Arrange events which will reassure staff that new location is good for them as well as the community.

- Arrange for individual tours for "problem" staff.

Stengel

- Stengel: "All staff will be given tour so they know where they are moving and the floor on which they will be located."
- Berra: "This move is no different for the more senior staff than the original move to 123 Main Street 15 years ago."
- Carlin: "Staff will see the quality of their new work space versus their 'old' work space."
- Miss Humphreys: "Newsletter will be published every eight weeks promoting the new location. Newsletter will continue to be published for up to two months after the move to tell people that they moved!"

Packing instructions

Equipment

- Paper clips, pencils, staplers, other loose items should be placed in an envelope, sealed, packed into cartons.
- Office machines (personal computers, electric date stampers, copiers, typewriters, etc.) are not to be packed. They will be moved separately.
- Office machine support items (typewriter pads and covers) should be packed into cartons.
- Telephones and related equipment are not to be packed.

Furniture

- Bookcases: Pack all books into cartons.
- Desks: Pack all contents, including work papers, books, desktop items, and letter trays, into cartons.
- File cabinets: Do not pack contents. Leave intact, tighten drawer holder to keep files in place.
- Security files: Leave intact, tighten drawer holder to keep files in pace. Lock and place a signed seal on each drawer.
- Storage cabinets: Pack all contents into cartons.

Personal Items

- Move small items (photographs, memorabilia, personal plants) yourself; do not pack into cartons.
- For larger items, request special moving carton or assistance from move captain.
- Coats and sweaters may be packed into cartons.
- Keys to your current desk, file cabinet, etc. should be tagged and taped to inside top/center drawer if it is *not* being relocated. For furniture that is moving, pack in sealed envelope.
- Hanging art work, bulletin/tack boards should be tagged but not packed into cartons.
- Odds and ends that are not breakable, should be placed in an envelope, sealed, and packed into cartons.
- Card files are to be secured and may be packed into cartons.

Tagging Instructions. Although tagging is normally performed by mover, facility manager, and move captains, the general instructions are important so that employees do not change, add, or remove tags. There are two labels generally utilized: moving and do not move. (See Figure 3.6.)

Moving tag

Directions

- Write your last name and room number on each end of every carton you utilize (tags occasionally disappear).
- Uniform placement of tabs:
  Cartons: two tags, directly below hand-hold on either end.
  Furniture: front, upper right corner of cabinets, and topside of desks.
  Equipment: front, upper right corner.

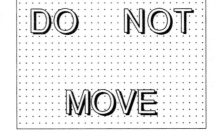

Figure 3.6 Sample moving tags.

Color-coding

- Each floor or quadrant of a floor is color-coded on furniture move plan and coordinated with a matching colored tag.
- This expedites the physical movement by quickly spotting which items belong on what floor or quadrant of a floor.

Floor number

- Serves as a double check to assure delivery to correct floor.
- In new buildings, the tenant floor number may be different than the construction floor number. For example, the floor above a three-story lobby would normally be construction floor 2, but may be tenant floor 4.

Room number

- The furniture move plan contains a preassigned room number.
- The individual room number should be written on each tag given to the corresponding person.

Piece number

- Used to count and number the various pieces physically being relocated to the room number.

- ✔ Beware the employee who wants something moved that should not be. Double-check the number of pieces agreed to be moved prior to final move.

Do not move tag

- Used for items that are not to be relocated to the new facility.
- Placed in visible location on furniture and equipment.

- ✔ Beware the employee who cannot bear to be without that favorite old piece of furniture. Somehow the Do Not Move tag falls off it!

Final checklist before the move

- Desk empty?
- Files tightened? Secured? Sealed?
- Bookcases, supply cabinets cleaned out?
- Hanging art, etc. tagged?

- Moving or Do Not Move tags on each item?
- Liquids drained from equipment?
- Questionable furniture conditions? Mover and yourself both agree on conditions and put it in writing.
- Color-coded signs hanging in new facility?
- Floors and walls protected with masonite or similar material in both old and new locations?
- Got the permits from the municipalities?
- Notified both building managers and secured truck dock and elevators?
- New stationery in new facility?
- Alerted telephone company of switch-over?
- Walkie-Talkies, beepers, and/or secured telephone lines in place to communicate with each move coordinator?
- Notified your insurance company?
- What are you waiting for, this is overtime for the movers!

First checklist after the move

- Welcome employees to new facility.
- Break down cartons as employees are finished unpacking.
- Promptly remove excess cartons.
- Check condition of all furniture and equipment with mover and move coordinators.
- Verify damage and keep a written list.
- Double-check that all equipment works.
- Assure that employees understand how their new furniture works: articulated keyboards, adjustable chairs, task lights, etc.

Complaints. Here is a memorandum from an irate client in Yourco. The names have been changed to protect the guilty. See Figures 3.7 and 3.8.

Case work study: Making the commitment
Yourco information
- UR Moving, a relocation consultant and low bidder three months ago, requests that you give them a firm commitment.

Yourco
123 Main Street
Yourville, Yourstate

Memorandum to: Facility Manager
          From: Mad customer
            Re: ABC Movers
          Date: September 1993

As you know, I did a move with ABC movers. ABC was scheduled to meet me at 123 Main Street at 9 am, pick up approximately ten pieces of furniture and move it to 789 Overpay Drive in Yourville. They were also scheduled to meet me at 3 pm that afternoon at 456 Park Street to pick up nine more pieces, also to be relocated to Overpay Drive. Below is a synopsis of what actually transpired.

•I arrived promptly at 123 Main Street at 9 am

•At 9:30 am I called ABC movers to inquire where the movers were. I was assured they would arrive any minute

•At 10 am I called again. This time they beeped the movers, and they were just pulling into the truck dock and should be upstairs within five minutes

•At 11 am, I called again. They were having trouble getting into the truck dock, the move wasn't listed with the dispatcher. I was told that it looked okay and they'd be up any moment

•At 12 noon, I left with a note of the items tacked onto the door, as the elevator arrived, so did the movers!

•Later that afternoon, I arrived promptly at 3:15 pm (I was late but I knew it wouldn't matter). I was right!

•After another round of phone calls to ABC movers, I realized that it was 4:30 pm before they arrived

Figure 3.7   Sample move complaint memorandum (Page 1).

- UR Moving's bid, $300,000, will increase by a previously announced 8 percent at the end of 90 days if no commitment is made.
- A commitment now will save $24,000.
- Increase will bring their price within $1,000 of next lowest bidder.
- Your project is dragging on.
- Your appropriation approval will not occur in time to get the save unless you give a verbal approval.

123 Main Street
Yourville, Yourstate

Memorandum to: Facility Manager
        From: Mad customer

•Luckily, they did not take a dinner break and moved the items I had tagged

•However, when they did arrive, one mover had on a 'walkperson', which was worn all night. At Overpay Drive, I instructed the 'walkperson' where each piece should go and its orientation

•I find it hard to believe that in a job where communications between people is important, that the union permits its members to wear a 'walkperson' on the job. Ten minutes later, 'walkperson' would ask me where those same pieces of furniture were going!

•Perhaps someone should tell 'walkperson' that he might be able to hear better if he took off his 'walkperson.'

•I have worked with ABC Movers for quite some time, and have never witnessed such insubordination, irresponsibility and inconsiderateness

•Obviously, Yourco has some sort of arrangement with ABC Movers and that's great if it works, but couldn't we also ask that we receive certain crews when doing our moves and not have to settle for the bottom-of-the-barrel?

Looking forward to hearing from you.

p.s. 1-We are still waiting for someone from ABC Movers to contact us about a facsimile machine that disappeared in our last move three months ago.

p.s. 2-When will our new stationery arrive?

Figure 3.8 Sample move complaint memorandum (Page 2).

■ Verbal approvals are definitely against Yourco policy.

Among the suggestions to be considered are:

■ Let Yourco purchasing worry about it.
■ Let your supervisor give the verbal approval.
■ See if you can get an exception from the auditors.

↙ What is your recommendation?

Give it to purchasing

- Yourco has centralized purchasing and they are used to this circumstance.
- Purchasing's supervisor can decide what to do with getting an exception.
- You have done your job in securing the bid and a 90-day guarantee.
- Even with price increase, UR Moving will still be low bidder.
- You need to concentrate on balance of project.

Let your supervisor give the verbal

- This is clearly a case involving Yourco policy.
- Your supervisor should handle this situation.
- You do not want audit looking into the rest of your project, they get in the way.
- You will have a note in file that your supervisor authorized this exception.

Go to audit

- This is clearly a case involving Yourco policy.
- No verbal orders are permitted.
- Let audit decide if an exception is warranted.
- You prefer going to audit, as you are project manager and it is your responsibility.

Analysis

Those who selected giving it to purchasing
- You are reactive.
- Regardless of central purchasing or not, you are the project manager.
- Purchasing always follows policy: no funding, no purchase order.
- Yourco created a centralized purchasing to avoid any conflicts.

↙ This is correct when Yourco policy is inviolate.

✔ This is correct when centralized purchasing absolutely issues all purchase orders. This may be especially true in governmental and educational agencies.

Those who selected letting your supervisor give the verbal

- You are reactive.
- This is why you have a supervisor: to review and decide on issues that are "above your level."
- Yourco policy exception approval shouldn't be done by the same person seeking the exception.

✔ This is correct when Yourco policy can have an exception if properly authorized.

✔ This is correct if your supervisor or departmental policy so states a procedure.

Those who selected going to audit

- You feel you are being proactive by going to audit.
- You may feel that audit will note your concerns for adherence to corporate policies.
- Your project file will include your CYA (cover your asterisk) memorandum.

✔ This is correct when Yourco policy exceptions can be approved only by the audit division.

✔ There are some views that audit should review adherence to policy, not set policy nor grant exceptions.

And those who selected...?   Proactive project managers

- Would go back to UR Moving and request patience and an extension of the price freeze
- Would note that if pricing changes, Yourco may have to rebid entire project
- Would document situation for their records
- Would not want to violate Yourco policy

4

Managing
Beyond Occupancy

Introduction

In building management, as in sports, there always seem to be two or more sides to an issue. No one route consistently leads to success.

What is consistent in sports?
Highest score wins?

- Golf—it's low score that wins the cup.
- Horse racing—it's the fastest (lowest) time that takes the purse.

Home team advantage?

- Basketball—it helps but doesn't guarantee a victory.
- ✔ Ask the 1990–1991 Los Angeles Lakers about home team advantage—they lost.
- Football—the Super Bowl is usually held at a neutral stadium.

Team with more players?

- It's usually an even match.
- Hockey—temporary loss of teammates during a penalty doesn't guarantee losing.
- ✔ Ask the goalie about giving up a short-handed goal.

Rules and regulations?

- Yes, and they are usually well monitored

- Not to "catch" someone cheating, but to ensure a fair game

In sports, the number of referees, judges, and umpires is directly proportionate to the number of players on a side (about one referee for each two players). In addition, in some sports, the referees have additional helpers.

Baseball

- Four umpires for nine players on a team
- Helpers: one scorer to determine hits and errors

Basketball

- Two referees for five players on a team
- Helpers: timekeeper

Boxing

- One referee for the two boxers in the ring
- Helpers: three judges to score match, one timekeeper

Football

- One referee, several linespeople for eleven players per team
- Helpers: timekeeper, three instant-replay judges, several sideline personnel to mind the number of downs played and to mark the yardage

Hockey

- One referee and two linespeople for five skaters plus the goalie per team
- Helpers: timekeeper and penalty box "keepers"

Tennis

- One umpire for each one or two players per team
- Helpers: two linespeople, a net-minder, and "cyclops"

Building management

- One building manager for all tenants
- Helpers: dozens of porters, cleaners, security guards

The referee is the building manager or building superintendent. When the function is not performed by the landlord, the building manager is designated as the landlord's agent. The building manager is empowered with all the duties and responsibilities of the landlord. The building manager is directly responsible for maintaining the rules and regulations of the building.

Building staff provide daily cleaning, moving, and minor repairs. The staff (helpers) either are directly employed by the landlord or more likely are employed by the cleaning consultant. The landlord retains the cleaning company to provide these services. This relieves the landlord or building manager of day-to-day concerns with staffing. The building manager's role is to supervise the daily activities of the landlord's property.

Sounds like great odds, all those tenants in the building and only one building manager. The role includes responsibility to ensure adherence to all terms of the Yourco lease, as outlined in Chapter 2, and to ensure compliance with the building rules.

Building rules? In addition to building standards, there are rules to abide by every day. While they appear to be rather mundane and may be easy to live with, they have a tendency to become nuisance items at critical times in your operation or future renovation work.

You may get to the point of deferring maintenance or other operational changes just to avoid the hassle of dealing with the building rules. An article in *Building Operating Management* magazine (February 1990) stated that as the 1990s began the extent of deferred maintenance expenses in public and elementary school facilities was $41 billion. Colleges and universities have over $60 billion in maintenance, renovation, and new construction that has been deferred.

You cannot afford to defer your maintenance and operating expenses. If you defer your project now, what are the chances of getting funding in the future for the deferred maintenance *and* the new maintenance items?

Therefore, be familiar with the building rules, how they are applied by your particular building manager, and how far you can go in bending or stretching them.

Contracts

By now you have been through the management goals to achieve in contract negotiations with landlords, architects, engineers, and the like. This chapter finishes your education with cleaning and maintenance contract samples.

As a tribute to your new learned contractual skills, my favorite cartoon regarding contracts is presented in Figure 4.1. Of course, it is Peanuts, featuring "Good ol' Charlie Brown."

Figure 4.1 PEANUTS. (*Reprinted by permission of UFS, Inc.*)

Maintenance and Operations

Building rules

Advertising

- Landlord shall have the right to prohibit advertising that in landlord's opinion impairs the reputation of the building.

- Canvassing, soliciting, and peddling are not permitted.

✔ This is usually fine, as it protects you from other tenants' misbehavior.

Alterations

- No tenant shall mark, paint, drill into, or deface any part of the building.

- No boring, cutting, or stringing of wires without prior landlord approval.

- No tenant shall install any resilient tiling except in a manner approved by the landlord.

✔ Be sure to add that landlord approval shall not be unreasonably withheld.

Cleaning

- Any tenant whose premises are situated on the ground floor of the building shall at tenant's own expense keep the sidewalk and curb directly in front of said premises clean and free from ice and snow.
- Tenant shall, at its expense, provide light for landlord's contractors while performing janitorial or other cleaning services.
- Use of exterminators must be approved by landlord and are at tenant's expense.
- No tenant shall clean any window from the outside in violation of Yourstate labor laws.

✔ The first point is applicable if you have a store front, not office space.

Clear passage

- Sidewalks, entrances, passages, elevators, vestibules, stairways, and corridors of the building shall not be obstructed or encumbered or used for any purpose other than ingress and egress.

✔ Great idea, make sure that landlord adheres to the rule, too.

Combustion

- No tenant shall bring or keep any inflammable, combustible, or explosive material, chemical or substance.
- No cooking without the approval of the landlord.
- No tenants shall cause or permit unusual odors to emanate from their premises

✔ Does your microwave in the employee lunch area qualify?

✔ Check it out with the landlord and seek exemption.

Employment

- No tenant shall use or occupy any space to be used for barber shop, public stenographer, manicure shop or employment bureau, shoe shine, restaurant or any other occupation which predominately involves direct patronage of the general public.
- No tenant shall engage or advertise for laborers giving this building's address.

✔ This is fine if you are leasing office space.

Light rights

- Skylights, window, doors that reflect or admit light and air into the halls or other public places shall not be covered or obstructed.

- Windowsills shall be kept clear of parcels, bottles, or other articles.

- ✔ Easier written than enforced. It's difficult to convince your staff that the windowsills/convectors are not an extra work surface.

- ✔ Landlord usually doesn't check either unless the complaint comes from you regarding lack of air circulation.

Noises

- No tenant shall make unseemly or disturbing noises.

- No tenant shall interfere with other tenants or neighboring buildings by the use of musical instruments, radio, television, unmusical noise, whistling, singing or in any other way.

- ✔ Great idea—make sure that landlord adheres to the rule too.

Removals

- All removals from the building or carrying into building of any safe, freight, furniture or bulky matter must take place at such time and manner as landlord determines.

- Landlord reserves the right to inspect all freight and to exclude any such freight that violates building rules.

- Nothing shall be thrown out of any doors or windows.

- ✔ Remember this rule the next time you are scheduling any alteration or new equipment delivery.

Security

- No tenant shall add or change any locks or bolts.

- Tenant must, upon termination of lease, restore to landlord all keys.

- Landlord reserves the right to exclude from building, between 6:00 P.M. and 8:00 A.M. on business days, and all hours on weekends and holidays, any persons without a building pass.

- Tenants are responsible to lock all entrances to their premises.

- Any hand truck or other means of conveyance shall utilize rubber tires, rubber side guards, and other safeguards as landlord may require.

- No tenant shall place any object on the floor that exceeds the floor load per square foot for which such floor was designed to carry and is allowed by law. Landlord reserves the right to prescribe the weight and placement of such heavy items.

✔ In general, these rules serve you well. Check on the passes. You may want to insist, in writing, that your corporate identification card is sufficient for a pass during off hours.

Services

- Tenant requirements will be attended to only upon application at the building office.
- Building employees shall not perform any services without specific instructions from the building office.
- No tenant shall purchase spring water, ice, food, beverage, lighting, maintenance, cleaning, towels, or similar services without landlord's approval.

✔ Be sure to add that landlord's approval shall not be unreasonably withheld.

Signage

- No sign, advertisement, object, notice, or lettering shall be exhibited on any outside or inside premises without prior written consent of landlord.
- Any sign, lettering, etc. must be of a quality, type, design, color, and style approved by landlord.

✔ Be sure to add that landlord's approval shall not be unreasonably withheld.

Usage

- No tenant can bring in or keep any bicycles, vehicles, or animals.
- No manufacturing or storing merchandise for auction.
- Premises shall not be used for lodging, sleeping, or any immoral or illegal purposes.

✔ Does the landlord provide bicycle racks for staff that may require them?

Washrooms

■ The water and washrooms and other plumbing fixtures shall not be used for any purposes other than those for which they were constructed.

✔ This is only a problem when such fixtures don't work and you need building staff to repair them.

Window treatment

■ No awning or other projection shall be attached to the outside wall or window.

■ No curtains, blinds, shades, or screens shall be attached to or hung in any window or door without prior written consent of the landlord.

■ Such awnings, projections, curtains, etc. must be of a quality, type, design, color, and style approved by the landlord.

✔ If your corporate standard for window treatment is required, seek approval during lease negotiations.

Yourco-owned building provisions

You'll note that the paragraph headings are the same as for a leased facility. However, the same message is delivered differently. In addition, certain clauses are not necessary, as Yourco corporate policies would apply.

Advertising

■ No signs or advertisements are permitted without the consent of Yourco public relations and Yourco building office.

■ Yourco-approved solicitations will be the only canvassing permitted (Blood Drive, United Way, etc.).

Alterations

■ Yourco facility management will be responsible for all alteration projects.

Cleaning

■ Yourco facility management will be responsible for all cleaning per the attached cleaning schedule.

■ Cleaning over and above what is scheduled will be charged directly to Yourco department charge-back code.

Clear passage

- Sidewalks, entrances, passages, elevators, vestibules, stairways, corridors of the building shall not be obstructed or encumbered or used for any purpose other than ingress and egress.

Combustion

- Yourco department shall not bring or keep any inflammable, combustible, or explosive material, chemical, or substance.
- Microwave ovens are permissible with the location to be jointly approved by Yourco department and facility management.

Employment

- Only Yourco employment office may engage or advertise for workers giving this building's address.

Fire and safety

- Yourco building safety officer is responsible for adherence to fire and safety regulations.

Light rights

- Skylights, window, or doors that reflect or admit light and air into the halls or other public places shall not be covered or obstructed.
- Windowsills shall be kept clear of parcels, bottles, or other articles.

Noises

- This clause is probably not necessary.
- Use skill in stacking the building to place potential "noisy" departments near each other or in the basement.

Removals

- All removals from the building or carrying into building of any safe, freight, furniture, or bulky matter must take place at such time and manner as jointly determined by Yourco department and facility management.

Security

- Yourco building office will maintain a master key for all locks.

- Yourco building office will add or change any locks or bolts as required.
- Yourco identification card will admit employees to the building at any time.
- Visitors will be required to display a building pass issued by the concierge guest desk.
- Any hand truck or other means of conveyance shall utilize rubber tires, rubber side guards and other safeguards.
- Objects that may exceed the floor load per square foot allowed by law will be placed within Yourco department as jointly determined with Yourco engineers.

Services

- Yourco building office will have staff available at all times to attend to Yourco departmental needs.
- Yourco building employees shall not perform any services without specific instructions from the building office.
- Yourco building office shall purchase spring water, ice, food, beverage, lighting maintenance, cleaning, towels, or similar services as requested by Yourco department (and charged to appropriate departmental code).

Signage

- Any sign, lettering, etc. must be of a quality, type, design, color, and style befitting the image of Yourco.

Usage

- Bicycle racks are provided adjacent to side entrance to building
- Yourco security shall monitor the bicycle rack.

Washrooms

- Water and washrooms and other plumbing fixtures shall not be used for any purposes other than those for which they were constructed.

Window treatment

- Curtains, blinds, shades, or screens shall be attached to or hung in any window or door by Yourco building office.

Typical cleaning contract

Cleaning services vary from building to building and town to town.

The best you can do is write some clause into the original lease regarding a review of cleaning a few months after initial occupancy to evaluate the effectiveness of the service. Ask the other tenants to outline what general cleaning and extra cleaning services they receive. Ask the tenants to rate the quality of the cleaning and how they arrived at the rating.

Below are typical building cleaning schedules. Unless otherwise indicated, services listed are nightly. Nightly means that it will be performed five nights each week, Monday through Friday, except on legal holidays. Check which holidays are observed by the cleaners versus the holidays your staff works. If the schedule is not listed, and you require cleaning, it will be at an extra charge. Inquire for rates and any minimum charges that may apply.

Leased space: General cleaning schedule

Building lobby

- Sweep and wash flooring.
- Machine-scrub flooring once a month.
- Vacuum all carpeted mats, when necessary.
- Clean all cigarette urns, replace sand or water, as necessary.
- Floors in elevator cabs are to be washed, waxed and polished or vacuumed, if carpeted.
- Dust and rub down walls, metal work, elevator doors, mail chutes, etc.

✔ This ensures you that the facility is maintained properly.

Draperies

- Clean building standard draperies annually.
- Any draperies furnished and installed by tenant are to be cleaned by tenant.

✔ This is usually the norm for tenants.

Flooring

- Sweep all stone, tile, marble, terrazzo, and other types of flooring
- Damp-mop ceramic tile, marble, and terrazzo flooring in entrance foyer.
- Vacuum all carpeted areas and rugs once a week—moving light furniture other than desks or file cabinets.

- Sweep or vacuum all private stairways as often as necessary.

✔ You should define "as often as necessary" and you do pay extra if you make the request.

High dusting

- Shall be performed every three months
- Shall include pictures, frames, charts, walls, ventilating louvers, lighting fixtures, overhead pipes, sprinklers, venetian blinds, and window frames not reached in nightly cleaning

✔ Remember to check that this service is performed; get the schedule.

Lavatories

- Sweep and wash all flooring.
- Wash and polish all mirrors, powder shelves, piping, hinges, etc.
- Wash both sides of all toilet seats.
- Wipe clean all toilet tissue, soap and towel dispensers.
- Wash and disinfect all basins, bowls and urinals.
- Dust all partitions, tile walls, etc.
- Wash all partitions once every three months.
- Empty and clean paper towel and sanitary disposal receptacles.
- Remove wastepaper and refuse to designated area in the premises.
- Fill toilet tissue holders, soap dispensers, etc. Tenant to supply material for soap and towel dispensers.
- Machine-scrub flooring once a month.

✔ You may want to check unit pricing of supplies of landlord against your own leverage contracts.

Office areas

- Empty and clean all wastepaper baskets, ashtrays, receptacles; damp-dust as necessary.
- Clean all cigarette urns and replace sand or water as necessary.
- Remove wastepaper and waste materials to a designated area in the premises.
- Remove all finger marks, smudges, and other marks from metal partitions as necessary.

✔ Landlord furnishes sand or water.

✔ Designated area should not be in your space.

Surfaces

- Dust and wipe clean all furniture, fixtures, and window sills.
- Dust all glass furniture tops.
- Dust all chair rails, trims, as necessary.
- Dust all baseboards and remove stains, as necessary.
- Wash clean all water fountains.
- Maintain locker and slop sink rooms.

✔ You should define "as often as necessary" and you do pay extra if you make the request.

Leased space: General cleaning costs

Benefits paid by Yourco

Basis	52.2 weeks per year
Funds	Annuity, pension, welfare, training
Holidays	Ten
Insurance costs	All
Payroll taxes	All
Sick leave	Two weeks
Time off	Bereavement, birthdays, and jury duty
Unused sick leave	$100 per day not taken
Vacation	Two weeks

Rates per hour

	Straight time	Overtime
Porter, head	$29.00	$41.00
Porter or matron, day	21.00	30.00
Porter or matron, night	21.00	30.00
Loading dock attendant	21.00	30.00
Move coordinator	23.25	32.60
Window cleaner	27.25	37.00

✔ Based on approximate 1992 New York City local union rates.

✔ Negotiate no night-time differential.

✔ Less expensive to start a night porter than to extend a day porter into an overtime situation.

✔ Not all benefits are subject to one and one-half times multiple when computing overtime rate

Yourco-owned building: Cleaning schedule.   This is similar to the leased space cleaning schedule. Some schedules are done more often and are all inclusive, since building and tenant are one and the same.

Building lobby

- Sweep and wash flooring.
- Machine-scrub flooring once a month.
- Vacuum all carpeted mats, when necessary.
- Clean all cigarette urns, replace sand or water, as necessary.
- Floors in elevators cabs to be washed, waxed and polished or vacuumed, if carpeted.
- Dust and rub down walls, metal work, elevator doors, mail chutes, etc.

Draperies

- Clean all draperies annually.

Flooring

- Sweep all stone, tile, marble, terrazzo, and other types of flooring using an approved chemically treated cloth.
- Damp-mop ceramic tile, marble, and terrazzo flooring in entrance foyer.
- Vacuum all carpeted areas and rugs nightly, moving light furniture other than desks or file cabinets.
- Sweep or vacuum all private stairways as often as necessary.

High dusting

- Shall be performed every three months
- Shall include pictures, frames, charts, walls, ventilating louvers, lighting fixtures, overhead pipes, sprinklers, venetian blinds, and window frames not reached in nightly cleaning

Lavatories

- Sweep and wash all flooring.
- Wash and polish all mirrors, powder shelves, piping, hinges, etc.

- Wash both sides of all toilet seats.
- Wipe clean all toilet tissue, soap, and towel dispensers.
- Scour, wash, and disinfect all basins, bowls, and urinals throughout all lavatories.
- Dust all partitions, tile walls, etc.
- Wash all partitions once every three months.
- Empty and clean paper towel and sanitary disposal receptacles.
- Remove wastepaper and refuse to designated area in the premises.
- Fill toilet tissue holders, soap dispensers, etc.
- Building office to furnish all material for soap and towel dispensers.
- Machine-scrub flooring once a month.

Office areas

- Empty and clean all wastepaper baskets, ashtrays, receptacles; damp-dust as necessary.
- Nonsmoking building (if you can do it); therefore, it is not necessary to clean all cigarette urns and replace sand or water.
- Remove wastepaper and waste materials to a designated area in the premises.
- Remove all finger marks, smudges, and other marks from metal partitions as necessary.

Surfaces

- Dust and wipe clean all furniture, fixtures, and windowsills.
- Dust all glass furniture tops.
- Dust all chair rails and trims, as necessary.
- Dust all baseboards and remove stains, as necessary.
- Wash clean all water fountains.
- Maintain locker and slop sink rooms.

Leased space: Building day porters. In addition to the nightly cleaning routines outlined above, the building office always maintains full-time staff for various tasks during the day. Generally, porters are scheduled in a manner that they are available seven days a week, 24 hours a day. These individuals may be directly employed by the building manager or through a cleaning consultant. The normal duties of porters are listed below.

Building cleaning

- Clean all windows inside and outside every two months.
- Clean first-story exterior window wall every month.
- Exterior spandrel glass (if applicable) is to be cleaned once a year.
- All mullions (if applicable) are to be cleaned once a year.
- Clean entrance doors twice a day.
- Clean lobby glass and directory once a day.

✔ Building image is important for you, your staff, and your clients.

General cleaning

- Clean and maintain basement corridors and utility areas.
- Set out mats during inclement weather.
- Clean and maintain building air conditioning, fan, and machine rooms.
- Clean stairways, etc.
- Clean roof setbacks and clear roof drains as necessary.
- Sweep and hose sidewalks, remove snow, etc. (may not apply to tenants with a retail store front).
- Clean standpipes and sprinkler siamese connections once a week.
- Polish and maintain exterior metal work, marble, etc.

✔ Absolutely necessary and is covered somewhere in your rent.

Lavatories

- Fill toilet tissue, soap, sanitary napkin, and towel dispensers as may be required during the day.

✔ Check out if the porters come at the same time each day, or upon request.

Security

- Police lobby, elevator cabs, lavatories, and building employees' locker rooms.

✔ Security officers are not armed individuals; the idea is just for them to be seen and keep their eyes open for unusual occurrences.

Yourco-owned building: Day staff. In addition to the nightly cleaning routines outlined above, the building office should also maintain full-time staff for various tasks during the day. The normal duties of porters are listed below.

Building cleaning

- Clean all windows inside and outside every two months.
- Clean first-story exterior window wall every month.
- Exterior spandrel glass (if applicable) to be cleaned once a year.
- All mullions (if applicable) to be cleaned quarterly.
- Clean entrance doors twice a day.
- Clean lobby glass, directory twice a day.

General cleaning

- Clean and maintain basement corridors and utility areas.
- Set out mats during inclement weather.
- Clean and maintain building air conditioning, fan and machine rooms.
- Clean stairways, etc.
- Clean roof setbacks and clear roof drains as necessary.
- Sweep and hose sidewalks, remove snow, etc.
- Clean standpipes and sprinkler siamese connections daily.
- Polish and maintain exterior metal work, marble, etc.

Lavatories

- Fill toilet tissue, soap, sanitary napkin, and towel dispensers as may be required during the day.

Moves

- Yourco department moves, box deliveries, etc. may be done with day staff.
- Notification of 24 hours is required to guarantee availability.

Security

- Yourco security department will be responsible for building security.

Case work study: Building rules

Yourco information

- Yourco facility management has always handled out of town alterations.
- A sales office in another city has decided to do its own construction management.
- It is within Yourco's decentralized mode to allow such local authority.
- The local sales manager is a hot-shot success in generating income.
- You know that the building's landlord absolutely sticks to the rules, no exceptions.
- You have developed a good working relationship with that building's manager.

Among the suggestions to be considered are:

- Let the local office handle it; you'll take over when problems arise.
- You'll make an issue of this one and take it to senior management.
- Call the sales office to offer your assistance.

✔ What is your recommendation?

Discussion

Let the local office handle it

- Why should this hot-shot success run your alteration project?
- Facility appears to be easy; let the manager discover the difficulties in managing a project.
- The manager will never want to tackle a facility project again.
- You will be the conquering successful facility manager when you save them after the project runs into trouble.

Take it to senior management

- You have been waiting for a good test case of centralized versus decentralized control.
- If the news of this local group doing facilities spreads, you may be out of work.
- This is an intrusion into Yourco facility management turf.
- You wouldn't think of running their sales office.

Offer your assistance

- You all work for the same company.
- You wouldn't hesitate to offer a new customer to the sales manager.
- Offering your advice will display your team approach.
- You may not want to run every small alteration project everywhere.

Analysis

Those who selected letting the local office handle it

- You are vengeful but realistic.
- You may be losing sight of the corporate goals.
- Check your turf issues at the door: What about working together?

✔ This is correct when Yourco is truly decentralized.

✔ This is correct when your workload is beyond your capacity.

Those who selected taking it to senior management

- Yourco may be decentralized for businesses but should not be for support services.
- Previously, projects run by nonprofessional facility managers have resulted in extra costs for Yourco.
- Senior management needs to give Yourco facility management a mandate to perform all alteration work.

✔ This is correct when senior management holds Yourco facility management responsible for alteration work.

✔ This is correct when nonprofessionals have spent corporate funds trying their hand at a facility project.

Those who selected offering your assistance

- Regardless of centralized or decentralized, Yourco suffers when you do not offer your experience with this building's manager.
- The local sales manager may not be familiar with Yourco facility management.
- This would be a good opportunity to meet with the sales manager to explain your role.

✔ This is always the correct solution.

✔ Offering your assistance and explaining the complexities may result in working together.

Preventive Maintenance

Preventive (adjective)   Anticipating or serving to prevent; same as preventative

Maintenance (noun)   Being maintained, upkeep, support

Maintaining your facility is much like the rush job for your supervisor. Inevitably, you rush through the job to meet some tight time frame. You make a mistake. And all of a sudden there is sufficient time to redo it. In other words, there is never enough time to do it right, but always enough time to do it over.

Preventive maintenance provides you with an opportunity to do it right, a little each year. If you defer maintenance, you will not be able to get sufficient funds to do it over. The key to preventive maintenance is ongoing contracts and agreements with firms that supply this service. If you do not out-source this service, then your staff's performance appraisal should reflect specific preventive maintenance goals.

Some day-to-day services that must be maintained are:

1. Elevators/escalators
2. Exterminators
3. Fire alarm system
4. Heating, ventilation, air-conditioning machinery
5. Landscaping
6. Lighting
7. Rubbish removal
8. Window washing equipment

Here are typical contractual terms to ensure the ongoing safety of Yourco employees—and your employment.

Elevators/escalators

Boilerplate. These are typical terms with a maintenance company, not with the manufacturer of the equipment.

Access

- Yourco must provide free and safe access to equipment to staff.
- Agreement is for repairs, replacements, or adjustments of parts due to wear and tear—not vandalism, accidents, or misuse.

- No repairs, replacements, or adjustments due to vandalism, accidents, or misuse unless specifically authorized.
- Repairs, replacements, or adjustments made by Yourco staff or others may result in termination of contract by us within ten days.

Acts of God

- Not responsible for acts of God, war, strikes, labor troubles, fire, lockouts, disputes, et cetera, that cause a delay in our repairs or availability of materials or supplies.
- Deadline dates agreed to will be extended accordingly by the length of such act of God delays.

Liability

- When requested, we will cooperate in the defense of suits brought jointly against maintenance company and Yourco due to accident involving equipment.
- Liability is limited to the price of this agreement.
- Yourco is responsible for advising passengers on how to use equipment.

Price

- Price increased or decreased each year is based on the Producer Price Index for Metals and Metal Products published by the U.S. Department of Commerce, Bureau of Labor Statistics.
- Rate changes effective (date of occupancy).
- ✔ Rule of thumb for 1992—about $1,200 per month per elevator or escalator.
- ✔ A building with two banks of elevators (six elevators per bank), two freight elevators and two escalators would cost Yourco about $19,200 per month for preventive maintenance. That totals about $230,400 per annum. Sales, use, excise, and other taxes are additional as applicable.

Service hours

- Agreement based on service during regular working hours (usually 9:00 A.M. to 5:00 P.M.)
- Any work beyond regular hours to be billed at straight-time plus overtime premium and travel time and expenses

Terms

- October 1, 1993 through September 30, 1998 (five years).

- Service charge of 18 percent per annum (1½ percent) per month or the legally highest allowed rate due on all payments that are 30 days over-due.

- Successive late payments give us the option to cancel agreement upon 30 days' written notice.

- Either party may cancel agreement after notifying other party of reason for agreement default; and, notified party does not commence action to rectify reason for default.

Outline of services

Periodic traction elevator maintenance
Clean, inspect, adjust, lubricate, et cetera:

- Alarms
- Brake and brake shoes
- Control cables
- Controller parts or components
- Door closers and other operating devices
- Elevator machines
- Guide rails
- Motor generators
- Solid-state motor drive components

Periodic escalator maintenance

Clean, inspect, adjust, lubricate, et cetera:

- Belts, chains, sprockets
- Comb-plate
- Controller parts or components
- Escalator machines
- Handrail
- Drive unit
- Rollers
- Step links and treads
- Tracks

Exterminators (pest control program)

✔ This section is not for the squeamish!

Boilerplate

✔ Similar to above.

Outline of services

Advise and consent

- Advise Yourco building management of potential vermin and rodent sites.
- Recommend expedient extermination solution.
- Pests are defined as mice, rats, roaches, silverfish, and water bugs.

Pest control phases

1. All below-grade floors, main floor, and first 25 percent of tower
2. Remainder of tower floors
3. Twice a week surveillance and follow-up program

Price

- $150 per floor (phases 1 and 2)
- $250 per visit (phase 3)
- Time and materials for all other visits

Service hours

- Normal working hours are 9:00 A.M. to 5:00 P.M.
- Emergency requests responded to within 2 hours if called within normal working hours

Terms

- October 1, 1993 through September 30, 1996 (three years).
- Either party may cancel agreement after notifying other party of reason for agreement default; and, notified party does not commence action to rectify reason for default.

✔ It is a good idea to stagger the expiration of your agreements to allow yourself negotiating time without burdening your workload.

Fire alarm system

Boilerplate

Acts of God

- Not responsible for acts of God, war, strikes, labor troubles, fire, lockouts, disputes, et cetera, that cause a delay in our repairs or availability of materials or supplies.
- Deadline dates agreed to will be extended accordingly by the length of such act of God delays.

Insurance

- Contractor is not an insurer.
- Liability is limited to 10 percent of annual contract service charge.
- Liability insurance may be obtained through contractor at an extra service charge and separate rider.

Maintenance

- Yourco authorizes contractor to maintain in good working order all items listed in outline of services.

Price

- First year: $25 per rentable square foot in the building
- Eight percent increase each subsequent year

Service hours

- Normal working hours are 9:00 A.M. to 5:00 P.M., regular business days
- All other times, Saturdays, Sundays, and holidays are considered overtime and will be billed accordingly if testing was requested by Yourco

Terms

- October 1, 1993 through September 30, 1997 (four years)
- Either party may cancel agreement after notifying other party of reason for agreement default; and, notified party does not commence action to rectify reason for default

✔ It is a good idea to stagger the expiration of your agreements to allow yourself negotiating time without burdening your workload.

Testing

▪ Yourco is responsible for notifying staff when system is out of service because of testing.

Outline of services

Check/test for proper operation

▪ Bells
▪ Controllers
▪ Door holders
▪ Heat detectors
▪ Pull stations
▪ Water flow switches

Remove, disassemble, clean, replace, test, reinstall

▪ Air duct detectors
▪ Ionization detectors

Weigh, check pressure, test

▪ Carbon dioxide (CO_2) cylinders
▪ Halon cylinders

Heating, ventilation, air-conditioning machinery

Boilerplate. Most terms are similar to those above. A few specific items:

Inspections

▪ One per calendar quarter

Price

▪ Comprehensive coverage for services outlined below is $25,000 (based on an office facility of 1 million square feet).
▪ Coverage is payable $6,250 per quarter.

Terms

- May be canceled by contractor if equipment is relocated or altered without consent of contractor.
- If equipment is abused by Yourco.
- For nonpayment of bills older than 30 days.
- Yourco may not assign agreement.
- Agreement excludes water treatment, which is highly recommended.
- Agreement applies only to equipment, not to any hardware, ducts, plumbing, wiring, et cetera, connected to equipment.
- Contractor is not liable for any loss of revenue or profit arising from damages or delays to equipment.

Outline of services

Check, tighten, change, calibrate

- Freon
- HVAC system motor
- Magnetic starter
- Oil pump
- Operating controls
- Purge compressor
- Safety controls
- System pressure/leaks
- Tubes: absorber, condenser, evaporator

Miscellaneous

- Operator training
- Safety checks on all starter components
- 24-hour emergency service

Landscaping
Boilerplate
✔ Same as above

Outline of services

Guarantees

- All trees and plantings are guaranteed by the contractor for one full year commencing the day of planting, except for acts of vandalism.
- Contractor will be responsible for all replacement expenses.

Pricing

- ✔ Too many variables, but segregate initial tree and planting expenses from ongoing maintenance program.
- ✔ Many trees and plants are priced by their size, fullness, or caliber (diameter of the trunk)—not necessarily the time required to plant.

Terms

- Contractor will maintain plantings with at least two visits per week.
- Contractor will fertilize, prune, water, and weed.

Lighting

Boilerplate

Hours

- 8:30 A.M. to 4:30 P.M.
- All other times are overtime hours (1.5 times normal hourly rate).
- Double overtime is applicable Sundays and holidays (2.0 times normal hourly rate).
- Only one-half hour is allowable for lunch.

Rates per hour

	Straight time	Time and one-half	Double time
Mechanic	$22.50	$33.75	$45.00
Helper	16.25	24.37	32.50

- All bulbs and materials are the responsibility of Yourco.
- Bulbs shall be *ABC* only, no substitutes.

✔ Prices are based on New York City labor rates, circa 1992.

✔ Negotiate another manufacturer's bulbs in for your own peace of mind.

Staffing

- Two full-time local union electricians will be required: one mechanic and one helper.
- Prevailing labor rates apply.

Outline of services

Inspect and replace burned-out bulbs

- Elevators
- Exit and emergency lights
- Lobbies
- Rest rooms
- Stairwells
- Tenant areas

Respond to lighting-related requests

- As directed by building manager
- After daily inspection outlined above

Rubbish removal

Boilerplate

✔ Same as above

Price

- All prices are per pull.
- Prices are based on paper waste only.
- Any mixture of wet and compacted or with plastic bags will result in a 10-day warning period.
- If rubbish warning is not met, price increases by 5 percent.
- Removal cost:

Cubic yard, compacted $50.00

Cubic yard, wet $17.00

✔ Negotiate up to 20 percent off these rates on the basis of volume.

■ Recycling income:

Computer paper: 110 percent of *Fiber Market News* price per ton

Cardboard: 100 percent of *Fiber Market News* price per ton

✔ Negotiate up to 15 percent higher price per ton.

Window-washing equipment

Boilerplate

✔ Same as above

Price

■ Varies with number of rigs, building location, and condition.

✔ Typical cost for office tower is under $1,500 per service call.

Outline of services

Clean, check, lubricate, replace

■ Brakes
■ Cables
■ Electrical controls
■ Fittings
■ Fuses
■ Gearbox
■ Mechanisms
■ Pins: cotter, spring
■ Rail system
■ Rollers
■ Roof anchors
■ Safety switches
■ Wiring

Managing Your Performance Appraisal

The underlying meaning of performance appraisal terms

We have all been subject to reading our own performance appraisal. Some of us are managers and have struggled over the exact words and phrases to utilize in appraising staff.

Here are some of *your* key traits as written by your supervisor and their humorous or hidden meanings:

As written	True meaning?
Articulate	Obnoxious
Cooperative	Agrees to work, does nothing
Devotes overtime hours to work	Spends all day goofing off
Expressive	Talks back to everyone
Gets along well with others	A social butterfly at the office
Intelligent	Gets out of doing assignments
Motivates others	Tom Sawyer approach to work
Punctual	In before the late arrivers
Pays attention to detail	Likes to split hairs
Quantitative	Recalculates weekly paycheck
Rationale approach	Gets someone else to do work
Record keeping is excellent	Covers errors well
Reliable	Comes back from lunch break
Self-starter	Makes coffee on own
Technically proficient	Knows how to turn on computer
Writes well	Hard to ruin a vacation memo

Sample performance appraisals

The performance appraisal is competed in two distinct time periods. At the beginning of the appraisal period (usually the calendar year), basic information about you and your various project and personal objectives are completed. Both you and your supervisor sign or initial your agreement to these objectives. After the appraisal period is completed, you fill in your results against these objectives; and, your supervisor evaluates your performance against these objectives.

These components are made up of the following:

Basic Information about you

- Group/division/department/unit
- Your name
- Corporate title
- Functional position description
- Date in position
- Personnel/social security number
- Date of the appraisal
- Period covered by the appraisal

At the beginning of the year

- Your project objectives for the year, including a brief description of the project and its target dates
- Your development plan for personal goals and achievements
- Your career interests and career path goals
- Your signature or initials and date of acceptance of these objectives
- Your supervisor's signature or initials and date of acceptance signifying that the objectives are achievable

After the end of the year

- Results achieved against each project objective
- Results achieved against development plan for personal goals and achievements
- Supervisor's review of your performance against all of your objectives and a summary of your overall performance
- Supervisor's review of your career interests and career path goals
- Your comments on your supervisor's appraisal of you
- Optional: higher management's comments
- Your supervisor's signature/date of completing the appraisal
- Higher management's signature/date, if applicable
- Your signature/date of acceptance of the appraisal

Sample performance appraisal analyzed

Figures 4.2, 4.3, and 4.4 depict a completed Yourco performance appraisal. The top of all forms is the same. In this sample, the appraisal period is calendar year 1993.

Page 1 (Figure 4.2)

1 Project objectives and target dates

- Completed by you at beginning of appraisal period, reflects all known projects and estimated target dates or milestones.
- Goals are accepted as signified by your initials and date.

Yourco Performance Appraisal	Date: January 4, 1994
Name/Title Your Name	Identification No. 123-45-6789
Functional Title Facility Resource Manager	Date in Position 26-Oct-88
Group/Division/Department/Unit Corp Ops/Real Estate/Resource Mgmt/Facilities	Appraisal Period Jan. 1, 1993 - Dec. 31. 1993
1. Project Objectives and Target Dates	2. Achievements and Comments
1. Relocate Credit Div. to 789 Overpay 8/93 Extensive renovation of site, building, mechanical, and electrical systems	Successfully completed the relocation on time and under budget
2. Refurbish corporate residence, London 8/93 Requires selection of furniture, furnishings and finishes for Yourco Senior officer	Completed in September due to delay in customs Project was on budget
3. Renovate Trading conference room 8/93 Expand room to accomodate additional seating	Project was reassigned to another staff member
4. Complete space plan for 123 Main Street 9/93 Restack plan of existing facility to be implemented after relocation to Overpay Drive	Due to senior management extensive reviews, space plan was completed in October
5. Implementation of Space Plan Ongoing Work with various departments towards restacking Start implementation in October after relocation to new facility at Overpay Drive	Implementation was started on time despite delay in space plan approval
Goals Accepted: Y. N. 1/6/93 (your signature/initials) date Goals Achievable: Y. S. 1/6/93 (supervisor's signature/initials) date	

3. Supervisor's Review of Overall Performance
Your Name has successfully completed the relocation of the Credit Division to 789 Overpay drive to the complete satisfaction of our clients (users). Your Name clearly demonstrated dedication to Yourco by the numerous hours required to complete this project. The renovation of the London residence is another example of a satisfied client. The Trading room was reassigned due to the extensive time required to complete the space plan. Your Name continues to be an asset to our department.

Figure 4.2   Performance appraisal. (Page 1 of 3.)

Yourco Performance Appraisal	Date: January 4, 1994
Name/Title Your Name	Identification No. 123-45-6789
Functional Title Facility Resource Manager	Date in Position 26-Oct-88
Group/Division/Department/Unit Corp Ops/Real Estate/Resource Mgmt/Facilities	Appraisal Period Jan. 1, 1993 - Dec. 31. 1993
4. Development Plan 1. Increase knowledge of construction process 2. Improve knowledge and duties in space planning 3. Be assigned independent projects with total project management responsibilities	5. Achievements and Comments 1. Achieved by attending two construction seminars 2. Achieved as evidenced by senior management's acceptance of space plan for 123 Main Street 3. Achieved by sole management of relocation of Credit Division to Overpay Drive
6. Strengths Assessment 1. Personal traits include self-motivation, uses logic, conscientious 2. Good knowledge of project scheduling 3. Good understanding of financial control 4. Excellent design skills	7. Strengths Enhancements 1. Additional traits include thorough and good client interpersonal skills 2. Good understanding of interrelationship of disciplines required for successful project 3. Same 4. Enhanced with sensitivity to finishes and costs without loss of quality
8. Career Goals and Interests 1. Be promoted to Senior Resource Manager 2. Manage in-house project management staff 3. Work on new building complex	9. Career Achievements 1. Achieved, Your Name was promoted in October in recongnition of fine project abilities 2. Not achieveable this year, but possible in the near future 3. Was responsible for relocations into our new building at 789 Overpay Drive

10. Supervisor's Review of Development and Career Goals
Your Name has shown excellent development in both project and construction managment. Additionally, Your Name successfully managed the highly complex relocation of Credit to our new facility at Overpay Drive. In addition to Your Name's promotion to Senior Resource Manager, Your Name is under consideration for the project management head position.

Your Supervisor   1/4/94

Signature   Date

Figure 4.3   Performance appraisal. (Page 2 of 3.)

- Goals are agreed to by your supervisor as signified by supervisor's initials and date.

✔ Don't put in goals that you cannot possibly achieve.

2 Achievements and comments

- Completed by you after appraisal period with your own commentary.
- Projects that were reassigned are noted.
- New projects, not previously assigned, would be added when applicable (there are none in this sample).

Yourco Performance Appraisal	Date: January 4, 1994
Name/Title Your Name	**Identification No.** 123-45-6789
Functional Title Facility Resource Manager	**Date in Position** 26-Oct-88
Group/Division/Department/Unit Corp Ops/Real Estate/Resource Mgmt/Facilities	**Appraisal Period** Jan. 1, 1993 - Dec. 31. 1993

11. Comments of Higher Management
Your Name has set a fine example for resource managers.

Senior Manager   1/5/94

Signature   Date

12. Mobility Comments
Are there any other departments that you feel that you would like to be considered for in terms of transfers?

No.

13. Your Name's Comments

I concur with appraisal.

Your Name   1/5/94

Signature   Date

14. Divisional Reviews

Division Head   1/12/94   Human Resource Manager 1/13/94

Signature   Date   Signature   Date

Figure 4.4   Performance appraisal. (Page 3 of 3.)

✔ Achieve your goals as a minimum goal.

3 Supervisor's review of overall performance

■ Completed after appraisal period by your supervisor.

✔ Good supervisors have already told you this information throughout the year—they do not wait for the annual review.

Page 2 (Figure 4.3)

4 Development plan

■ Completed by you at the beginning of appraisal period

5 Achievements and comments

- Completed by you after appraisal period

6 Strengths assessment

- Completed by you at the beginning of appraisal period

7 Strengths enhancements

- Completed by you after appraisal period

8 Career goals and interests

- Completed by you at the beginning of appraisal period

9 Career achievements

- Completed by your supervisor after appraisal period

10 Supervisor's review of development and career goals

- Completed by your supervisor after appraisal period

Page 3 (Figure 4.4)

11 Comments of higher management

- Completed by your higher management (usually two levels above you) after the appraisal period

12 Mobility comments

- Competed by you after appraisal period

✔ You have an opportunity to request a transfer.
✔ Most people feel if they fill in another department, and they do not get transferred, it is "held against them."
✔ And, most people might be right! It depends upon the corporate culture.

13 Your name's comments

- You have an opportunity to air your feelings for the record.

✔ The response most often placed in this box: "I concur with appraisal."

14 Divisional reviews

- When required, senior management would review, might comment, and then date the form.
- In all cases, human resources would review and date the form.

✔ You do not get to comment on these reviews.

✔ You do see these reviews when you get your copy back for your records.

How to ensure favorable performance reviews

As one of my staff says: "This is a no brainer: Do a good job. Yes, that is the minimum. But it is not enough."

Unfortunately, the squeaky wheel gets grease syndrome comes into play. You need to emphasize to your colleagues and your supervisor your triumphs during the year. But do not be obnoxious about it.

Unsolicited memoranda from your clients are very helpful. (Even when you hint to them about writing a note to your supervisor.) You are only as good as your last project! Make sure you end the appraisal period in style!

Remember *Sic transit gloria mundi.* How quickly fame fades.

Overcoming corporate management misunderstanding of performance

It's your job to lose. Earlier in this chapter, there was a discussion on sports. If you follow professional football, you will remember that the New York Giants just barely edged the Buffalo Bills, 20–19 in Super Bowl XXV. Many sport fans consider this the closest and most exciting game.

If you remember some of the details of the season, Phil Simms was the Giants quarterback until he was injured late in the season. Jeff Hostetler took over and guided the team on to the Super Bowl victory. Yet, in the very next season, the "talk" was which of the two quarterbacks will start the season. Each will be given an equal opportunity during practice games.

Barring any injuries, the feeling was in fact that Simms was the incumbent—which means that it was his job to lose. Think of yourself as the past season's seasoned quarterback. Your injury is the one job that did not get completed on time or within budget.

As you get ready for your annual review, remember that it is your job to lose. You can control most factors on a job. (Yes, it is easy to blame everybody or anybody.) Yourco gives you, the quarterback, the game ball for successful work. Don't lose it. (Incidentally, Phil Simms did lose out to Jeff Hostetler.)

Each year your supervisor should be reviewing your performance. Your supervisor may also be required, quite independent of how you performed against certain tasks, to rate your skills.

Skills evaluation matrix

The Skills Evaluation Matrix is the generally accepted format. This scores your specialty skills and managerial skills and "pits" them against your peers.

In the economic crunch of this decade, your skills assessment is usually more critical than your annual appraisal. In *Corporate Facility Planning* the Functional Evaluation Matrix or weighted analysis was used to help you benchmark which vendor offered the best product for computer-aided design. The same type of analysis is used by human resources to evaluate which employee is best overall when there are so many variable aspects to the job.

Filling out the matrix

- Step-by-step instructions are below.
- See Table 4.1 for an example of the completed matrix.
- See Table 4.2 for the matrix summary.

Attributes

- Select all the appropriate skills that are outlined in the position description of the individuals.

- ✔ Twenty-two skills are listed, including technical skills, report writing, reliability, resourcefulness, and financial control.

- Sort the skills into major categories of attributes.

- ✔ Four categories appear: education/experience, managerial, interpersonal, and financial reporting.

- Assign a priority of importance to you, as a manager, of each skill in each category.

- ✔ Under Financial Reporting, both analysis and control are of equal weight.

- The sum of the weights in each category should total to one (1).

TABLE 4.1   Functional Skills Matrix

Skills	Weight	Employee #1		Employee #2		Employee #3	
		Score*	Ex-ten-sion	Score*	Ex-ten-sion	Score*	Ex-ten-sion
Education/Experience							
Degree in arch./fac. mgmt.	0.15	5	0.75	3	0.45	4	0.60
Design experience	0.15	5	0.75	5	0.75	4	0.60
Five-years experience	0.20	5	1.00	5	1.00	3	0.60
Space planning ability	0.25	4	1.00	5	1.25	4	1.00
Technical skills	0.25	4	1.00	3	0.75	4	1.00
Total	1.00		4.50		4.20		3.80
Managerial							
Construction management	0.10	4	0.40	4	0.40	5	0.50
Mgmt. of external consultant	0.10	3	0.30	2	0.20	5	0.50
Multiple assignments	0.15	3	0.45	2	0.30	5	0.75
Organizational skills	0.10	3	0.30	3	0.30	4	0.40
Problem solving	0.25	4	1.00	3	0.75	5	1.25
Project/facility management	0.25	5	1.25	5	1.25	5	1.25
Report writing	0.05	4	0.20	4	0.20	2	0.10
Total	1.00		3.90		3.40		4.75
Interpersonal							
Customer satisfaction	0.20	4	0.80	5	1.00	5	1.00
Oral presentation skills	0.20	3	0.60	5	1.00	4	0.80
People management	0.25	4	1.00	3	0.75	5	1.25
Reliability	0.15	4	0.60	4	0.60	5	0.75
Resourcefulness	0.10	4	0.40	4	0.40	5	0.50
Tact	0.10	3	0.30	2	0.20	4	0.40
Total	1.00		3.70		3.95		4.70
Financial Reporting							
Accuracy of reports	0.15	3	0.45	3	0.45	2	0.30
Financial analysis	0.35	3	1.05	3	1.05	4	1.40
Financial control	0.35	4	1.40	3	1.05	4	1.40
Timeliness of reports	0.15	4	0.60	3	0.45	1	0.15
Total	1.00		3.50		3.00		3.25

*Scoring key: 5 = exceptional; 4 = constantly exceeds criteria; 3 = meets position criteria; 2 = improvement is needed; 1 = unsatisfactory.

✔ Each of the four categories totals to one (1).

■ Scoring criteria can be on a 10 or 5 scale. The higher the number, the better the individual performs that skill.

✔ Scoring legend at the bottom of the chart is a 1-to-5 scale, with the definition of each level clearly defined.

TABLE 4.2 Functional Skills Matrix Summary

Skill	Weight	Employee #1	Employee #2	Employee #3
Education/experience	1.00	5.00	3.25	3.00
Managerial	1.00	2.80	4.85	4.90
Interpersonal	1.00	2.45	4.05	4.90
Financial reporting	1.00	4.85	4.85	2.55
Grant total	4.00	15.10	17.00	15.35
Average	1.00	3.78	4.25	3.84

- Usually in a weighted analysis you assign the highest score to the best product and compare the other products to the top choice. In employee evaluations you do not score an individual with the highest score unless it is earned.

✔ Under Interpersonal, no employee scored a 5 for exceptional performance in Tact.

- Multiply the score for the employee for each skill times the weight assigned and enter under "extension."

✔ Under Managerial, the extension for Employee #1 for Multiple Assignments is 0.45.

- Total the four attributes and enter onto a summary page (Table 4.2).
- Divide the total by the number of categories (four) and evaluate the averages.

Evaluation.   In reviewing the skills matrix, you would note the following about these employees.

Employee #1 3.78

- Excels in education and experience category
- Excels in financial reporting
- Below par in managerial
- Serious problem in interpersonal skills

Employee #2 4.25

- Excels in managerial skills
- Excels in financial reporting
- High performance in interpersonal skills
- Acceptable performance in education and experience

Employee #3 3.84

- Excels in managerial skills
- Excels in interpersonal skills
- Acceptable level in education and experience
- Unacceptable level in financial reporting

If you were required to release (fire) one of the employees, which one would you select?

You would undoubtedly retain Employee #2 as the highest rated individual. In addition, Employee #2 had scores of three or higher (meets position criteria). The harder choice remains. The scores are close enough for you to further evaluate individual skills.

For example, if attitude as reflected in People Management is important to the position, then Employee #1 only scored a 2 versus a 5 for Employee #3. If Financial Reporting, in general, is more important, Employee #1 clearly is superior to Employee #3.

Finally, a table of statistics cannot reflect some of the intangibles that you as a manager feel in interacting with the employee each day. Also the personal habits—dress, punctuality, neatness, attentiveness, etc.—are difficult to score.

Case work study: Performance versus reality

Yourco information

- A project was approved for $1,000,000 on January 5.

- Your annual performance review is in December.

- After 10 long months, you have finished the project, paid the last invoice, and proudly inform the managing director of an $80,000 save.

- Upon hearing of the save, the director "requests" several new items to be purchased, which total $80,000.

- The director's approval level is $250,000.

Among the suggestions to be considered are:

- Proceed with the extras; after all, Yourco already approved the full $1,000,000. You want to take credit for the completed project for your performance appraisal.

- Close the project and refuse to purchase extras. Request a new project form be submitted. You will take credit for a completed project and starting a new project as well.

- Write a memo to your supervisor prior to the annual performance review. Outline your save and document that you are continuing on the project as requested by the director.

✔ What is your recommendation?

Discussion. There is no question that the funds were originally approved for the full $1,000,000. And that the director is authorized to spend the $80,000. There is also your concern to get through your performance appraisal without the director complaining to your supervisor that you are holding up the completion of the project.

Proceed with the extras

- Yourco authorized $1,000,000 for the director's project.
- Director could stir up troubles and can easily authorize the new expenditure.
- Why create problems at review time?
- Why create extra paperwork with a new project request form?

Close the project

- Your performance appraisal included getting the project being completed on time (10 months) and on or under budget.
- You want full credit in your review for accomplishing both.
- The authorization from Yourco was for up to one million dollars based on specific business and facility needs.
- You met all needs and for $80,000 less. Yourco did not authorize these extras. The project is completed and should be closed.
- You feel that if the director complains, you have a solid business rationale to support your posture.

Document your save/buy the extras

- Your performance appraisal included getting the project being completed on time (10 months) and on or under budget.
- You want full credit in your review for accomplishing both.
- Yourco authorized $1,000,000 for the director's project.
- Director could stir up troubles and can easily authorize the new expenditure.
- Your supervisor will treat you harshly in your review if you create "waves."

Analysis

Those who selected proceed with the extras
- Obviously, you are reactive and take the course of least resistance.

- You probably never will close a project.
- You need to review Yourco policies regarding continuous expenditures.
- The audit division is a good place for you to review the proper procedures.

✔ This is correct if Yourco policy concurs with full expenditure of previously approved amounts.

✔ Governmental and some educational facility units frequently face this: use it or lose it within the fiscal year.

Those who selected close the project

- You are the proactive facility manager.
- You really are doing the proper accounting and facility move.
- Your supervisor should note this in your performance appraisal.
- You do have a fiduciary interest to watch the capital expenditures of Yourco.

✔ This is correct in most corporate environments.

✔ This may not apply within governmental or educational agencies.

Those who selected document your save/buy the extras

- You might as well write your own performance appraisal, too.
- This attitude of CYA (covering your asterisk*) is getting out of hand.
- You shouldn't be concerned that the director will alert your supervisor.

✔ This is correct if Yourco policy concurs with full expenditure of previously approved amounts. But, why write the CYA?

✔ Governmental and some educational facility units frequently face this: use it or lose it within the fiscal year. But, why write the CYA?

Headhunters, Resumes, Career Paths, and Beyond

Executive search firms (headhunters)

I Heard It Through the Grapevine was a big hit in the past. In the past, the grapevine was used for finding someone to fill a position. Now the professional version of grapevines is the executive search firm. Executive search firms go by the nickname "headhunters."

If you could foretell the future, you would probably be rich. Another view, you might do things differently today to alter what you did then. Here is your opportunity. When headhunters work with you and need to synthesize your resume into a paragraph, they tend to oversell you. They tend to add spice, zest, and zip into your quest for a position. You are about to read *your* future headhunter paragraphs below. You can do something about it now to change these descriptions.

Headhunters do bulk mailings to senior facility professionals. These mailings list all available unemployed facility staff handled by that headhunter. The synopses listed below may appear to you as "made-up," "unreal," "totally ridiculous."

✔ I would agree with you.

✔ However, they *are* real text and mailed to thousands of professionals like me about available professionals like you!

Bulk headhunters. These firms handled virtually any facility professional who walks into their offices. The bulk mailings all show creative talent in describing the otherwise unusual talents of these individuals.

- Reflect actual statements used by the headhunters

Designer/draftsperson, asking low $30's

- A contemporary thinker who has an intellectual range coupled with an inspirational design ability
- Is an industrious designer with fortitude and a very friendly disposition
- Catch this rising star

Field representative, asking upper $30's

- Is a well rounded and enterprising individual
- Shows a true pride through the quality of their (sic) work
- Has ingenious ideas
- Can make the vital connection
- A level-headed and flexible person

Job captain/designer, asking $35,000

- A gifted, aesthetically aware individual with superb design and technical flair
- Is highly skilled in conceptualizing and planning of vast-scale and in-depth projects
- Is a great communicator
- Has strong credentials for long-range potential

Junior interior designer, asking $20,000

- This young design novice is a class act!
- Is low key, yet gets the point across
- Has a discerning eye and exquisite taste
- A flourishing talent with sights set high

Registered architect, asking $45,000

- This design professional's work is of undeniable distinction
- Has incredible determination and stamina
- Has a portfolio that will turn heads
- Looking for a long-term commitment with a builder or real estate developer
- Has what it takes to reach the top
- A winning choice

Space planner/designer, asking $35,000

- You could hire this person on personality alone
- Is an awe-inspiring co-worker who is ready to face new challenges within the corporate world

Specialty headhunters. These firms tend to handle only the more seasoned facility professionals. They also do bulk mailings but the text tends to be more mature. Salaries are not included in the one paragraph descriptions. A single page mailing contains an average of eight profiles per side.

Construction manager

- With a proven track record as an Owner's representative for an international real estate developer
- Background in trust administration and lease negotiations

- Degree in construction management and license in architecture
- Uniquely qualified for many real estate construction and property management positions

Corporate architect

- Registered architect with an MBA in finance
- Recipient of several prestigious fellowships
- Member of the properties and real estate division of a major financial institution
- Performs a variety of architectural and financial functions related to real estate acquisition
- A highly competent and personable individual with a straightforward personality

Director of facilities

- As a department head of a major corporation, this individual manages 20 professionals and is responsible for varied projects costing up to $100 million
- He is currently involved in selecting sites, establishing budgets, and in assigning project managers
- A major player in the corporate facilities world

Junior project manager

- Has a Bachelor of Science from an Ivy League school plus four years' experience
- Is highly focused and goal oriented
- Experience thus far has centered on small-scale, detailed projects for branch renovations
- Seeks responsibility and a growth-oriented position

Zoning analyst/owner's representative

- Registered architect with a masters in architecture from Harvard
- Excellent business skills
- Proficient in applying both disciplines to the development sector
- Does zoning and market analyses, prepares financial feasibility studies and pro forma

Bulk-Specialists. These firms combine the best (and worst) of the two types of firms above. They tend to list both seasoned professionals and relative new comers. These firms segregate corporate applicants from the rest of the bunch. The applicants are assigned case numbers and are listed as such in the bulk mailings. See Figure 4.5 for an example of this mailing. One creative firm has gone so far as to include a coupon worth $500 toward the placement fee of any of their candidates within the enclosed mailer.

And they get paid for finding you.   The manner in which headhunters are paid falls into two basic categories: retainers and contingencies.

Retainer

- Yourco retains the headhunter to fill a specific position
- Yourco pays the fee either upfront or over a specific time period
- Headhunter works until the 'right' candidate is accepted by Yourco
- Headhunter has the exclusive search to fill position

✔ Yourco advantage is that it only has to deal with one headhunter firm.

✔ Yourco would normally go this route to fill a senior position

✔ Yourco disadvantage is that the fee is almost always paid in advance before a candidate is actually hired

✔ Headhunter incentive is to fill position as soon as possible for maximum profit and satisfaction of Yourco

Number	Position	Salary	Education	Commentary
15109	CADD Operator	low $30's	BS Arch Tech	•5 years CADD experience •Coordinate construction for corporate facilities •Good applicant
21268	Jr. Architect	$20's	BS/Arch	•2 1/2 years experience in small office •On boards doing office renovations, rehabs •Credible lightweight
21369	Space Planner	$40's	B/Arch	•9 years exp. as Arch'l designer & space planner •All projects were corporate interiors •Nose to the grindstone type
21472	Security	mid $60's	BA MBA Exec Mgmt	•20+ years management security experience •Fire safety director, NYPD training •Hi-level interface •This is an outstanding candidate
21596	Mgr, Genl Services	$85K-$100K	BS Civil Engr	•PE with excellent experience in construction, general services and facility management •Responsibilities in long term planning, telecom real property, purchasing, P & L mgt, food services •A Pro!
21699	Dealmaker	$100K	B/Arch Design MBA Wharton	•Provides due diligence services for investment bank •Involved with real estate analysis •Really good background!!!

Figure 4.5   Headhunters bulk-specialty mailings.

Contingency

- Yourco announces position to be filled to several headhunters
- When a successful candidate is hired by Yourco, then headhunter is paid
- Yourco can request as many firms as it wishes to deal with to search for the candidate

✔ Yourco advantage is that no fee is due unless Yourco actually hires one of the candidates.

✔ Yourco is not limited to the resources of one headhunter.

✔ Yourco disadvantage is that headhunters send too many candidates hoping for a lucky strike.

✔ Headhunter incentive is to fill position to earn fee.

Fee

- Requested headhunter fees range from 25 to 33 percent of the hired candidate's first year salary
- Candidate pays nothing, Yourco bears the entire cost

✔ Negotiate, negotiate, negotiate.

Headhunters

Here are some convenient telephone numbers if:

- You are now encouraged to seek a move up the corporate ladder elsewhere
- You are fired for spending too much time at work reading this book
- You are curious about "what is out there"

There are hundreds of headhunters, but some of the examples reflected above came from these firms:

Comprehensive Marketing	(404) 884-3232
Edwards and Shepard Agency, Inc.	(212) 725-1280
Fine Personnel Associates	(212) 557-3737
Ruth Hirsch Associates, Inc.	(212) 758-4070
Helen Rauch & Associates	(212) 794-8557

Beyond Occupancy

Corporate career paths defined

Now that you have Yourco's strategic corporate facilities management responsibilities, you may add the following items to your position description.

- Alteration negotiations with the Landlord
- Answering complaints and compliments
- Asset management
- Budget preparation and approvals
- Financial control
- Fire and safety management
- Lease negotiations, payments, renewals, and escalations
- Maintenance and repairs
- Preventive maintenance
- Proficiency planning
- Relocation management
- Security management
- Signage
- Space planning
- Strategic business planning
- Tactical facility planning
- Workletter negotiations
- Writing a successful rationale
- Zoning issues

Keeping up with industry news. I suggest you keep up with the industry and economics by reading as much material as possible. I receive many, many periodicals; and, I read through all of them!

Non–trade periodicals

- *Consumer's Report*
- *Fortune Magazine*
- *Macworld*

- *Money Magazine*
- *The New York Times*
- *The Wall Street Journal*

Trade periodicals

- *Better Buildings.* Better Buildings, Inc., Harold Kelman, editor-in-chief, (212) 563-6460
- *Black's Guide.* Black Guide, Inc., A McGraw-Hill Information Systems Company, James F. Black, Jr., President, (201) 842-6060
- *Building Design & Management.* Cahners Publishing, Philip G. Schreiner, editorial director, (708) 635-8800
- *Buildings.* Stamats Communications, Inc., Linda K. Monroe, editor, (319) 364-6167
- *Building Operating Management.* Trade Press Publishing Corp., Dick Yake, editorial director, (414) 228-7701
- *Business Interiors.* Group C Communications, Inc., Susan C. Mutch, publisher, (908) 842-7433
- *Commercial Property News.* Gralla Publications, Mark A. Klionsky, (212) 869-1300
- *Constructor.* Associated General Contractors of America, William F. Heavey, (202) 393-2040
- *Designer Specifier.* North American Publishing Company, Miriam Furman, editor, (212) 620-7330
- *Expansion Management.* New Hope Communications, Inc., Doug Greene, editor-in-chief, (303) 939-8440
- *Facilities Design and Management.* Gralla Publications, Anne Fallucchi, editor-in-chief, (212) 869-1300

✔ Still my favorite

- *Garbage.* Old House Journal Corp., Patricia Poore, editor and publisher, (718) 788-1700
- *Modern Office Technology.* Penton Publishing, Inc., John B. Dykeman, associate publisher/editorial director, (313) 761-4700
- *The Office.* Office Publications, Inc., William R. Schulhof, publisher & editorial director, (203) 327-9670
- *Real Estate Forum.* Real Estate Forum, Inc., Gerald D. Schein, publisher, (212) 967-1498

Strategic Thinking Test Answer

Figure 4.6 shows the correct answer to the strategic thinking test. The answer always seems so obvious after you know it. The key here is that most people tend to connect the ring of outer dots quickly. Unfortunately, this leaves the middle dot unconnected. After that try, various lines are tried that always stay within the imaginary boundary of the eight outer dots.

The reason you may not have solved this test is rather simple. You set your own limits on yourself. There was no instruction that you could not go beyond the boundaries of the outer ring of dots. You'll note in the answer that the lines exceed the limits of that imaginary boundary. If you set your strategic plan as to answer all asset and facility inquiries, you are still missing the point. Go back and reread Chapter One.

✔ Put this book down, get out to your clients, and be proactive.

✔ To succeed in strategic thinking, do not limit yourself.

✔ Think globally.

✔ Your performance depends upon it.

✔ And, maybe, your career does too.

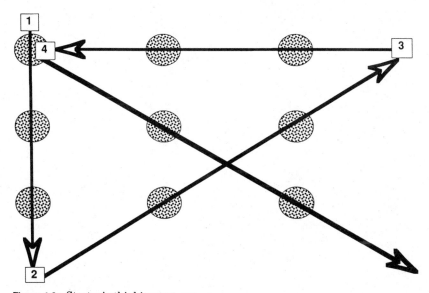

Figure 4.6 Strategic thinking test answer.

Next Steps: Your Personal Strategic Plan

- To provide strategic real property management services based on Yourco's business plans
- To provide a centralized resource for lease management of Yourco occupied properties
- To assure the highest and best use of Yourco space
- To assure Yourco facilities are managed through preventive maintenance
- To manage the procurement of quality facility products that maximize Yourco's leveraged contracts
- To evaluate, establish and maintain asset and facility standards that assure employee safety and comfort while enhancing productivity

✔ My strategic plan? Sounds like this last point should be my next book.

Conversion Tables

TABLE A.1 Linear Measure Conversion Table to and from the Metric System

Converting to the Metric System	
	1 inch = 2.5400 centimeters
12 inches =	1 foot = 0.3048 meters
3 feet =	1 yard = 0.9144 meters
5280 feet = 1 statute mile =	1,609.3 meters
3 miles =	1 league = 4.8300 kilometers

Converting from the Metric System		
0.3937 inch =	1 centimeter =	10 millimeters
3.9370 inches =	1 decimeter =	10 centimeters
39.3700 inches =	1 meter =	10 decimeters
393.7000 inches =	1 decameter =	10 meters
328.0833 feet =	1 hectometer =	10 decameters
0.6210 miles =	1 kilometer =	10 hectometers
6.2100 miles =	1 myriameter =	10 kilometers

TABLE A.2 Square Measure Conversion Table to and from the Metric System

Converting to the Metric System	
	1 square inch = 6.452 square centimeters
144 square inches =	1 square foot = 0.0929 square meters
9 square feet =	1 square yard = 0.8361 square meters
43,560 square feet =	1 acre = 0.4047 hectare
4,840 square yards =	1 acre = 0.4047 hectare
640 square acres =	1 square mile = 259 hectares

Converting from the Metric System		
0.1549 square inches =	1 square centimeter =	100 square millimeters
15.499 square inches =	1 square decimeter =	100 square centimeters
10.763 square feet =	1 square meter =	100 square decimeters
1.196 square yards =	1 square meter =	100 square decimeters
119.6 square yards =	1 square decameter =	100 square meters
2.471 square acres =	1 square hectometer =	100 square decameters
0.386 square miles =	1 square kilometer =	100 square hectometers

TABLE A.3   Volume Measure Conversion Table to and from Metric System

Converting to the Metric System	
	1 cubic inch = 16.387 cubic centimeters
1,728 cubic inches =	1 cubic foot = 0.0283 cubic meters
27 cubic feet =	1 cubic yard = 0.7646 cubic meters
Converting from the Metric System	
0.6102 cubic inches = 1 cubic centimeter	= 1,000 cubic millimeters
61.02 cubic inches = 1 cubic decimeter	= 1,000 cubic centimeters
35.314 cubic feet = 1 cubic meter	= 1,000 cubic decimeters

TABLE A.4   Currency Conversion Table to and from the United States Dollar (October 1991)

Currency	Per $1 U.S.*	Amount in U.S. dollars†
Argentinian austral	8700.000000	0.000114
Arubian florin	1.785710	0.560000
Austrian shilling	11.650000	0.085840
Australian dollar	1.223990	0.817000
Barbadian dollar	2.000000	0.500000
Belgian franc	34.000000	0.029140
Bermudian dollar	1.052630	0.950000
Brazilian cruziero	400.000000	0.029410
Bahamian dollar	1.020410	0.980000
Canadian dollar	1.120000	0.892860
Chinese renminbi	5.400000	0.185190
Danish kroner	6.400000	0.156250
Dutch gilder	1.870000	0.534760
Eastern Caribbean dollar	2.600000	0.384620
Egyptian pound	2.702700	0.370000
English pound	0.564020	1.773000
Finnish markka	4.030000	0.248140
French franc	5.640000	0.177300
French Pacific franc	102.000000	0.009800
German mark	1.660000	0.602410
Greek drachma	180.000000	0.005560
Hong Kong dollar	7.500000	0.133330
Irish punt	0.613600	1.630000
Israeli shekel	2.200000	0.454550
Indian rupee	26.000000	0.038460
Italian lira	1251.009100	0.000799
Jamaican dollar	12.500000	0.080000
Japanese Yen	133.000000	0.007520
Kenyan shilling	27.000000	0.037040
Mexican peso	2920.000000	0.000340
Moroccan dirham	8.850000	0.112990
New Zealander dollar	1.612900	0.620000
Norwegian krone	6.470000	0.154560
Portugese escudo	138.000000	0.007250
Scottish pound	0.569800	1.755000
Spanish peseta	104.500000	0.009570
Swedish krona	6.010000	0.166390
Swiss franc	1.460000	0.684930
Thai baht	23.000000	0.043480
Taiwanese dollar	26.500000	0.037740

*Amount of foreign currency you receive for each U.S. dollar.
†Amount of U.S. money you pay in exchange for a foreign currency.

Index

ABOUT THE AUTHOR

Stephen Binder is a vice president at Citibank where he serves as Director of Space and Occupancy Management, responsible for over 21 million square feet of office space in over 1000 different facilities with a portfolio value of $1 billion. He has more than 25 years of corporate management experience, has lectured and published extensively throughout the world, and is currently teaching at Pratt Institute's Graduate Program in Facilities Management. In 1987 the International Facility Management Association named Mr. Binder a Distinguished Member for his outstanding contributions to the field. He is the author of *Corporate Facility Planning*, also published by McGraw-Hill.